THE POLITICS OF COMMUNITY

To my parents

The Politics of Community

The Bangladeshi Community in East London

JOHN EADE
Department of Sociology and Social Administration
Roehampton Institute

Avebury

Aldershot · Brookfield USA · Hong Kong · Singapore · Sydney

Published by

Avebury

Gower Publishing Company Limited,
Gower House, Croft Road, Aldershot,
Hants. GU11 3HR, England

Gower Publishing Company,
Old Post Road. Brookfield, Vermont 05036
USA

British Library Cataloguing in Publication Data
Eade, John, <u>1946-</u>
   The politics of community: the Bangladeshi
   community in East London
   1. Great Britain.   Bangladeshi
   immigrants,   Social conditions.
   I. Title
   305.8'9'412'041

ISBN 0 566 05717 4

Printed and bound in Great Britain by
Antony Rowe Limited, Chippenham, Wiltshire

Contents

Acknowledgements

This book is the product of research undertaken between 1982 and 1986 for a doctoral thesis at the Department of Politics and Sociology, Birkbeck College, University of London. I would like to thank, first of all, Sami Zubaida for his patient encouragement during that time and Jo-Anne Robertson for her stimulating and provocative discussions during the early stages of research.

I am also grateful for the support given by my colleagues in the Department of Sociology and Social Administration, Roehampton Institute, especially Peter Hughes and Tom Selwyn. Thanks are due, too, to the staff of the Local History Library, Bancroft Road, London E.1, for their ready response to my many requests for assistance in the search for documentary evidence.

A special debt of gratitude is owed to Fina Mason for all the many hours spent on the various typing drafts over the years. I am also grateful to Shirley Hare for her typing of the final draft, to Karen Shelton for her preparation of the maps, to Stephan Feuchtwang for his vigorous advocacy of my research and to Sarah Ladbury for her patient advice during the preparation of the final draft.

I cordially thank Peter Saunders for giving me permission to publish extracts from Urban Politics: A Sociological Interpretation, Hutchinson, London, 1979 and Social Theory and the Urban Question, Hutchinson, London, 1981 and Deborah Phillips for permission to use material from What Price Equality?, GLC, 1986.

Finally, I would like to thank all my friends in Tower Hamlets who have patiently put up with all my requests for information. Among those I am particularly grateful to Tassaduq Ahmed for encouraging me to continue at a difficult stage of the research and to Sue Carlyle for helping me meet members of the Spitalfields Labour Party. Mark Adams and Richard Backes provided valuable help with contacting local community groups. Among the other Tower Hamlets friends who helped me I would like to thank especially Ala Uddin, Korom Ali (Ayyoub), Nurul Huque, Jill Cove, George Roberts and John Eversley.

My hope is that this book will throw some light on a period of vigorous community activity when there was considerable hope that local and central government might drastically improve local resources in a way which would help all local residents but particularly those in greatest need. Hopefully, my account will stimulate others to analyse developments since the May 1986 borough election when the Labour Party was defeated after decades of electoral success in the area. At least one interpretation of events between 1982 and 1986 is now available for discussion by those interested in the 'inner city' and in the people who contribute to what, clearly in the 'East End', is a highly dynamic and changing society.

Maps

MAP 1

<u>*TOWER HAMLETS WARDS*</u>

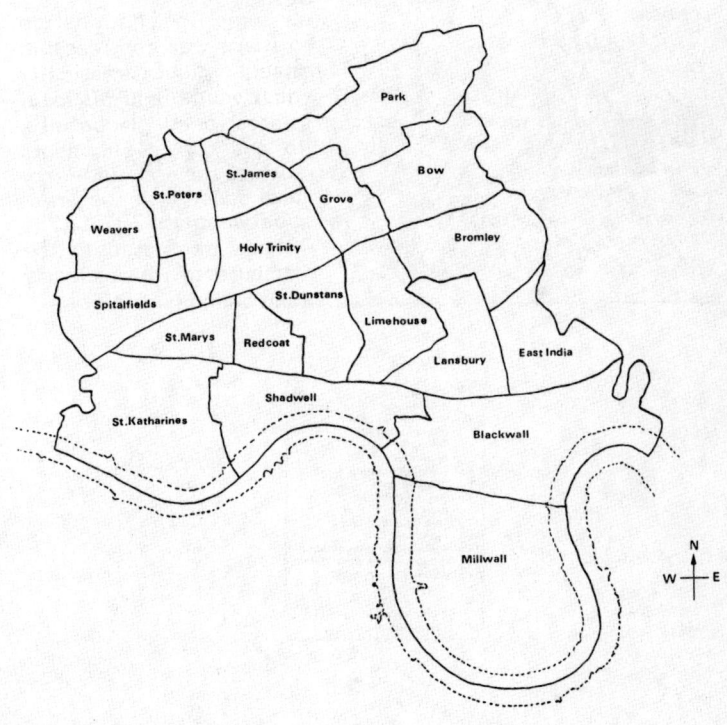

MAP 2

SPITALFIELDS WARD

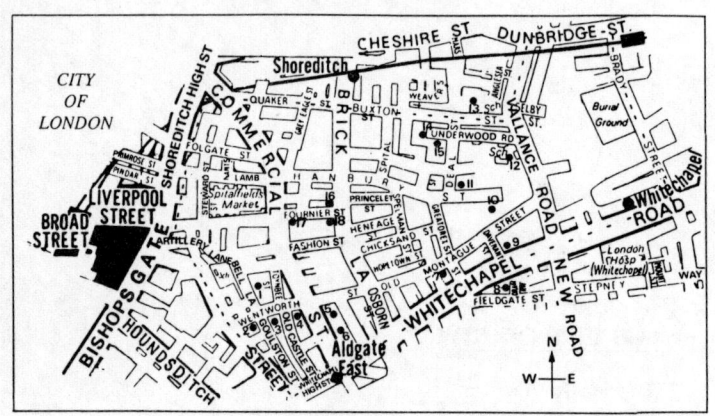

KEY

..	Ward Boundary
1	Holland Estate
2	Wentworth Dwellings
3	Brunswick Buildings
4	Denning Point
5	Toynbee Hall
6	Canon Barnett Primary School
7	Hopetown Hostel
8	East London Mosque
9	Booth House
10	Spitalfields 'Brady Centre'
11	Montefiore C.E.C.
12	R.Montefiore 2'y School (Closed)
13	T.Buxton Junior and Infant School
14	St. Anne's Primary School
15	St. Anne's Church
16	Jamme Masjid
17	Christ Church, Spitalfields
18	Christ Church Primary School

Introduction

(A) **SUBJECT OF STUDY**

The following account will focus upon the issue of political representation in the context of East London's Bangladeshi community. The research was undertaken in the London borough of Tower Hamlets between 1982 and 1986, a time when attempts were made to change drastically the relationship between political, administrative and community organisations and the strategies and practices which members of those organisations pursued at ward, borough and metropolitan levels. Before I proceed with an outline of the approach which informs my study a brief discussion will be provided of the major perspectives in order to clarify the context of my analysis.

1

(B)   **ETHNICITY AND THE POLITICAL REPRESENTATION OF ETHNIC GROUPS**

Communities with origins in the New Commonwealth and Pakistan in Britain have been studied mainly by anthropologists in terms of ethnicity, which 'refers generally to the perception of group difference and so to social boundaries between sections of a population'. [1] Cohen (1969) encouraged research into the political mobilisation of ethnic groups which were seen as competing with each other for scarce resources and manipulating their cultural distinctiveness in the process of political struggle. Substantive investigations have appeared during the last twenty years which have described the part played by ethnic minority leaders and community organisations in representing the interests of certain ethnic groups. The support given by ethnic minority voters to the major political parties and the political aspects of interaction between ethnic minorities and the majority population (Anwar, 1973, 1975, 1979, 1986; Saifullah Khan, 1976; Peggie, 1979; Sharma, 1980; Werbner, 1985).

Political representation of Britain's ethnic minorities has largely been analysed in terms of the interests which ethnic group leaders have sought to mobilise within the particular community and in the wider politial arena dominated by outsiders.   An issue, which has particular relevance to the discussion of political representation and ethnic minorities, was raised at an early stage by Saifullah Khan (1976). She questioned whether ethnic minority leaders' claims to represent 'their community' were related in any way to the interests of the majority of first generation settlers.   She went further to criticise the assumption that these leaders represented a minority community defined in terms of its country of origin and argued that such categories as the 'Pakistani community' reflected the interplay between community leaders and outsiders, such as state agencies, the media and academics. Attention should be paid, therefore, to the process whereby community was constructed within the wider arena of political representation.

Werbner (1985), in her study of Pakistani voluntary organisations in Manchester, has provided further evidence of how this process has developed through an analysis which criticised the notion that ethnic groups could be understood as united by some monolithic interest. Voluntary organisations compete with each other partly because of their different interests and their development has been affected by the influence of outside state and para-state

2

agencies which have funded certain community organisations and chosen particular community leaders as representatives of 'their commmunity'. Community leaders could manipulate the cultural symbols of both the ethnic group and 'host society' and the most successful manipulators were often to be found at the periphery of the community, They worked closely with outsiders but took care to maintain their ties with the ethnic group's centre by attending religious festivals and supporting community causes.

The analysis of community politics in terms of ethnicity has tended to assume that British society is composed of a plurality of social groups and that politics entails the struggle or competitive game between the articulators of different interests. Saifullah Khan (1982), Werbner (1985), Anwar (1986) and others have tried to respond to the criticism that this perspective, like other forms of pluralism, fails to consider adequately the issues of structural inequality between various groups, the power of the state and the part played by race, class and gender - see, for example, Solomos et al. (1979). The modifications which have so far been effected have failed to address themselves, however, to the theoretical problems surrounding the concept of interest which has played a key role within investigations of political representation among ethnic groups and within pluralist studies generally of British politics. These problems refer, for example, to the relationship betwen objective interests and the subjective perceptions of individuals, the distinction between interests and wants, the choice between alternatives and the social or individual basis of interests. [2] In failing to address themselves to these problems those examining the political representation of ethnic groups have usually reproduced conventional notions concerning 'democratic' social and political processes. It is necessary, therefore, to move beyond discussions of ethnicity to a consideration of other perspectives.

(C)   URBAN POLITICS - REX, PAHL, AND SAUNDERS

These three writers have made a major contribution to the understanding of the British urban political arena within which the representation of ethnic minority communities has been principally located. The first major sociological study of the relationship between urban social conflict and race relations was produced by Rex and Moore (1969). They tried to provide a new basis for urban sociology by showing how the life chances of individual social actors were determined by the housing market. They saw the housing class struggle as 'the central process of the city as a social unit'. [3] The

3

significance of their approach to the study of urban politics lay in their contention that individual actors sharing a common position in the housing market might organise politically to pursue their shared interests.

Their perspective towards urban politics formed the basis for an investigation of housing competition within Birmingham. The link between housing struggles and race relations was substantiated by their concentration on a particular 'twilight zone' of the city where the competition over housing as a scarce resource had resulted in the confinement of 'coloured immigrants' to this zone and to particular types of housing which were unattractive to white residents. Local government officials and councillors were insensitive to the constraints operating upon 'coloured immigrants', while the white residential majority generally enjoyed a more favourable position in the housing class struggle partly on account of the close relationship between political parties and white housing-class interests. The Labour Party, in particular, was associated with the provision of council housing and with white working class occupation of such housing.

In response to theoretical discussion and empirical evidence which demonstrated the limitations of the housing-class analysis, Rex, in collaboration with other colleagues, revised his position. His study together with Tomlinson and others (1979) of another working class area of Birmingham considered class in the context of struggles over education and jobs as well as housing. Black residents were seen as constituting an 'underclass', a term which indicated that they might be:

> systematically at a disadvantage compared with working-class whites and that instead of identifying with working-class culture, community and politics, they formed their own organizations and became in effect a separate underprivileged class. [4]

Attention was drawn to the role played by racial discrimination in the allocation of housing and in the creation and maintenance of racial segregation within housing. Black politics was to be understood in the context of the local 'communal and ethnic organisations' which were 'a means of protecting the rights of minority groups'. [5]

Although Rex wished initially to provide the basis for a new urban sociology his revisions led away from the study of urban inequality to general forms of social inequality and racial disadvantage. Moreover, while he wished to illustrate the deficiencies of Marxist understandings of urban social conflict in particular, his concentration on conflict between classes defined as status groups led him closer to the Marxist view that:

4

divisions grounded in different forms of housing consumption are important only at the levels of ideology in that the working class is fragmented by different types of provision, none of which alters the basic underlying class division between wage labour and capital.[6]

Despite the limitations of Rex's approach, however, the effect of his collaborative studies has been to encourage research into the competition between social groups across the city over scarce resources, especially housing, education and jobs and the participation of political parties, local government institutions and ethnic community organisations in such competition. The life chances of ethnic minority settlers were shown to be vitally affected by institutions located within urban political, administrative and occupational arenas, by the systematic advantages which white residents enjoyed therein and by the racial discrimination which permeated those arenas.

Although Pahl did not focus specifically upon New Commonwealth settlement, he built upon Rex and Moore's examination of urban social conflict and race relations and his discussion of urban managerialism highlighted a number of processes which played a key role in the struggle for scarce resources. Pahl's managerialist thesis was central to his attempt to establish an urban sociology:

concerned with the social and spatial constraints on access to scarce urban resources and facilities as dependent variables and the managers and controllers of the urban system which I take as the independent variable. [7]

Urban managers included politicians, local government officials, estate agents, property developers and those representing insurance companies and building societies. Urban social conflict could be generated by the unequal distribution of such scarce resources as housing evident within urban areas. Pahl wished to examine the role of urban managers in creating and sustaining that inequality and suggested that in the political arena campaigns for the reduction of inequality would focus on the workplace rather than housing.

In response to criticism Pahl later restricted the category of urban managers to local government officials whose actions were seen as limited to the allocation of scarce resources. The availability of housing and other scarce resources was controlled elsewhere - by the central government and the private sector, for example. Pahl's appreciation of the intimate relationship between central and local government also led him to consider the part played by

5

local government officers as urban managers within an increasingly centralised and hierarchical corporatist state. They still enjoyed 'considerable discretion either in determining the rules or in administering the rules determined elsewhere' and remained significant as mediators 'between the private sector and the welfare sector on the one hand, and between the central state and the local population on the other'. [8]

Pahl's research highlighted the power enjoyed by particular social actors within urban social systems. He also pointed to the significance of the relationship between the private sector of business and housing management, the public welfare sector and the incorporation of local government in a highly centralised and hierarchical state. An assessment of struggles over scarce resources between white and black residents of Britain's urban areas would have to ensure that these factors were carefully taken into consideration.

Saunders has built upon the study of urban managerialism and the corporate state to argue that local political struggles and political representation generally should be understood in the context of the state's dual character. The corporate sector at national and regional levels of government was distinguished from local government which produced 'social consumption policies in response to popular pressure but within an overall context of political and economic constraint'. [9] Social consumption referred to the state provision of social and welfare services including council housing and local government officials as urban managers were important as intermediaries between local and central state levels and through their involvement in the distribution of social and welfare services. Local government was considerably open to popular protests and struggles and radical politicians could gain control of certain local councils. Yet the subordination of social consumption to social investment policies concerned with capital accumulation at regional and national levels severely restricted the room to manoeuvre enjoyed by local councils committed, for example, to radical policies over social and welfare services.

Saunders proceeded to argue that conflcts over social consumption were based upon 'specific sectoral interests which may or may not coincide with class alignments'. [10] Urban struggles were 'typically isolated from the labour movement and strategically limited in their objectives'. [11] The fragmentation of urban conflicts, their concentration on local issues and loyalties and their potential isolation were

6

further obstacles in the path of linking urban and 'political class struggles' [12] These factors were appealed to by Saunders in support of his claim that social consumption interests 'cannot be dismissed as more ideological barriers to class solidarity'. [13]

Saunders' theoretical discussion was linked to a substantive account of urban politics in Croydon (1979). He exposed the intimate relationship between political, administrative and business institutions in a borough which saw little organised pressure on local decision-making from representatives of a manual working class which constituted almost half of Croydon's total population. Building on earlier discussions of local, politics, especially Dearlove's examination of the London borough of Kensington and Chelsea, (1974), Saunders pointed to the importance of the rules of access to local decision-making and the way in which councillors and senior council officers responded to some pressure groups but not to others. Saunders exposed a crucial link between 'interests, strategies and political power' and pointed to a major dilemma faced by those 'whose interests are opposed to the policies of powerful groups'.

> If they play by the rules of the game, there is no guarantee that their action will be deemed legitimate, and even if it is, they are likely to achieve little. If they flaunt the rules of access, their actions will be deemed illegitimate, and they will find themselves engaged in a battle which they are almost certainly doomed to lose. [14]

Saunders' work represents an attempt to establish the specificity of urban political and social processes outside the confines of pluralism and Marxism. He provides a general framework for the analysis of urban political struggles which is particularly relevant to my substantive investigation of political representation in Tower Hamlets. His writings reveal a refreshing openness to the applicability of different theoretical perspectives to the various aspects of urban politics and the state. [15] His eclecticism poses a challenge to all-embracing Marxist theories of politics and the state in particular and it is to these that attention will now turn.

(D) MARXIST PERSPECTIVES

(i) Instrumentalism - The approach of Miliband and Lojkine

Marxist interpretations of political representation and urban conflict have revealed a considerable divergence of opinion which reflected general debates among them as to

7

the character of the state within capitalism. The following discussion will focus on two highly influential perspectives - instrumentalism and structuralism - and certain writers in particular. The problems which their interpretations exposed can be seen as indicative of inadequacies to be found among Marxist analyses of politics and the state generally, however. Miliband contended that:

> Taken together, as they need to be, these three modes of explanation of the nature of the state - the character of its leading personnel, the pressures exercised by the economically dominant class, and the structural constraints imposed by the mode of production - constitute the Marxist answer to the question why the state should be considered as the 'instrument' of the 'ruling class'. [16]

In spite of the state's instrumental character Miliband distinguished between state power and class power and did not accept that the two were always inter-connected. The state was relatively autonomous from the ruling class and, therefore, members of the state's political constraints exercised by the mode of production and the pressures of the dominant class.

Miliband rejected the economic reductionist tradition within Marxism which saw economic forces and class interests as directly determining the development of political policies and struggles. He failed, however, to provide a theoretical explanation of the economic-political relation and, as a result, could not adequately explain the extent to which the actions of politicians were limited by economic constraints. [17]

A similar attempt to resolve the problematic relationship between economic and political factors was made by Lojkine. He explained the relative autonomy of the state in terms of class fragmentation and class struggle. The dominant economic class was divided into competing class fractions, although the monopoly capital fraction was pre-eminent and state policies reflected that pre-eminence. The state, however, sometimes responded to pressure from other class fractions and it could also act independently of the monopoly capital fraction. One of the reasons for such a situation was the system of poitical representation whereby subordinate groups could force the state to recognise their interests through urban protest movements or electoral gains at various levels of the representational structure. Leftist local councillors could influence state policies on behalf of the working class and state officials could respond to working

8

class demands even when their response adversely affected the interests of monopoly capital. Lojkine produced his own substantive investigation of urban development projects in two French urban areas to demonstrate the fragmentation of capitalist interests and the political agitation of pauperised shopkeepers against their traditional municipal council allies.

According to Saunders Lojkine failed to escape the problem which was also evident in Milband's instrumentalist analysis of the state: 'namely, how the relative autonomy of the state is to be theorised while retaining the argument that capital (or one fraction of it) remains in control of it'. [18] Lojkine's answer partly 'in terms of the balance of class forces' fails because working class success in municipal elections can affect state policies in which case the state is 'no longer the instrument of monopoly capital'. [19]

(ii)   Structuralism - Castells, the urban system and the local state
Castells (1976, 1977, 1977, 1983) attempted to adapt the perspective of Althusser and Poulantzas to an investigation of the urban system and political struggles. The urban system was presented in his earlier work as a part of the mode of production and consisted of a structure of political, ideological and economic levels which paralleled the structure of the mode of production. The political level referred to local state institutions and played the dominant role of co-ordinating the three levels thereby maintaining the cohesion of the urban system. Rather than merely replicating the wider structure of the mode of production, however, the urban system performed the particular task of reproducing labour-power through the means of collective consumption which referred, for example, to housing, social and welfare services, educational and recreational facilities. The local state at the political level played a crucial role in co-ordinating the urban system through its increasing importance in the provision of collective consumption, the arrangement of urban space and the reproduction of labour-power. Town planning was the policy through which the local state performed its function of systems maintenance and around which popular struggles clustered.

The heavily functionalist character of Castells' earlier formulations raised difficulties which he tried to resolve in later publications which were influenced by empirical research in Dunkirk. Urban planning came to be seen as involved with class struggle and class fragmentation. Local state intervention not only maintained the urban system but also produced new contradictions which were related to the disjunction between state support for the rising costs of

9

reproducing labour-power and private capital's enjoyment of the profit ensuing from that labour-power. A fiscal crisis of the state was produced leading to state cutbacks in the means of collective consumption.

Because collective consumption involved other sections of the urban class structure, a broad alliance could be established between the working class and other class fractions adversely affected by the urban crisis. In his later discussions of urban social movements Castells no longer saw class struggles and class relations as 'the only primary sources of urban social change' [20] In a welcome if belated recognition of the significance of non-class solidarities he noted that:

> The autonomous role of the state, the gender relationships, the ethnic and national movements, and movements that define themselves as citizen, are among other alternative sources of urban social change. [21]

Yet his later formulations still failed to provide an adequate sociological understanding of of:

> the nature and characteristics of social bases in the mobilisation process; of how a social base becomes, or fails to become, a social force. [22]

Moreover, Castells did not resolve problems bound up with the issue of human subjectivity and relative autonomy. He remained opposed to the concept of individual actors and human subjectivity which influenced the work of Rex and Pahl, for example. Yet, as Saunders has pointed out, in order to explain 'how class practices mediate structural contradictions, it seems necessary to understand how the members of diffferent classes came to interpret their objective situations'. [23] The urban crisis of collective consumption generated urban social movements but the way in which those movements politically developed depended upon certain practices which produced 'autonomous (though determined) effects that are not all contained simply in the deployment of structural laws'. [24] Castells' attempt to avoid the tradition of economic determinism through such a formulation failed nonetheless since the relationship between structural laws and contradictions, on the one hand, and political practices and class struggles, on the other, remained inadequately explained since 'structural contradictions may be seen as the conditions of existence, but not the causes. of class practices'. [25]

The difficulties encountered in the use of the relative autonomy to explain the correspondence between political and other levels of a mode of production have encouraged

10

some to argue for a necessary non-correspondence betweendifferent phenomena. Hindess, for example, has claimed that a choice has to be made between economic reductionism or an approach which confronts 'the real autonomy of political and ideological phenomena and their irreducibility to manifestations of interests determined by the structure of the economy'. [26] Hirst has also contended that the 'issues, the ideologies, the classes specified within the political arena are constituted there - one cannot read beyond it to some essential arena of class struggle beyond politics'. [27]

Substantive investigations of the local state and urban political struggles by Marxists in France and Britain have been caught up in the failure to provide an adequate theorisation of the relationship between the state and economic class. This inadequacy would also appear to undermine explanations of the local state by Duncan and Goodwin in terms of the interaction between economic class relations and 'the bureaucratic, apparently classless logic of the "state" form'. [28]

(iii)   Marxist discussions of class, race and racism.

The Marxist writers considered above did not pay close attention to the significance of racial or ethnic differences to their treatment of urban social movements and political struggles. The general problems evident in their formulation have not been resolved in Marxist discussions of class, race and racism within Britain - see, for example, Sivanandan (1976), Miles and Phizacklea (1977), Hall (1978), Solomos et al. (1982), Gilroy (1987).

Discussions of black participation in urban politics have usually sought to clarify the relationship of race and racism to the various levels and practices of the capitalist state and the capitalist mode of production. Although attention has been paid to the development of autonomous black organisations outside traditional working class institutions, Marxists have explained such activities with reference, for instance, to class fragmentation and the general pressures operating upon black and white members of the working class.

Miles and Phizacklea (1984), for instance, in their study of 'racism in British politics', recognised that the experience of black people was shaped by various forms of oppression. They conceded the special experience of black women in the face of both racist and sexist oppression but reminded their readers that:

11

by virtue of being a wage labourer, the West Indian or Asian migrant, whether male or female, also shares with other fractions of the working class, a range of economic, political and ideological pressures. [29]

Black and white workers were subject to the common exigencies of the capitalist mode of production. The political problem did not concern 'colour' or 'race' but the racism of a capitalist society where 'people and wealth are forced to migrate for the sake of profit alone'. [30]

Marxists usually explained the relationship between political struggles against racist, sexist and economic oppressions in the context of some totality, i.e. the mode of production or a particular social formation. Solomos et al. in their examination of an 'organic crisis' of British capitalism and race during the 1970s, for instance, attempted to provide an historical account of the interplay between 'economic, political, ideological and cultural processes' and of the way in which race 'has increasingly become one of the means through which hegemonic relations are secured in a period of structural crisis management'. [31] The autonomy of race and the discontinuous character of 'racial forms of domination' had to be recognised, but economic class still played a determinant role within the British capitalist social formation. [32]

These Marxist reformulations were a response to the challenge posed during the last twenty years by a variety of pressure groups and political campaigns which concentrated on single issues, viz. the rights of women, blacks and gays, and operated largely outside the major political parties and trade unions. Marxist critiques of economic reductionism have been accommodated within an updated understanding of the class struggle against capitalism and the state. Any attempt by state institutions to respond to these pressure groups has been viewed with deep suspicion. Gilroy's recent discussion of GLC anti-racist policies between 1981 and 1985, for instance, provided a fundamentally negative view of the initiatives which were introduced during those years and served to justify Gilroy's claim that the anti-racist potentiality of state institutions should not be assumed at central or local level -

> even where a progressive, radical local authority acts in the name of anti-racism its practices may reinforce the very ideologies it is seeking to challenge[33]

It is within the context of the studies examined above, therefore, that I will present my analysis of the relationship between the local state and those claiming to represent a particular ethnic minority community.

12

(E) POLITICAL REPRESENTATION AND THE BANGLA- DESHI COMMUNITY

Ambitious overall theorising, such as the various versions of Marxism, encounter considerable difficulties in explaining political representation. Studies of ethnicity, on the other hand, tend to reproduce conventional notions concerning political and social processes. The most searching examination of the major theoretical perspectives towards political representation and urban struggles has been supplied by Saunders in a discussion which had established the speficity of sectoral interests which 'may or may not coincide with class alignments' and the problems involved in linking together urban and 'political struggles'. [34] The fragmentation of urban struggles over social consumption has also to be seen in the context of the local state and the rules of access which members of the local state use in the process of local decision-making.

Yet the most relevant substantive account for my purposes has been produced by Ben Tovim et al. (1986) since they have examined two local authorities where the dominance of the Labour Party has helped representatives of local ethnic minorities to exert pressure on local state institutions to introduce anti-racist policies and reforms. In the context of Liverpool and Wolverhampton they have studied the interplay between the local Labour Parties, Community Relations Councils, local voluntary organisations and local and central government. Ben Tovim and his colleagues were particularly concerned with the policy implications of their research through their investigation of the positive aspects of anti-racist struggles and of the utilisation by local organisations of local and central government initiatives. Their work directs attention, for example, to local practices and policies which were involved with institutional racism and decision-making and which affected people's everyday lives through the provision of social and youth services, housing and education.

What is lacking in their account, however, is a sufficiently detailed exploration of the processes and practices operating within the localities chosen for research. What has been put forward is a programme for research rather than a profound analysis. My investigation will attempt to remedy this failure through an examination of the politics of community within another urban area - the London borough of Tower Hamlets and the Spitalfields ward in particular.

The focus will be upon Bangladeshi voluntary organisations, various 'umbrella' groups such as the local Community Relations institutions, the Labour Party, the borough council, the GLC and ILEA. Dramatic changes took place in the relationship between these organisations during 1982 and 1986 as they engaged in various anti-racist strategies and political decision-making and reforms were introduced by Labour Party regimes at borough and metropolitan levels. These initiatives improved delivery of social and welfare services, albeit in a limited form, to Bangladeshis who experienced generally the greatest disadvantages within the locality. The following chapters will analyse the processes and practices involved in the changes taking place between 1982 and 1986 so that an understanding can be attained of the limited gains which Bangladeshi residents gained before the demise of the GLC and the electoral defeat of the Labour Party in the borough elections of May 1986.

Care will be taken to avoid presenting the Bangladeshi community as though it were a single and cohesive entity. One of the striking characteristics of Marxist and non-Marxist discussions of political representation, as Feuchtwang has noted, is their tendency to 'assume at one and the same time, the singularity and cohesion of sexual, racial and class oppressions'. [35] If the categories of 'blacks', 'workers' and 'women', for example, are not seen as singular or as referring to some cohesive social group then the way is open for an investigation of the organisation and construction of those categories 'through definite and distinct differentiations'. [36] A critical approach will be taken towards the language of representation in order to explore the assumptions made by political community representatives concerning those whom they claimed to represent.

The discussion of statements will be combined, therefore, with a consideration of the various strategies pursued by local community groups, political activists and local government officials. Although community workers and councillors sought to combat racism through reforms of local government practices, for example, the analysis will not assume that racism was a unitary phenomenon nor that local state institutions were neatly integrated organisations in which decisions made at senior level were passed down in a straight-forward process to the lower and more local levels of each hierarchy. [37] Power will not be seen as located at the central or global level of the state but as operating at all levels of political and administrative systems. Local community groups will be seen as not solely engaged in

14

resistance to 'those in power' but as involved themselves in power relations at ward level through their representation of others and the public funding of at least some of their activities. [38]

Against a strong tendency within the perspectives outlined above to present communities and classes as political forces which spoke through their political representatives, it will be argued that communities and classes were constituted in political institutions and practices. [39] The 'Bangladeshi community', 'white' people and the 'working class', for instance, were differentiated in the context of political struggles and debates over the distribution of scarce material resources. The political construction of community and class was expressed through the ideological constituencies of anti-racism and socialism in particular as community workers and political activists sought to articulate the needs of others and related those needs to certain practices.

The issue of representation arose not because of some innate impulse within social collectivities to express their political will but because there were political forums which called for the representation of certain social categories. Conflicts and struggles involved different factions and personalities competing to articulate the needs of those who were to be politically represented. The political arena, therefore, produced the issues around which conflicts took place as well as the parties engaged in those struggles. The politics of community in Tower Hamlets has to be understood in terms of the constitution of political forces through the political process.

There is no intention to deny the existence of social ties and conditions which were described by local people in the language of community and class. An investigation of political representation, however, must be directed towards the construction of political constituencies from local ties and conditions. The 'Bangladeshi community', as a political constituency, was constructed in the political arena. Moreover, political struggles had a significant impact on local ties and conditions through their influence over the competition for scarce resources, especially in the area of state welfare services. Consequently, attention must be paid to the way in which political debates and reforms of local state practices affected the perception of social differences among residents and their pursuit of jobs, housing and education.

15

(F) THE SCOPE OF THE ACCOUNT, SOURCES AND METHODS OF RESEARCH

The substantive analysis of political representation and the Bangladeshi community will begin with an introduction to the borough and to Spitalfields in particular. The description of the community organisation in the ward will lead to a discussion in Chapters Two and Three of the various claims to represent the Bangladeshi community in the Spitalfields political arena. The focus will widen in Chapter Four to a consideration of Bangladeshi community representation and community relations at borough level, while Chapters Five and Six will concentrate upon the articulation of Bangladeshi needs in housing and education to other institutions as well, viz. the GLC and ILEA. The Conclusion will summarise the findings of the six chapters and will consider their relevance to the issues of political representation outlined above.

The study is based on research undertaken between 1982 and 1986. During the early stages of my research it became clear that there existed a wealth of material relevant to the politics of community which was being generated by local pressure groups, political parties, the borough council, the GLC and ILEA. My approach moved away, therefore, from an initial preoccupation with tape-recorded interviews with community workers and political activists to the collection and examination of English language written materials. Local government reports were available in the borough's Local History Library, Bancroft Road, and at County Hall but many of the leaflets, letters, reports and other documents used below were collected from local pressure groups and political organisations.

Most of my contacts were made through groups and individuals based at the Montefiore Community Education Centre, which became the liveliest centre within Spitalfields during my period of research, and the Spitalfields 'Brady' Centre nearby. As familiarity between myself and certain community workers and Labour Party activists grew I was able to observe closely the operation of several local pressure groups and the Spitalfields Labour Party. I was permitted access to the records of some community organisations, to attend ward Labour Party meetings and to observe the party's campaigns over local and more global issues at close hand.

Many of the links thus established were with second generation, male Bangladeshi community workers and white Left-wing party leaders. Their views and the material which they made available were supplemented, however, by information from other white and Bangladeshi community

16

workers and opponents of the Left-wing leadership both inside and outside the party. This information could not only be gleaned from written materials but also from the opinions expressed at public meetings where commmunity workers and local residents sought to bring pressure on Labour councillors within the borough council, the GLC and ILEA.

Although my research concentrated on the Spitalfields ward my contacts and material were not confined to that particular locality. The networks formed by community organisers and political activists radiated across the borough and beyond to pressure groups and Labour Parties elsewhere in London. What is presented below, therefore, is an examination of the politics of community in terms of the interplay between local and more global levels of political and administrative institutions.

NOTES

[1]   Wallman, S., (ed.), Ethnicity At Work, Macmillan, London, 1979, p.ix.
[2]   Khan, V.S., 'Pakistanis in Britain: perceptions of a population', New Comunity, vol.5, no.3, Autumn 1976, pp. 228-9.
[3]   Rex, J., and Moore, R., Race, Community and Conflict, O U P, London, 1979, p. 273.
[4]   Rex, J., and Tomlinson, S., Coloured Immigrants in a British City, R K P, London, 1979, p.275.
[5]   Ibid., p. 157.
[6]   Saunders, P., Social Theory and the Urban Question, Hutchinson, London, 1981, p. 146.
[7]   Pahl, R.E., Whose City?, Penguin, London, 1975, p. 210.
[8]   Pahl, R.E., 'Socio-political Factors in Resource Allocation', in Herbert, D., and Smith, D., (eds.), Social Problems and the City, O U P, London, 1979, p. 39.
[9]   Saunders, P., 'Community Power, Urban Managerialism and the "Local State"' in Harloe, D., (ed.), New Perspectives in Urban Change and Conflict, Heinemann, London, 1981, p. 45.
[10] Saunders, P., Social Theory, op. cit., p. 275.
[11] Ibid.
[12] Ibid., p. 276.
[13] Ibid.
[14] Saunders, P., Urban Politics: A Sociological Interpretation, Hutchinson, London, 1979, p. 64.

[15]   See, in particular, his article in Harloe, op. cit.
[16]   Miliband, R., Marxism and Politics, O U P, London, 1977, p. 74
[17]   Saunders, P., Urban Politics, op. cit., p. 162.
[18]   Ibid., p. 165.
[19]   Ibid.
[20]   Castells, M., The City and the Grassroots, E. Arnold, London, 1983, p. 291.
[21]   Ibid.
[22]   Lowe, S., Urban Social Movements: The City After Castells, Macmillan, London, 1986, p. 52.
[23]   Saunders, P., Social Theory, op. cit., p. 201.
[24]   Ibid., p. 202.
[25]   Ibid., p. 201.
[26]   Hindess, B., 'The Concept of Class in Marxist Theory and Politics', in Bloomfield, J., (ed.), Class Hegemony, Party, Lawrence and Wishart, London, 1977, p. 104.
[27]   Hirst, P.Q., 'Economic Classes and Politics' in Hunt, A., (ed.), Class and Class Structure, Lawrence and Wishart, London, 1977, p. 131.
[28]   Duncan, S.S., and Goodwin, M., 'The local state: functionalism, autonomy and class relations in Cockburn and Saunders', Political Geography Quarterly, vol. 1, no. 1, Jan. 1982, p. 94. They argued that: 'The "problem of local government" can be seen as the problem of imposing the "state form" - bureaucratic citizenship - onto local consciousness of class relations; local government can be one way of reducing local class relations and class-based action to the legal relations of individual abstract citizens'. Ibid., p. 92.
[29]   Miles, R., and Phizacklea, A., White Man's Country: Racism in British Politics, Pluto, London, 1984, p. 172.
[30]   Ibid., p.176.
[31]   Solomos, J., et al., The Empire Strikes Back, p. 11.
[32]   Ibid., n. 4, p. 37.
[33]   Gilroy, P., 'There Ain't No Black in the Union Jack', Hutchinson, London, 1987, p. 25.
[34]   Saunders, P., Social Theory, op.cit., p. 275.
[35]   Feuchtwang, S., 'Socialist, feminist and anti-racist struggles', M/F, no. 4, 1980, p. 42.
[36]   Ibid., p. 41.
[37]   'Local government' wil be used to refer to the local elective institutions of the borough and the GLC, for example, as well as their related administrative bureaucracies. These institutions will be seen as part

of a local state which incorporated a variety of non-elected bodies, viz. local police forces, J Ps, local offices of central government departments as well as local adminstrative institutions.

[38]   Although my analysis of the various levels of the state, of strategy, practice, power and resistance initially drew inspiration from the formulations of Michel Foucault as expressed in Gordon, C., (ed.), Power/Knowledge: Selected Interviews and Other Writings 1972-1977, Harvester Press, Brighton, 1980, my approach towards the relationship between power and resistance and my investigation of knowledge did not eventually pursue the directions explored by Foucault.

[39]   The following interpretation follows closely that advanced by Zubaida, S., and developed in depth in his book, Islam, the People and the State, R K P, London, forthcoming 1988.

1 Tower Hamlets and community organisation in Spitalfields

(A) **TOWER HAMLETS**

The London Borough of Tower Hamlets was established ion 1965 through the amalgamation of the three boroughs of Stepney, Poplar, Bethnal Green and Bow. In common with other boroughs in the inner ring of the Greater London metropolitan area, Tower Hamlets experienced a complex set of inter-related forces - rapid industrial change, concentrations of poor housing, a declining population and high rates of unemployment - which resulted in a disproportionately high burden on welfare state service. [1] Although the borough's residents had benefitted from the general increase in affluence after the Second World War, recession during the 1970s and repeated cuts in public spending have increased the vulnerability of a significant minority in the borough who failed to prosper to the same extent as other residents. Bangladeshis, like many other migrants before them, were obliged to settle in areas of the borough where there were some of the worst environmental, residential and working conditions.

The borough's population was predominantly working class in terms of occupation. In 1981 official estimates claimed that only 36.5 per cent of Tower Hamlets actively employed residents, aged 16 or over, were engaged in managerial, professional and other non-manual jobs compared with the Greater London average of 57.0 per cent.[2] A substantial part of the borough's manual work force had been employed in the Port of London Authority's docks and in associated industries until the gradual closure of the docks during the last twenty years. The southern wards of the borough - St. Katharine's, Shadwell, Blackwall and Millwall - still housed concentrations of families in the public authority council estates with a tradition of working in the docks. The dockland area was rapidly changing as the London Docklands Development Corporation redeveloped the old docks and surrounding neighbourhoods modifying locally the general social and economic character of the borough. Manual work jobs could also be found in the Lea Valley industrial estates to the north-east of the borough covered by the Bow, Bromley and East India wards. Other industrial enterprises were located in the western wards of St. Katharine's, St. Mary's, Spitalfields and Weavers where large breweries, garment factories, furniture and and paper businesses were located. Employment in these various industrial enterprises had been severely restricted by recession and the tendency, evident in other parts of London's 'inner city', for firms to move out to more attractive locations in the suburbs or new towns. To a limited degree the decline in industrial jobs had been offset by the expansion of the service sector through office development and employment in public services, i.e. hospital, transport and council operations. The City of London also provided opportunities for manual and white collar employment but, even so, Tower Hamlets, like other 'inner city' boroughs, experienced higher than average rates of unemployment. The 1981 Census revealed that the borough had 'the highest level of male unemployment in London at 19.2% and the second highest level of female unemployment at 11%'. [3]

Another striking characteristic of Tower Hamlets' population was its dependence on public authority housing. Over 80 per cent of the borough's inhabitants occupied housing controlled by the GLC or the borough council and, in some wards, the proportion of the total population in council housing was well over 90 per cent. [4] The metropolitan and borough councils had played a crucial role, therefore, in redevelopment and rebuilding after the Second World War and council officials were extremely important agents in the process of allocating and maintaining public housing in Tower

21

Hamlets. The greater vulnerability of the borough's residents to unemployment since the 1970s has been combined with the heavy burden of public spending cuts on housing and welfare state services. Despite the great improvements in living conditions and the increase in affluence since the end of the Second World War, Tower Hamlets has been affected by a set of forces which have led, as in other boroughs of London's 'inner city', to far greater deprivation than in the outer suburbs of the metropolis.

(B) **SPITALFIELDS WARD**

Spitalfields shared with other western wards in the vicinity of the City of London a number of characteristics which distinguished it from the more central and eastern wards. It contained a relatively high proportion of small industrial, wholesale and retail units - evidence, in particular, of the garment industry which had developed in the area during the nineteenth century, and the shopping outlets associated with the industry. There were also larger industrial, commercial and office units along the main arteries of the Middlesex Street, Commercial Street, Brick Lane, Whitechapel High Street and Whitechapel Road, for example, the Spitalfields Fruit and Vegetable Market on Commercial Street, Truman's Brewery in Brick Lane and the Black Lion development on Whitechapel Street. Along Middlesex Street and Wentworth Street there ran the famous street market, 'Petticoat Lane', which drew customers from far afield.

The relatively high density of economic activity brought the problems of noise, rubbish clearance, traffic congestion and poor retail amenities for local residents who were also confronted with comparatively worse housing conditions than wards in the centre and the east of the borough. [5]

Numerous reports had drawn attention to the poor housing situation in Spitalfields and other western wards during the 1970s and early 1980s. Slum clearance of privately rented accommodation and the refurbishment of older, dilapidated council housing, largely by the GLC from the late 1970s up to 1985, has considerably improved the situation but pockets of poor housing still remain along Brick Lane, in the Fournier Street conservation area and the GLC Holland estate, for instance. Even though steps have been recently taken to improve the physical condition and the resources of buildings in the ward, the pressure of in-migration, primarily from Bangladeshis, has helped to maintain a high level of over-crowding in publicly and privately rented accommodation alike.

For the purposes of generally describing the ward, three broad areas can be distinguished - West Spitalfields lying between Middlesex Street and Commercial Street, Central Spitalfields between Commercial Street and Brick Lane and East Spitalfields stretching from Brick Lane to the ward's eastern border.

(i)   West Spitalfields

The area had been heavily affected by its proximity to the City of London. Its population had fallen much more rapidly during the 1970s than the rest of the ward as slum clearance and office development encouraged out-migration. The community life and shopping services of what had been a thriving Jewish community had long been in steep decline and the largest concentration of the ageing Jewish population was concentrated in and around the high rise council block of Denning Point on Commercial Street. The older, dilapidated Holland estate contained a mixture of old white residents and more recent Bangladeshi settlers. The rest of the inhabitants were scattered in smaller blocks of housing association accommodation and privately rented accommodation or were engaged in 'gentrifying' properties in the small conservation areas of Artillery Passage and Brune Street.

Doubts surrounding the future of the Spitalfields Fruit and Vegetable Market and proposals concerning the redevelopment of land between the Market and the British Railway Liverpool Street Station raised fears of a further increase of office building in the area.

The area contained a mix of commercial and office units. Wholesale and retail shops lined Middlesex Street, Wentworth Street (flanked by the 'Petticoat Lane' street market), Commercial Street and Whitechapel High Street. These shops dealt not only in textile goods, produced by the garment industry locally and further afield, but also in consumer goods such as watches, videos and shoes. The Spitalfields Market occupied a large site opposite the Fruit Exchange. Offices were scattered across the area forming small concentrations in the conservation areas. The only other large buildings besides the White's Row car park built during the 1970s were the hostels for homeless people near the Spitalfields Market.

23

(ii) Central Spitalfields

This area contained a similar mixture of office buildings and commercial outlets. More of the wholesale and retail shops were involved in the sale of textile goods and in the streets between the main thoroughfares of Commercial Street and Brick Lane the small 'sweat shops' and manufacturing units of the garment industry were located. The redevelopment of the Fournier Street conservation area had forced many of these industrial enterprises to move into neighbouring streets during the last ten years but the close network of industrial and commercial units using cheap local labour persisted. Flanking the clothes shops on Brick Lane in particular were Asian restaurants, patronised mainly by white customers, and the tea shops and general stores where local Bangladeshis stopped for snacks and provisions.

Central Spitalfields contained a number of other commercial and industrial units. Yet by far the largest site in terms of size and labour force was Truman's brewery on Brick Lane, although most of its employees came from outside the ward.

The area had also been affected by slum clearance and office redevelopment but the opening of the Flower and Dean village during 1984 and 1985 offset the rapid decline in the population. Most of the tenants on the Flower and Dean estate were Bangladeshis, as were those in dilapidated, privately rented accommodation along Brick Lane and in the Fournier Street conservation area. Some of the residents in the Fournier Street conservation area, however, were wealthy, white owner-occupiers who were engaged in the gentrification of the locality.

Central Spitalfields contained a number of community centres, educational institutions and public authority offices serving the local inhabitants. The site of Toynbee Hall, an old East End 'settlement', was used for public meetings and provided facilities for a Citizens Advice Bureau, a play centre and lodgers. Its housing association had been involved in the establishment of the Flower and Dean village, which boasted a new Health Centre, and it also owned a residential block for single people near Denning Point in West Spitalfields. Two primary schools were located on Commercial Street and Brick Lane respectively; they were attended predominently by Bangladeshi children. On the corner of Fournier Street and Brick Lane there stood the Great Mosque (Jamme Masjid) which had previously been used as a synagogue, a Methodist chapel and a place of worship for the Huguenot settlers for whom it had been built in 1742. [6]

At the western end of Fournier Street a more celebrated religious monument faced the busy Commercial Street and Spitalfields Market - Christ Church, Spitalfields, designed by Nicholas Hawksmoor and completed around 1729. [7]

(iii)   East Spitalfields

The most residential area of the ward lay to the east of Brick Lane. Housing redevelopment had been at its most intense in this area with the GLC opening up the Hopetown Street and Davenant Street estates between 1979 and 1985 as well as smaller blocks elsewhere and facilitating the refurbishment of parts of the large Chicksand Estate.   The borough council's inability to develop its property between Underwood Road and Hanbury Street resulted in the erection of an owner-occupier estate on the site during the late 1970s. Across Vallance Road lay further council estates on Fulbourne Street and Collingwood Street.   Most of the privately rented accommodation was located in the streets immediately adjoining Brick Lane, while on Old Montague Street and Whitechapel Road the Salvation Army had built hostels for homeless people. As in the other areas Bangladeshis were heavily concentrated in the dilapidated privately rented housing and in the older council blocks. The occupants of the owner-occupier estate were mostly whites as were the residents of the Salvation Army hostels.

Wholesale and retail shops connected with the garment industry lined Whitechapel Road and Vallance Road, while 'sweat shops', restaurants, general stores and tea shops surrounded a survivor of the furniture industry in the area - A.L. Epstein and Co. - on Hanbury Street close to Brick Lane. Elsewhere shops supplied provisions to local inhabitants on the council estates.

The lower level of industrial, commercial and office development in East Spitalfields made it more similar to other wards in the centre and east of Tower Hamlets. Large open spaces had been provided along Buxton Street and Vallance Road while the large Selby Street site awaited redevelopment and provided hope for more local authority housing.

East Spitalfields contained the largest number of community centres and educational institutions. The Montefiore Community Education Centre, had been established in the premises of an old ILEA primary school during the mid-1970s and had become a prime focus for adult education courses and community groups.   Further along

25

Hanbury Street stood the Spitalfields (Brady) Centre which had been built for Jewish youth activities but, again during the 1970s, it had been turned into a recreational centre for all borough residents. Both centres provided accommodation for youth groups and various organisations concerned with the provision of resources to local residents.

Further east on Vallance Road another ILEA property, the old Robert Montefiore Secondary School, provided accommodation for a Schools Council mother-tongue project and, during 1985-6, a new primary school was established to alleviate the pressure on local schools caused by the increasing proportion of young Bangladeshi children in the area. Bangladeshi children formed the majority of children at the ILEA primary schools on nearby Buxton Street whereas white and Afro-Caribbean children mainly attended the Roman Catholic primary school adjacent to the nineteenth century Roman Catholic church of St. Anne's, Underwood Road.

(C) BANGLADESHI SETTLEMENT IN SPITALFIELDS

Bangladeshis have been the most recent of a long line of poor migrants to the area - Huguenot refugees during the seventeenth century, Irish peasants in the 1840s, Polish and Russian Jews during the late nineteenth century, Maltese and Cypriots after the Second World War.[8] Before the recent redevelopment programmes Spitalfields contained a relatively high proportion of privately rented accommodation which newcomers were obliged to enter if they could not buy property or were ineligible for council housing. Throughout the period of large-scale Bengali migration during the 1960s and early 1970s, a predominantly male population of settlers occupied the privately rented sector in Spitalfields and found similar accommodation in the neighbouring wards of St. Mary's, St. Katharines and Weavers.

The distribution of Bangladeshi settlers has gradually spread as people have moved into other wards and have begun to take up council accommodation. Moreover, the pattern of migration has changed as wives and dependants have joined male settlers, although there is still a striking imbalance in the male/female ratio of the borough's residents who had been born in Bangladesh.[9] The initial tendency for male migrants to live together, therefore, has largely given way to the establishment of nuclear families, although the pressure on housing and kinship obligations ensured a relatively high proportion of extended family units and a demand for larger than average household accommodation.

By the time of the 1981 Census, Tower Hamlets contained by far the largest proportion of Bangladeshis in the metropolis. Estimates of their numbers in the borough varied from an official figure of between 14,000 and 18,000 (10 per cent to 13 per cent of Tower Hamlets' total population) to claims of up to 24,000 by local activists. [10] A survey undertaken by one local pressure group in 1979-80 argued that those of Bangladeshi 'ethnic origin' constituted 46.9 per cent of Spitalfields' population[11] and official figures showed substantial proportions of Bangladeshis and other New Commonwealth or Pakistani settlers not only in St. Katharine's, St. Mary's and Weavers but further afield in Shadwell, St. Dunstan's, Bromley and St. Peter's wards. Although there were pockets of migrants from other countries to be found in the boroughs - Chinese, Irish, Cypriots, Somalis, Afro-Caribbeans and Pakistanis, for example, Bangladeshis were by far the largest ethnic minority. [12] Yet despite the growth of pressure groups in Spitalfields which helped to highlight the problems encountered by residents in the ward, especially Bangladeshis, some of the worst conditions were now experienced in other wards such as St. Mary's and Grove. Moreover, only 23 per cent of the borough's Bangladeshi population lived in Spitalfields - as one official report noted, 'the east side of the Borough has almost as many Bangladeshis as does Spitalfields'. [13]

The vast majority of Bengali settlers came from one particular district, Sylhet, and through the process of chain migration a substantial number appeared to come from particular villages or rural localities within Sylhet. They spoke various forms of Sylheti dialect and the first generation at least had a low standard of literacy in standard Bengali. Most were Muslims of the Sunni persuasion.

The settlement of Bangladeshi migrants came at a time of rapid decline in the local population. In Spitalfields the number of inhabitants fell by over half between 1951 and 1981 - from 13,870 to 6,415. The completion of slum clearance projects and the opening of new estate between 1981 and 1985 stemmed the decline and led to an increase from the 1981 figure to 6,958 according to one local pressure group. [14] Slum clearance projects and transfers to council accommodation elsewhere affected white and Bangladeshi residents alike but the steady rise of the Bangladeshi proportion of the ward's total population indicated a greater pressure among Bangladeshis than whites to live in Spitalfields.

As in other urban areas of Britain with large concentrations of ethnic minorities Bangladeshis appeared to be taking over space that white residents did not want or wanted less keenly than space elsewhere.[15]

The flows of in- and out-migration resulted in a highly mobile population. The major fixed element in the ebb and flow of settlers was composed of elderly white council tenants who decided to end their days in Spitalfields. Many of these residents were the remnants of the old Jewish community and as they died their places were frequently taken by young Bangladeshi families. Young white families occupied the more desirable council blocks in East Spitalfields, the owner-occupier estate on Underwood Road and the gentrified houses in the conservation areas.

Bangladeshi settlers were mainly confined to council blocks from which white residents had moved or to the quickly disappearing privately rented accommodation in Central Spitalfields and the streets immediately east of Brick Lane in particular. Bangladeshis had begun to move into new accommodation which may have been attractive to whites such as the Flower and Dean village, but only because of a favourable allocations policy by the housing association administering the development.

Pressure by local groups and GLC co-operation had resulted in a greater provision of large units to cater for Bangladeshi families. However, these were limited gains for Bangladeshi settlers and did not significantly alleviate the overcrowding in comparatively inferior private and local authority accommodation.

The Bangladeshi population in Spitalfields, then, was highly mobile, predominantly young and largely located in different sectors of the housing structure from white residents. With the rapid diminution of the privately rented sector Bangladeshis, like most of their white neighbours, had become council tenants and their community leaders came to appreciate the significance of the political and administrative control of local authority housing. The arrival of wives and dependants from Bangladesh and the marriage of young Bangladeshi settlers led to particular demands on local statutory educational, health and welfare services. ILEA's primary schools in the ward and the Church of England school on Brick Lane, for example, had become predominantly Bangladeshi and new facilities were provided in the old Robert Montefiore Secondary School, East Spitalfields, to deal with the demand for primary school places. White children of primary school age were represented in significant numbers only in St. Anne's Catholic primary school - older white children, like their Bangladeshi counterparts, had to travel to secondary schools outside the ward after the closure of the Robert Montefiore Secondary School on Vallance Road.

The broad separation between whites and Bangladeshis in housing and education was also to be found in the economic sphere. Bangladeshis were mostly employed in the local garment industry, catering trade and small shopkeeping sector. White working class residents who had not yet retired, found employment outside those areas of economic activity and often outside the locality, i.e. in local authority services or skilled and semi-skilled manual jobs in the borough and the City of London. Little is known of the occupational background of those in the new owner-occupier estate on Underwood Road or those engaged in the gentrification of property in the conservation areas but, like the few white teachers and others involved in the 'professions', it may be reasonably assumed that most were employed in middle class occupations across the borough and in the City of London. The life-style of the Bangladeshi and white residents contrasted sharply with the world of the unemployed white hostel dwellers in the ward. [16]

(D) COMMUNITY ORGANISATION IN SPITALFIELDS

Spitalfields was similar in many respects to other western wards along the borough border with the City of London but the impact of poor environmental and housing conditions, industrial decline and rapidly increasing proportion of Bangladeshi settlers was felt most acutely in Spitalfields during the 1970s. The area could be seen as a particularly dramatic illustration of 'inner city' decline evident elsewhere in London and other British urban centres. As such Spitalfields could be included in central government schemes designed to alleviate inner city problems.

Although the borough council repeatedly insisted that deprivation in Spitalfields had to be related to the wider context of similar wards and the borough in general, it supported an 'area deprivation action-research project' in 1975 in conjunction with the GLC and the Home Office. The scheme, funded largely by central government, was to last five years and had the following aims:

(i)   to co-ordinate and bring forward local authority programmes

29

(ii)   to carry out action programmes to meet
            the special needs of the area

(iii)   to improve communication between the
            residents, local authorities and statutory
            agencies

(iv)   to involve the public and mobilise their
            active participation, and

(v)   to carry out research in order to learn
            lessons of general application. [17]

The project was far more successful in mobilising local participation, encouraging the establishment of community groups and promoting debates about local 'needs' than in introducing local authority programmes, undertaking action programmes and carrying out research. Through the formal structure of the Project's Steering Group and Consultative Committee, local activists were able to engage in formal discussions with each other and with councillors and local government officers over housing, education, street parking, refuse collection, recreation, health and local commerce, for example.

Although local activists were often united in efforts to pressurise the GLC and borough council to undertake improvement schemes, especially with regard to housing, they were also frequently divided by competing interests and different definitions of need. The major source of conflict was the competition between representatives of white and Bangladeshi pressure groups. The Spitalfields Project encouraged the growth of Bangladeshi organisations, particularly tenants associations and youth groups. The clash between competing interests was revealed, for example, in the minutes of the Steering Group on June 1, 1977. During a discussion over the rehabilitation of property in Spitalfields, Mr Cohen, the representative of Holland Estate Tenants Association,

> pointed out that reference is continually being made
> by the authorities to the Asian community and their
> problems. In his view, they were not the only people in
> Spitalfields who have special problems and it should be
> remembered that Spitalfields is made up of all sorts of
> people with different problems. [18]

30

A borough council senior official from the Planning Department replied that -

> he appreciated (Mr Cohen's) statement but, nevertheless, the Asian community has a very special problem and the point made in the report (on rehabilitation of property) is that it would be possible to pursue policies and provide accommodation for them. [19]

By the end of the Spitalfields Project in 1980 Bangladeshi community organisations were beginning to reflect the varied interests of settlers who, by then, constituted almost half of the ward's residents. Besides the Bangladeshi community a variety of white groups had received financial assistance as well as organisations intended to serve local residents with specific needs. Despite the wide range of community groups and funded projects, however, not every social category was catered for. Project officers drew attention to the specific needs of local hostel-dwellers but plans to fund a day-centre, for example, foundered in the face of local opposition.

Approximately £1,000,000 was spent through the Spitalfields Project between 1975 and 1980. After the conclusion of the scheme the borough council continued to spend over £200,000 a year on local organisations and activities, although 75 per cent of the money came once more from central government sources. The Steering Group was replaced by a Spitalfields Local Committee which could itself allocate a small proportion of the Spitalfields Urban Programme money to local groups. Most of the revenue was allocated at the higher level of the borough council and central government, although a Spitalfields Working Party of councillors, officials and local representatives acted as a link between the Spitalfields Local Committee and the borough council. During 1983/4 the Spitalfields Working Party recommended grants totalling £216,200 to the Spitalfields Project Office, the Community Fund, the Spitalfields Farm, the Playground Workers, the Kobi Nazrul Centre and the Bangladesh Youth Programme. [20]

The Kobi Nazrul Centre, named in honour of a renowned Bengali poet, had long been planned as a Bangladeshi community centre. It opened in October 1982 but soon ran into management difficulties and was closed during 1984. The Bangladeshi Youth Programme included six groups - the Asian Unemployment Outreach Project (AUOP) and five youth organisations. They all provided help to Bangladeshis in

31

the areas of housing, employment, social and welfare services, for example, although the youth groups also organised recreational activities of their members.

Local groups in receipt of public funds were crucially affected, therefore, by central government reductions in local authority spending. They were ready to pressurise the borough council to safeguard their interests and sometimes challenged borough council decisions through publicity and demonstrations. The Spitalfelds Housing and Planning Rights Service (SHAPRS), established during the last year of the 1975-80 Spitalfields Project, was a case in point. It criticised the borough council's housing record in the ward, particularly through two publications - New Houses in Spitalfields: The Big Sleep?, October 1979. and What's happening to West Spitalfields?, May 1980. The borough council, in conjunction with the GLC and the Department of the Environment, withdrew its funding and SHAPRS only survived through the Labour victory in the 1981 GLC election and a subsequent GLC grant.

The money available to Spitalfields before the GLC election of 1981 came mainly through the Traditional Urban programme run by the Department of the Environment. The Labour Majority Group at the GLC, by a more vigorous use of central government funding available through Section 11 of the Local Government Act 1966 and the Inner Area Programme, was able to increase its funding of posts attached to community groups in Tower Hamlets. During 1983 it also set up a Race and Housing Action Team in the borough, employing several Bangladeshi community workers, at its District Housing Office and began to develop empty sites for council housing. Spitalfields Bangladeshi groups benefitted the most from GLC schemes, even though three-quarters of the funds came from central government agencies in many cases. Another source of support for Bangladeshi community groups between 1981 and 1985 was the semi-autonomous Education Committee of the GLC and its administrative apparatus, the Inner London Education Authority (ILEA). Approximately £1,500,000 was spent by ILEA between 1983 and 1985 through the Tower Hamlets Initiative - an attempt to improve educational resources for Bangladeshis and other ethnic minorities in Tower Hamlets, with particular emphasis on Spitalfields. [21] A Bangladeshi co-ordinating organisation, Bangladeshi Educational Needs in Tower Hamlets, (BENTH), was formed to negotiate with ILEA over the allocation of new posts to Bangladeshi community groups.

32

By 1985, therefore, a wide range of community groups had developed in Spitalfields to an extent unrivalled by any other ward in the borough. Bangladeshi settlement across the borough had led to the creation of Bengali community groups in most wards, but the focus of most Bangladeshi community activity still remained in Spitalfields. Moreover, despite the creation of pressure groups by other ethnic minorities, such as the Somalis, Chinese and Afro-Caribbean settlers, Bangladeshis were represented by far the largest number of community organisations. The most comprehensive list of groups in the borough concerned with ethnic minorities was drawn up by ILEA during the Tower Hamlets Initiative. [22] Almost a half of the 112 listed organisations were based in Spitalfields and most of the Spitalfields groups were largely involved with Bangladeshi clients and their interests.

The Spitalfields community groups were a mixture of organisations run exclusively by members of a particular community and units employing people from various communities and trying to represent the differing interests of those communities. The work of these two types of organisation frequently overlapped as they proposed schemes in areas of mutual concern, i.e. housing, education, health, employment, women's rights, recreation and community relations.

Thirty-four of the 112 groups listed by ILEA were led by Bengalis in Spitalfields. Many had established their own management committees and hierarchy of elected officers. They were required to observe detailed administrative procedures if their activities were partly supported by funding as many were by 1985. Disputes over the management of community group affairs, especially revenue, led to the closure of some organisations or the secession of disaffected members and the formation of new bodies. Some of the groups listed by ILEA were not in operation by early 1986 or were hardly active. Yet most were making a vigorous contribution to the representation of local Bangladeshi interests and several claimed to speak for Bangladeshis across the borough and even further afield, i.e. the Bangladesh Welfare Association (the oldest Bangladeshi community organisation in Tower Hamlets), the Federation of Bangladeshi Youth Organisations and Bangladeshi Educational Needs in Tower Hamlets.

The majority of Bangladeshi activists were second generation males, but over the last five years, with support from the GLC Women's Committee and ILEA in particular, a small number of Bangladeshi women established their own groups in Spitalfelds and other wards and have criticised their male colleagues for a lack of sensitivity to the specific needs

33

of Bengali women. Nevertheless, the politics of community representation has been virtually the exclusive domain of first and second generation males among the Bangladeshi population and the issue of Bengali women's interests was barely acknowledged in the debates which form the basis of my analysis.

The representation of Bangladeshi interests was not confined to Bengali pressure groups, however, A number of organisations in Spitalfields were run by white and Bangladeshi activists and catered for the needs of the local population in the area of housing, employment, health and welfare services, youth and recreational facilities or the environment, for example. There were also some groups which were staffed and supported principally by white residents who were able thereby to express their particular interests in housing, recreation, welfare services and religion.

The expansion of local voluntary organisations' activities during the 1970s and up to 1986 had been encouraged by the provision of public authority funding. Since the election of a Labour Majority Group at the GLC level of local government, more money was made available to community organisations which were able to engage in consultation with GLC committees and with ILEA over the needs of various categories of people, i.e. ethnic minorities and women in particular, given the context of Spitalfields community organisations. Bangladeshi activists benefitted most from this period of expansion and some of the most vocal and well patronised were not those run solely by Bangladeshis but groups which employed both whites and Bengalis and which were formally committed to serving local residents in general.

(E) **SPITALFIELDS COMMUNITY AND STATUTORY ORGANISATIONS**

The kind of work in which community groups were involved considerably overlapped with the operations of central and local government agencies. The public funding of community group posts and the employment of community activists as 'outreach workers' [23] and as junior officials in statutory bodies were criticised by some local groups for creating a poorly trained section of welfare state workers with limited and insecure career prospects. The grants and jobs made available during the last few years have gone mainly to second generation Bangladeshi males who gained experience in voluntary youth work during the late 1970s. They have been largely responsible for developing contacts between Bangladeshi residents and welfare state institutions, explaining procedures, application forms and statutory

34

provisions to their clients and negotiating between their clients and white officials, for example. Although Bangladeshis could go directly to the local DHSS offices, council housing departments, Citizens Advice Bureaux or London Hospital, for instance, many sought the assistance of local community groups at some stage.

Although community activists have become involved in the complex practices of state administrative institutions and have to observe formal bureaucratic procedures in their own organisational operations, they could also generate local support by criticising government agencies for failing to satisfy the varying grievances of Spitalfields inhabitants. Activists pressurised state officials through formal meetings, public demonstrations, petitions, legal action and the threat of dire consequences if grievances were not satisfied. Another avenue consisted of the political processes of local government and, as Saunders (1979) has shown, in borough councils the administrative and political levels were intimately related. As Bangladeshi community activism grew in Spitalfields so male Bangladeshi activists came forward to take a prominent role in local politics.

(F)   **BANGLADESHI COMMUNITY STRUGGLES**

The rapid expansion of Bangladeshi groups did not proceed without conflicts among Bangladeshi community organisers and their networks of supporters. The struggles usually focused around the leadership of community groups and elections to official positions at annual general meetings (AGMs). The conflicts were skilfully fought out by the use of official procedures, the formation of electoral slates, the mobilisation of support through kinship, village, occupational and community group ties, for example, and the use of gossip and innuendo. Among the many struggles which occurred between 1980 and 1985 those involving four organisations in particular will be briefly discussed - the Bangladesh Welfare Association (BWA), the Federation of Bangladeshi Youth Organisations (FBYO), the Bangladeshi Needs in Tower Hamlets (BENTH) and the Kobi Nazrul Centre.

The BWA was the oldest and most prestigious community organisation among Bangladeshis. Before the creation of Bangladesh it was known as the Pakistan Welfare Association and moved into its current premises in Central Spitalfields during 1965. [24] Elections to its officer posts attracted wide interest especially among first generation businessmen who were reputed to spend large sums of money on mobilising support for the periodical elections during the 1970s. At the 1980 AGM in the Brady Centre the second generation community workers entered the BWA electoral arena for the first time on an agreed slate and were elected to officer positions after two older businessmen had gained the posts of President and General Secretary. During 1980 the foundation of a national Bangladeshi youth group, the FBYO, diverted the second generation activists' electoral energy into competition for positions on their own National Executive Committee in 1981. When a dispute broke out at the 1982 AGM of the BWA over the election of the President, youth leaders took opposing sides in a conflict involving two older businessmen, Walid Ali, the disputed President, and the General Secretary, Hajji Abdul Hamid. [25]

The divisions between second generation community leaders, which were exposed during the 1982 BWA leadership dispute, were also revealed in conflicts over the management of the FBYO and a new community organisation, BENTH, established during 1983 to negotiate with ILEA over the improvement of educational resources for Bangladeshis in the borough. There was a certain degree of overlap between the three disputes since the BWA Secretary, Hajji Abdul Hamid, co-operated with the youth leaders of the FBYO and BENTH whose position was challenged by rival youth workers. These conflicts also embroiled the Kobi Nazrul Centre, which was opened during October 1982 but soon ran into electoral conflict at its first AGM a year later when the other three disputes were in full swing. By the summer of 1984 the Kobi Nazrul Centre in Central Spitalfields, which had taken almost eight years to estabish, was closed while the public authorities decided what to do with the building.

The focus of my research precluded a detailed analysis of Bangladeshi community factionalism and the networks between Bengali residents. Nevertheless, some general comments can be made. Informants pointed to the loyalties between residents in Spitalfields who, through the process of chain migration, had come from certain areas of the Sylhet countryside, i.e. Balaganj, Jagganathpur, Golapganj and Beanibazar. Despite the creation of Bangladeshi youth groups, kinship and village ties linked first and second generation settlers together. Involvement in local institutions across Spitalfields, St. Katharine's ward and other wards was important too. Hajji Abdul Hamid, the BWA General Secretary, had set up a travel agency in St. Katharine's ward where he could develop patron-client relationships with local Bangladeshis from various parts of Sylhet. Yet he also operated near the youth group, the Bangladesh Youth Movement, whose prominent member, Habib Ullah, relied on his support in the BENTH dispute.

The two St. Katharine's organisers found themselves opposed to Spitalfields businessmen who had acted as intermediaries between Bangladeshi settlers and outsiders before the advent of community groups and who now sought the support of young second generation activists opposed to Habib Ullah and other youth organisers. They were confronted by another first generation businessman who had long competed wth them - Muhammad Reza, a restaurant owner from the Paddington area of London. He had encouraged the formation of the FBYO and had supported the FBYO and BENTH youth leaders in their disputes with their opponents. He collaborated with another first generation community organiser, Abdus Samad, in the management of other local groups, especially the Spitalfields Housing Co-operative and the Spitalfields Small Businesses Association. During 1984 Muhammad Reza became even more involved in local activities as a tutor on an educational scheme for Bangladeshis at the Montefiore Community Education Centre.

The conflicts among members of the BWA, FBYO, BENTH and the Kobi Nazrul Centre were based upon loyalties created in Bangladesh and in Tower Hamlets. Ties could be established across generation, locality and voluntary organisation, while personality clashes also fed the flames of dissension. Positions of authority in the borough could be used to generate support, helping non-Sylhetis such as Nurul Huque and Ashik Ali, who became councillors in the May 1982 borough elections to intervene in the disputes. Intra-communal conflicts involved public authorities such as the borough council and ILEA, while closer ties between Bangladeshi community organisers and the Spitalfields Labour Party between 1982 and 1985 resulted in a certain overlap between intra-communal and party conflicts. This overlap will be examined in greater detail in the next two chapters.

NOTES

[1]   See Coleman, A. 'The Death of the Inner City: Cause and Cure'. The London Journal, vol.6, n.1, 1980, pp. 3-22; Damesick, P., 'The Inner City Economy in Industrial and Post-Industrial London', Ibid., pp. 23-35; Howick C. and Key, T. The Local Economy of Tower Hamlets, An Inner City Profile, Centre for Environmental Studies, Research Series, 26, 1978.

[2]   See London Borough of Tower Hamlets (hereafter referred to as LBTH) Directorate of Development, The London Borough of Tower Hamlets, 1981 Census Analysis, p.14.

[3]   LBTH, <u>1981 Census Information and Analysis. 8, Tower Hamlets within its Inner London Context.</u>

[4]   LBTH Policy Committee, item 6.5, 5 June 1981, noted that 'In Tower Hamlets as much as 97.6% of dwellings are council dwellings as compared with an average of 56% for London as a whole'.

[5]   See GLC Public Information Branch, New Service, <u>Putting the Heart Back Into Spitalfields,</u> Oct. 6. 1977, no.396: LBTH Directorate of Development, <u>Towards a Local Plan for Spitalfields, Interim Report,</u> vol.2, Feb. 1977: Lomas, op. cit., p.12.

[6]   See Fishman, W.J. <u>The Streets of East London</u> London, Duckworth, 1987, p.134.

[7]   Ibid., p.135.

[8]   For a discussion of immigration to the borough see Leach, J. 'Bengali Immigration in East London: The Historical Background and the Situation Today', B.Sc. project, Polytechnic of South Bank, 1976; Bermant, C. <u>Point of Arrival,</u> Eyre Methuen, London, 1975; Carey S. and Shukur, A. 'A Profile of the Bangladeshi Community in East London', <u>New Community,</u> vol.12, no.3, Winter 1985-6; Fishman, op. cit., chapter 4.

[9]   See LBTH Directorate of Development, <u>A Short Report on the Asian Population of Tower Hamlets,</u> Feb. 1984, p.40 (hereinafter referred to as <u>A Short Report on the Asian Population.</u>

[10]   The official figure was provided by <u>A Short Report on the Asian Population</u> p.10. The 1981 Census only recorded 9,808 people born in Bangladesh but the 1984 report expanded the figure to include such factors as under-enumeration and 'Bangladeshis born outside the New Commonwealth or Pakistan'.

[11]   See SHAPRS and Catholic Housing Aid Society, <u>The Spitalfields Survey: Housing and Social Conditions in 1980,</u> 1981, p.5.

[12]   The 1981 Census claimed that 'Asian-born' people constituted 8.2% of the borough's population, while those born in Bangladesh formed 7.0% of the total population. The next substantial categories of foreign-born inhabitants were Afro-Caribbeans (2.4%) and those from the Republic of Ireland (2.3%). See <u>A Short Report on the Asian Population.</u> op. cit., p.3.

[13]   Ibid., p.iii.

[14]   See SHAPRS, Adams, M., <u>Blight Caused By Office Development, Panel of evidence on Tower Hamlets Borough Plan Office Policy,</u> May 30 1984.

[15]   See Jones, P.N. 'Coloured minorities in Birmingham, England', Annals of the Association of American Geographers, vol.66, no.1, 1976; Cater J. and Jones, T. 'English residential space: the case of the Asians in Bradford, Tijdschrift vor Economische Sociale Geografie, vol.70, no.2 1979.

[16]   The Spitalfields Survey noted that 545 residents lived in hostels across the ward, i.e. only 7.8% of the estimated total population in 1980, Ibid., p.3.

[17]   Crawley, I., 'The London Borough of Tower Hamlets and the Greater London Council's Spitalfields Project, Pt.2, The Case Study', M.A. dissertation, City of London Polytechnic, 1979, p.91.

[18]   Spitalfields Local Committee, Interim Report by the Spitalfields Project Steering Group, 1 June 1977, (v), p.2.

[19]   Ibid., p.3.

[20]   See LBTH Development Committee, Report of the Spitalfields Working Party. Spitalfields Urban Programme Grants 1983/84.

[21]   See Report by Education Officer, Tower Hamlets Initiative - Community Education Projects, ILEA 3296, 14 June 1983, and Report by Education Officer, Tower Hamlets Inner Area Programme - 1985-86. ILEA 4540, 10 Oct. 1984.

[22]   Ibid.

[23]   As the name suggests their job was to provide a link between the local offices of statutory bodies and Bangladeshi residents by going out to contact local people. Their posts were often funded by grants which were for limited periods.   Most activists had not received much education in Britain but some were able to benefit from the various training programmes initiated especially through the 1983 ILEA Tower Hamlets Initiative.

[24]   The Pakistan Welfare Association was formed in 1952 at a cafe in Cable Street, St. Katharine's ward. See Bangladesh Welfare Association, Annual Report 1981-83, p.2.

[25]   Pseudonyms will be used for those who were not public figures, i.e. those not engaged in elections or in high public office.

2 Spitalfields ward politics and community Bangladeshi representation, 1977-1982

(A) **INTRODUCTION**

Like other East London boroughs in the 'inner city' area, council policies had long been dominated by the Labour Party and by the mid-1970s public participation in the party's affairs had reached a very low ebb in the borough.[1] The demise of the Communist Party challenge in the central wards of Stepney at the 1971 borough election had eliminated all opposition from outside the party in the council chamber. Conflict between the Majority Group leadership and its critics was contained within the party, which exercised tight control over its members.

Contact with local community groups was maintained through the recruitment of community activists to the party, but when ward councillors attempted to defy Majority Group decisions the leadership was able to isolate them and undermine their political bases. An intimate relationship had long been forged between the Majority Group leadership and senior borough officials in the three boroughs of Stepney, Poplar, Bethnal Green and Bow before the creation of Tower Hamlets in 1965. What evidence there is suggests that the intimacy was maintained despite a change of Majority Group leadership after the three boroughs joined together.[2]

The new leadership which emerged in the early 1970s produced a Majority Group leader, Paul Beasley, whose virtual full-time commitment to council affairs gave him a decisive advantage over his colleagues for whom council duties had to be accommodated with their jobs and other commitments. Beasley's skillful use of intimate knowledge of council business and close contact with borough officials was supported, however, by fellow councillors from the old Poplar borough who created the initiative from former Stepney borough representatives.

Local pressure groups were dealt with by Paul Beasley largely on a personal basis. He took a keen interest in the emergence of Bangladeshi community groups in Spitalfields and encountered Spitalfields activists formally through the Spitalfields Project between 1975 and 1979 and the allocation of council monies to Spitalfields community groups. Yet, like council leaders in boroughs elsewhere, he preferred to work through informal links with local activists and wanted local groups to lobby the council discreetly. Strident public demands for more resources and attacks on Majority Group policies by Spitalfields activists were resented by Beasley and other senior councillors as unhelpful and insensitive to the constraints within which they were operating.

The electoral dominance of the Labour Party at borough council level was repeated in the election of local representatives to the GLC and Parliament. From 1968 the same two Labour councillors, Sir Ashley Bramall and John Branagan, were returned to the GLC while Ian Mikardo and Peter Shore won repeated victories in the parliamentary constituency elections. Between 1974 and 1977 the Labour Party provided the leadership of the borough council, GLC and central government, during which time Sir Ashley Bramall was Chairman of the Education Committee, Inner London Education Authority (ILEA), and Peter Shore held ministerial office.

Peter Shore, who represented the borough's southern constituency of Stepney and Poplar between 1974 and 1983, played an important role in the shaping of the Labour government's economic policy and in attempts to tackle the inner city problems of boroughs like Tower Hamlets. He was reported to be a popular figure within the Bangladeshi community, partly on account of his support for the Bangladeshi independence struggle, and he maintained close links with ther first generation leaders of the BWA. When Bangladeshi community organisers became involved in massive demonstrations after the murder of a young Bangla-

41

deshi garment-worker at a time of considerable disquiet about National Front activities, he chaired a police liaison committee which attempted to calm Bangladeshi fears and included Bangladeshi community representation.

The 1978 council election and the 1979 general election saw the demise of National Front electoral aspirations and undermined the challenge of Far Left organisations such as the Socialist Unity and Socialist Workers parties. At the same time dissatisfaction with the Labour Party encouraged the electoral fortunes of the Liberal Party, which had been building up local support through vigorous leafletting and close association with local grievances and community groups. Liberals concentrated on territory which had a tradition of Liberal support - parts of Bethnal Green - and won seven seats there in 1978. Their strategy of building up local support in Bethnal Green wards and criticising the Majority Group for failing to satisfy local grievances appeared to have attracted further disgruntled voters in the 1982 council election where Liberal candidates swept away Labour Party representation across the rest of Bethnal Green, increasing their seats from seven to eighteen. The Liberal challenge to Sir Ashley Bramall and Ian Mikardo in the GLC and parliamentary elections for Bethnal Green and Bow did not result in their defeat, but it established the Liberal candidates as the Labour party's main rivals.

Majority Group control of the borough council was also threatened by changes within the Labour Party during the late 1970s. A younger generation of more radical members began to join the ward parties and their ranks were swelled by those who had supported the Far Left parties during the mid-1970s but had realised their electoral limitations. The moribund ward parties across the borough were rejuvenated by these new recruits, who often came from outside the blue collar trade unions and occupations which had previously formed the backbone of party activists. They were largely involved in white collar jobs and the expanding public sector trade unions which had taken the initiative from the declining trade union lodges of the TGWU and NUR, for example, in the borough. Their commitment to local activism paralleled that of the Liberal Focus Team, and their regular attendance of monthly ward meetings and skillful use of formal procedures enabled them to advance to ward office and to gain entry to the next level of the borough party structure, the General Management Committee (GMC). Criticism of Majority Group policies came to be voiced at GMC level during the late 1970s, and young radical nominees were inserted by the GMC on to the panel from which ward parties could select their candidates for council elections. The clash between the 'Right' and 'Left' within the borough party led to the departure of some councillors from the party and into the new Social Democratic Party (SDP).

The assault on the Majority Group leadership was carried forward during the preparation for the 1982 council elections by the adoption of a more radical policy programme by the Tower Hamlets Labour Party, the replacement of senior party officers by younger radicals and the de-selection of long established councillors. After the 1982 council elections the Majority Group leadership could muster only twenty-two reliable votes on certain occasions because of temporary alliances between nine 'rebel' councillors within the party, eighteen Liberals and one Independent.

Even though ward party membership increased during the late 1970s and early 1980s, and the proportion of electors bothering to vote in council elections rose from 18.3 per cent in 1974 to 31.1 per cent in 1982, [3] regular participation in Labour Party affairs was still limited to a small number of activists and council seats were won by a relatively small amount of votes. Although councillors saw themselves as representing their constituents at a decision-making body, the borough council, they played a very limited role in the wider structure of decision-making which involved the Majority Group leadership, council officials and other institutions, such as the GLC and central government. In many cases their work as councillors was only part of a range of activities involving, for instance, local community organisations, trade union lodges, various levels of the borough party structure and metropolitan, regional and national organisations of the party. Conflict between 'Right' and 'Left' within the borough was consequently related to similar struggles elsewhere, especially within the GLC after the Labour Party victory in the 1981 metropolitan election.

(B) **POLITICAL CHANGES IN THE SPITALFIELDS WARD, 1977-82**

The Spitalfields ward had formed part of the Stepney borough before the creation of Tower Hamlets in 1965. From 1964 two Labour councillors were regularly returned by the ward - Annie Elboz and Bill Harris. Annie Elboz had served on the Stepney council since before the Second World War. Her Jewish background and long residence in the area enabled here to maintain close ties with the ageing Jewish population. She concentrated her council committee activities in the new Tower Hamlets borough on social services issues which closely affected her supporters. She lived with other elderly

43

Jewish residents in Denning Point, a relatively new, high-rise block on the edge of West Spitalfields and close to Toynbee Hall where she held her surgeries during the late 1970s and where the ward party convened its monthly meetings.

Bill Harris, a Catholic blue-collar worker, lived in the new section of the Chicksand council estate in East Spitalfields. By the late 1970s he had risen to high office within the borough Labour Party as its secretary and had become Chief Whip of the Majority Group in the council. After the resignation of the third Spitalfields Labour councillor, a Jewish businessman who had emigrated to the USA, they were joined by a young teacher, Geoff White, who was new to the area. He was made a member of the council's Development Committee, of which he became Vice-Chairman between 1978-9 - the customary process by which new party councillors became acquainted with council business and co-operation with borough officials.

This triumvirate, which easily defeated its rivals in the 1978 council election, had broken up before the next election was held in May 1982. The growing strength of radicals in the party had resulted in Bill Harris losing the post of secretary of the borough party and in the refusal of his own ward party to nominate him for the 1982 contest. Geoff White resigned from the party during 1981 and campaigned as a SDP candidate in Spitalfields a year later. Annie Elboz retained her nomination from the ward but had to fight the election in the company of two young radicals, Sue Carlyle and Steve Corbishley, both of whom lived outside the ward.

The Labour Party faced a challenge from the SDP not only in Spitalfields but also in other wards outside Bethnal Green which were not contested by the Liberals. The SDP did not win any seats but it gained a sizeable share of the vote, was easily the main threat to the Labour Party in the old Stepney and Poplar council areas, and came close to victory in the Shadwell and Blackwall wards.

Another striking characteristic of the 1982 election in the western wards of the borough was the significance of Bangladeshi voters and candidates. The St. Katharine's Labour Party entered the first Bangladeshi Labour candidate in the borough, Ashik Ali, who came top of the poll in the ward. The SDP, in its turn, chose two Bangladeshis to fight in the Spitalfields and St. Mary's wards, but the first Bangladeshi to defeat a Labour candidate was an Independent, Nurul Huque, who came first in the Spitalfields ward election. Steve Corbishley, a young radical newcomer to the ward Labour Party, suffered the indignity of being pushed into fifth place by another Bangladeshi Independent,

44

Syed Nurul Islam, who was a young community organiser. Indeed, Islam came within twenty-seven votes of defeating the second young Labour newcomer, Sue Carlyle.

Altogether nine Bangladeshis contested the 1982 borough council elections, concentrating on the four western wards with large settlements of Bangladeshis - Spitalfields, St. Katharine's, St. Mary's and Weavers. Spitalfields attracted the greatest competition, as five Bangladeshis (four Independent and one SDP candidate) joined five white contestants who represented the Labour Party and the SDP.

(C) BANGLADESHI PARTICIPANTS IN THE SPITALFIELDS WARD ELECTION 1982

(i) Introduction

The experience of the five Bangladeshi candidates in the ward election illustrated some of the differences between older and younger Bangladeshi community representatives discussed in the previous chapter. Nurul Huque, Golam Mustafa and Abdul Gofur were aged between forty-five and fifty-five. Golam Mustafa was the most experienced commmunity activist, coming to the area in 1959 and being elected secretary of the Bangladesh Welfare Association in 1963. He was a founder member of the Jamme Masjid Trust in 1976 and, during the racial violence of 1978, he became a member of the Bengali Liaison and Police Liaison Committees which were set up to tackle problems highlighted by events during that year. He operated a leather wholesale business on Hanbury Street, while Abdul Gofur in 1982 was running a general stores shop not far away near the Chicksand Estate. Gofur had little experience of community representation with the prominent white politicians and officials whom Mustafa had come to know. Most of his energies had been expended in contesting positions at the Bangladesh Welfare Association elections.

Unlike Mustafa and Gofur, Nurul Huque neither came from Sylhet nor was he a businessman. He had arrived in Spitalfields comparatively recently and had concentrated on community campaigns concerning education and housing. With his wife he had established a Bengali-medium school in West Spitalfields, the East End Community School, and had joined homeless Bangladeshi families squatting in a derelict council block in East Spitalfields. After a brief period as Acting Deputy Director of the Montefiore Community Education Centre, he had found a permanent job as an ILEA employee by the time he was interviewed (20.8.82) in his new home on the owner-occupier estate near the Montefiore Community Education Centre.

45

Sherajul Huque and Syed Nurul Islam, on the other hand, were relatively young men who had attained prominence as youth leaders. Sherajul Huque had been a founder member and general secretary of the Bangladesh Youth Front (BYF), established during 1978. He had worked closely with officers of the Spitalfields Project from 1978 to 1981 and found ready support from Paul Beasley, the leader of the Majority Group in the borough council. During a visit in 1980 to Bangladesh with Paul Beasley and other white activists, he was voted out of office by members of the BYF executive committee. Despite the formation of a rival organisation - the Bangladeshi United Youth Front - Sherajul Huque failed to outmanoeuvre his opponents and, by the time of the interview (26.8.82), he was more involved in running a clothing shop on Brick Lane than in youth work.

Syed Nurul Islam had helped to build up a youth group, the Bangladesh Youth Approach, outside Spitalfields among families settled on the Ocean Estate, St. Dunstan's ward. However, during 1980-81 he worked for the Asian Unemployment Outreach Project in Spitalfields as an 'outreach worker' and, like Sherajul Huque, he took a keen interest in elections at the Bangladesh Welfare Association and the new, potentially rival group, the Federation of Bangladeshi Youth Organisations (FBYO) established during 1980. Although Islam was unemployed at the time of the interview (20.8.82) he was later appointed as a GLC Housing Officer with special reference to the borough's Bengali-speaking tenants.

The greater electoral success enjoyed by Nurul Huque and Syed Nurul Islam compared with the others suggested that age, Sylheti origins or a business background were not decisive factors in the voting for Bangladeshi candidates. Nurul Huque and Islam were publicly supported by many of the voluntary organisations which had developed in the ward and as nominees of a campaign organisation formed by these groups and called the People's Democratic Alliance (PDA), they were able to present a formidable challenge to the Labour Party, SDP and the two other Bangladeshi Independent contestants. During interviews with Nurul Huque and Syed Nurul Islam the formation of the PDA and the election campaign were discussed but, before considering these two events, the dissatisfaction of those interviewed with the Labour Party will be described.

(ii)   Bangladeshi dissatisfaction with the Labour Party

Nurul Huque, Sherajul Huque and Golam Mustafa claimed to have been members of the Labour party. All

46

three were involved in the protest meetings and campaigns after the murder of a young Bangladeshi garment-worker, Altab Ali, on the night of the May 1978 borough council poll. Golam Mustafa attended meetings of the Bengali Liaison Committee, chaired by Peter Shore who was then Minister for the Environment, while Sherajul Huque campaigned for the borough's two Labour MPs, Peter Shore and Ian Mikardo, in the 1979 general election.

Golam Mustafa blamed all the major political parties for ignoring Bangladeshi and other ethnic minorities:

> all these political parties have neglected the ethnic communities. They have never welcomed them, They have never given the ethnic communities the chance to develop their ideas and to take part in politics . . . Because these communities have been neglected for a long time their explosion came in the last election. In 1978 I tried to get a Labour Party nomination but no-one wanted to know.

Sherajul Huque referred to the 1979 general election campaign in his criticism of the Labour Party in particular:

> the Labour MPs (Peter Shore and Ian Mikardo) held a meeting in Toynbee Hall where they said that they wanted our support and things like that. I said, 'O.K. Let's work with the Labour Party then. The Labour party is the only party where our people can find support . . .' We called a meeting and they promised a lot of things but in practice we had nothing at all after the election . . . I always wanted to see the Labour Party emerging as a party of the Tower Hamlets ethnic minorities and especially of the Bangladeshis.

The failure of the Labour Party to take steps to solve the various problems encountered by ethnic minorities locally was explained by Nurul Huque in terms of white racism. Recounting a meeting held in the Montefiore Community Education Centre by the Bangladeshi Youth League in the later part of 1978, Huque explained that,

> after my speech Ian Mikardo, Paul Beasley and Geoff White walked out. And they were calling me a racist because I was asking for Bengali doctors, social workers and teachers. They said, 'Look, Mr Huque. You pretend to be a socialist and a progressive but you are a racist . . . You want everything on the basis of race. We want the best doctors, not Bengali doctors. We want to give you the best social workers: the best teachers, not Bengali teachers.' But they knew what I

47

was aiming at . . . I said, 'You will not outwit me that way. There are good Bengali doctors. On racial grounds you are refusing jobs to us.'

(iii)   Bangladeshi youth activists and an autonomist political campaign

The political events surrounding Altab Ali's murder and subsequent attacks on Bangladeshis and other South Asian residents and shops in Tower Hamlets and Hackney involved more than just the older generation of businessmen and community representatives like Golam Mustafa. Young Bangladeshis were engaged in the street demonstrations and public meetings held between May and September 1978 and youth organisers like Sherajul Huque began to dispute the pretensions of older Bangladeshis to represent the community. In 1980 the various youth groups formed a national platform through the formation of the FBYO and some youth leaders decided to test the effectiveness of their support by fighting the BWA election during the same year.

The younger generation of community workers emphasised the importance of British rather than Bangladeshi politics. Dissatisfaction with the major political parties' attitudes towards ethnic minorities, especially the Labour Party locally, encouraged some young activists to argue for an autonomous campaign. During the 1980 BWA election Sherajul Huque claimed to have been involved in writing a manifesto for the state of young candidates which argued that:

> when our group will be elected we will look into the political problems of our community in Tower Hamlets and elsewhere. Wherever there are concentrations of Bangladeshis we will put some candidates there in the (borough council) election and show united opposition to the political parties . . . not particularly the Labour Party but every political party will realise that we have no faith in them, so they will begin to take up what we are looking for.

(iv)   SDP and Bangladeshi representation

The withdrawal of one of the ward's Labour Party councillors, Geoff White, from the party during early 1981 and his entry into the emergent Social Democratic Party later in the same year encouraged some Bangladeshi representatives to seek SDP nominations in the following May 1982 council elections. Golam Mustafa joined the new party at about the same time as his friend, Geoff White, and the BWA was approached by the SDP, according to Geoff White, in order to gain Bangladeshi nominees.

48

In Nurul Huque's opinion the SDP generally hoped to benefit from Bangladeshi disenchantment with the Labour Party. The Labour Party leaders in Spitalfields had not encouraged the recruitment of Bangladeshi residents into the party. Although the ward party experienced considerable changes during 1981 with newer, more radical members taking positions of responsibility, no Bangladeshi was nominated by the ward party to contest the 1982 council election.

(iv)   The People's Democratic Alliance

During the winter of 1981-82 public meetings were held to discuss the community's approach to the forthcoming contest. At a meeting of community workers in the Montefiore Community Education Centre an autonomous strategy was agreed upon with the campaign organisation, the People's Democratic Alliance, (PDA), comprised of delegates from every validated community group interested. Nominations were invited and a Selection Panel was set up to decide on the candidates to be proposed. A dispute quickly developed over how far reaching the strategy should be.

Sherajul Huque claimed to have regarded the campaign as a means to raise the political consciousness of Bangladeshi residents. Bangladeshis would be actively engaged in British electoral politics for the first time and would be diverted from useless preoccupations with Bangladeshi politics. Consequently as many candidates as possible should enter the council election. If only a few were elected, they would have to resign because of the dangers of political isolation in the council or of being won over by untrustworthy political parties.

The adventurous strategy which Sherajul Huque claimed to have advocated during the winter of 1981-82 raised a number of teasing questions for Bangladeshi activists. The plan of contesting the council elections on an independent basis excited public interest among Bangladeshis and over thirty applicants filed their nomination papers to the PDA Selection Committee. The applications came mainly from community workers living in various wards of the borough, since the PDA was composed only of delegates from accredited Bangladeshi community groups.

Sherajul Huque's suggestion that twelve to fifteen candidates be chosen went much further to satisfying these applicants than a more restricted strategy which entered only a few contestants in wards with large concentrations of Bangladeshi candidates. The less adventurous strategy would also increase the likelihood of disappointed activists standing

49

as Independents outside the PDA or campaigning for other parties like the SDP which were prepared to nominate Bangladeshis. The strategy was being discussed, moreover, at the same time as the SDP officially approached the BWA over the issue of recommending Bangladeshis for SDP nominations. The SDP's chances of beating Labour in Spitalfields and other wards outside the Liberal strongholds would be more harmed by Huque's strategy than by a more restricted campaign. In Spitalfields, for example the entry of two rather than all three PDA candidates could help the chances of Geoff White being elected. Geoff White worked closely with a number of Bangladeshi community representatives, such as Golam Mustafa, and his experience as a local councillor made him appear a formidable candidate.

A further consideration which was raised by Sherajul Huque and others was the possibility of winning council seats. Sherajul Huque's suggestion that if only a few PDA nominees were victorious they should resign, did not appeal to others who perceived advantages in representing the Bangladeshi community at council level. The two who eventually fought in Spitalfields as Independents, supported by the PDA, spoke of the attractions of success. Syed Nurul Islam, who came close to defeating Susan Carlyle, contended that the PDA was confident of victory in Spitalfields if no other Bangladeshi candidates were put up against the PDA nominees -

> The Alliance was a hundred per cent sure. I was a hundred per cent sure because, even if I don't go to any door I will pass automatically . . . because there were supposed to be three candidates . . . and we were only two. Therefore, all the Bangladeshi vote will come to us . . . When the Alliance thought about the other wards it thought, 'There is no point if we put a candidate in Shadwell ward where there are no Bengalis living.' Two candidates were proposed (in Spitalfields) because this was the first time . . . We decided to try first Spitalfields ward where we are a hundred per cent sure of success, try one seat in St. Katharine's and one in Weavers.

Islam's victorious colleague, Nurul Huque, refused to resign his seat after the election on the grounds that he could represent his community at the borough council despite being outside the Labour Majority Group or the Liberal Party. He claimed that his electoral success was based on 'the demand of the . . . Bangladesh community that somebody from them should represent and should talk on their behalf.' [4]

The Selection Committee refused to accept Sherajul Huque's adventurous electoral strategy or to nominate him as one of the two PDA-supported candidates in the Spitalfields ward. His rejection was bound up with the complex rivalries among community leaders and Bangladeshi organisations. Significantly, the Selection Committee chose a young Sylheti community worker prominent within the FBYO and briefly a Vice-President of the BWA during 1980 to stand with an older man, Nurul Huque, a non-Sylheti who ran his own Bengali-medium community school in West Spitalfields and had stayed out of BWA politics. Sherajul Huque decided to contest the Spitalfields election despite his rejection and joined forces with another older man, Abdul Gofur, who ran a small shop near the large Chicksand Estate, East Spitalfields, and had eagerly engaged in BWA conflicts. Yet the official support of community workers through the PDA appeared to have convinced voters more than the personal appeal of a rejected Sherajul Huque and his colleague, Abdul Gofur, judging by the number of votes cast in favour of the two PDA-supported candidates and their Independent opponents. [5]

The SDP only picked up two Bangladeshi candidates during the pre-election manoeuvrings. Golam Mustafa contested Spitalfields for the party, while Rafique Ullah, who had replaced Sherajul Huque as General Secretary of the BYF, represented the SDP with a white colleague in St. Mary's ward. Any hopes that Bangladeshi community workers may have nurtured about the delivery of a united appeal to Bangladeshi voters were also dashed by the nomination of Ashik Ali as a Labour Party contestant in St. Katharine's ward. His nomination may have prevented his Bangladeshi Independent rivals from presenting themselves as the sole representatives of their community and in a ward with a much smaller proportion of Bangladeshis than in Spitalfields, Bangladeshi Independents did not pose a serious threat at the polls.

(vii)   Community Representation

The general assumption among those interviewed was that they represented the Bangladeshi community and that Bengali voters would support them as community representatives. They did not raise the question of whether Bangladeshi voters had other considerations in mind, such as general political and economic issues which were not directly involved with distinctions of community. Studies of voting behaviour indicate that electors took many factors into consideration and that social solidarities based on class, for example, had a relatively small impact on voting choices.[6] Although research into other ethnic minorities revealed the ways in which voters could be mobilised by community leaders to vote for certain parties, [7] Bengali activists were not united in their political efforts nor was there any reliable evidence available concerning their ability to mobilise Bengali voters in support of certain candidates and political platforms.

In the particular circumstances of Spitalfields during 1981 and 1982, however, a sufficiently large number of voters, presumably Bangladeshis, were willing to vote for the two PDA Independents. At the same time, contestants recognised the strength of support among Bangladeshi residents for the Labour Party and saw the party as the most attractive arena for pursuing Bangladeshi interests. The 1982 election results could be beneficial if the party learned from its mistakes and became more open to Bangladeshi grievances. Nurul Huque, for instance, argued that -

> One thing has gladdened me very much that so many Bengali candidates participated (in the elections). Everyone will think (about us) in future elections - the Labour Party not only here (in Spitalfields) but in Weavers, St. Katharine's and other places will try to nominate Bangladeshi candidates. So we have started this process by contesting the election . . . that is the success - that we participated in politics directly, even sometimes outside the Labour Party. That speaks of the confidence of the community, of the people who put them up as candidates.

In Spitalfields, at least, community workers had reason to be confident to some extent of their ability to mobilise electoral support among Bangladeshi voters during 1981-82. Significantly, the two most successful Bangladeshi candidates were not businessmen, like Golam Mustafa and Abdul Gofur, but virtually full-time community workers supported by local community groups. Yet despite Sherajul Huque's prominent role in community organisation and politics, his embarrassingly low level of electoral support revealed the limitations of his appeal to local Bangladeshi voters.

Prominence in community organisation was no guarantee of popularity among local Bangladeshi residents and community activists were engaged in vigorous competition among themselves. However, both Nurul Huque and Nurul Islam explained their electoral support in terms of their involvement with the Bangladeshi community and its problems. Nurul Huque described the work undertaken by himself and his wife in the following terms -

In the field of housing I have told you about this squatting movement (in Pelham Buildings 1979-1980). Definitely I was one of the people who worked with the community hand-in-hand, lived with them in the squat . . . We were in the business of doing something. I did not do it as a mercy - I thought it was a duty. I thought it was a part of my life . . . I did not contest the election to have political status or to go up socially. No. I know the suffering of the people so far as their housing problems are concerned. I myself was unemployed for more than four years here . . . And about education, the two of us have tried in our humble capacity to do something . . . And about safety (from racist attacks) we were in the forefront of any movement on Brick Lane or in the area and we never hesitated to tell the truth.

Other candidates made similar references to their record as community workers and here they were at one with white contestants as we shall see later. The theme of moral rectitude evident in Nurul Huque's description of his credentials was also touched on by Nurul Islam -

People decided to give their votes to the right persons . . . (to those who) were honest, who were right and good persons for the community.

The Selection Committee set up by the PDA had to take into consideration the moral conduct of those seeking PDA nominations, according to Nurul Islam. Candidates' personal lives could not be discussed in the public meetings -

We can't discuss about . . . who goes into pubs, who has got a girlfriend and this and that. That's why we thought that 'Let's have representatives from the community in the Alliance - from the mosque, from voluntary organisations - and the Interview Panel (Selection Committee) can discuss about people's private lives'.

Both Nurul Huque and Nurul Islam were prepared to contend that their selection as PDA candidates and their electoral popularity reflected their probity as community workers and, implicitly or explicitly, the poor credentials of their Bangladeshi rivals.

53

(D)   **POLITICAL   STATEMENTS   -   ELECTORAL
ADDRESSES 1977-82**

(i)   Introduction

The political organisations which contested the 1982
borough council election in the Spitalfields ward fought the
contest partly by distributing to local residents their
electoral addresses. These statements provided a rich vein of
information about the communities which the various
organisations claimed to represent and about the
constituencies related to those communities. The electoral
addresses can also be analysed with reference to factional
struggles within each party and to ideological debates
between parties. To facilitate such an analysis reference will
be made to some of the addresses published in earlier ward
elections.

(ii)   Spitalfields Labour Party electoral addresses, 1977-78

As other studies have noted, dominant political groups,
long accustomed to managing borough council affairs in
alliance with senior administrative officials, emphasised the
achievements enjoyed under their regime and blamed
inadequacies upon outside agencies such as central
government.[8] Local pressure groups which publicly attacked
the ruling party were presented as failing to take a wider
view of the issues or to appreciate the constraints with which
the party was contending. Members of the ruling group
usually concentrated on the 'bread and butter' issues of local
government and Majority Group leaders tried to avoid
ideological debates within their party or between political
parties. They frequently appealed to local pride and
traditions and to the trust between local people and their
political representatives within the ruling group.
Nevertheless, in Tower Hamlets, as elsewhere, the growth of
community organisations, single interest pressure groups and
a more effective opposition within and without the party over
the last decade produced a lively challenge to the
managerialist position adopted by the Majority Group
leadership in the borough council.[9] Labour Party statements
between 1977 and 1982 reflected the changes wrought by this
challenge.

In 1977 Geoff White entered a ward by-election as the
new Labour Party nominee. The ward party was dominated
by the two senior councillors, Annie Elboz and Bill Harris,
and the address not surprisingly reflected the views of the
Majority Group leadership. The document concentrated on
what the party had achieved for local people. From pointing

54

out the advances made by the Majority Group in tackling problems across the borough, the address proceeded to explain the specific achievements within the ward, viz. the work of the Spitalfields Project and local improvements in housing, unemployment, traffic management, welfare services and youth provision. The borough council was presented as trying 'since 1964 to put their Socialist beliefs into practice and create reasonable living conditions for as many people as possible'. The address concluded that while 'the job of improvement is not yet completed, we are sure that with your help we can build a community of which we can be proud.'

There was no attempt to explain what socialism entailed, although the concentration on practical achievements and material problems facing the ward suggested that the socialist pretensions of the party referred to the improvement of living conditions for the local 'community'. Again, the local community remained unspecified. There was no mention of the evocative phrase, the working class, but specific categories of people were suggested, i.e. the unemployed, the elderly, council tenants, home-owners and young people.

Significantly, there was no reference to the Bangladeshi population despite the rapid increase in their numbers during the 1960s and 1970s in the ward. The explanation appears to lie in the general reluctance among Majority Group leaders to establish formal links with local community organisations claiming to represent the Bangladeshi community, even though informal ties were established between the Majority Group leader, Paul Beasley, and certain Bangladeshi activists and funds were administered by the council committees for Bangladeshi organisations. The only suggestion in the 1977 address that Geoff White's personal experience mght equip him to deal with the new settlers seemed to come in the description of the candidate as someone who 'has travelled widely in the Middle East and Asia, and believes in a fair deal for all citizens regardless of age, race or creed'.

Community was defined by the 1977 election pamphlet in terms of locality and the improvement of the material deficiencies in the ward would be attained by co-operation between an active new councillor and the community which he represented in a spirit of fairness to all. The building of 'a community of which we can be proud' would be the result of this co-operation. In the final paragraph of the address the relationship between a concerned, active councillor and the community was supported by the promise of regular 'surgeries'.

55

Whilst recognising the very real problems afflicting the area, he is very much impressed by the strong community spirit. If elected he plans to hold regular 'surgery' sessions in the ward to try and deal with the many problems prevailing.

The themes evident in the 1977 document were repeated in the 1978 address produced for the borough council election. The issues of housing, social services, employment, recreation and leisure were discussed in terms of what the Majority Group in the borough council could achieve as the introductory section illustrates:

The past four years may not have given us all that we hope for, but given the very difficult economic climate, and our determination to maintain our services at as high a level as possible, we think that Tower Hamlets Council has done a pretty good job. We've never made promises we cannot keep (we leave that to others). All we ask is that you consider our record and judge us on that.

Annie Elboz was described as needing 'no introduction to older Spitalfields residents having served Spitalfields as a Councillor since before the War', while Bill Harris's political experience and party seniority was established. The address asserted that 'Annie, Bill and Geoff make a good team well capable of representing the ward and fully aware of its problems'. The use of first names further emphasised the intimacy between the ward party's candidates and long established residents.

(iii)   Far Left electoral addresses, 1978

The advocacy of issues directly relevant to Bangladeshis and other ethnic minorities was pursued in the Spitalfields ward election by the Far Left Socialist Workers (SWP) and Socialist Unity parties in their criticism of both the Conservative and Labour parties and the National Front. The SWP pamphlet referred to entry restrictions on Asian dependants and physical attacks on 'black people' - 'Meanwhile, the stench of the gas chamber is in the air because the Nazi party is rebuilding itself', a reference presumably to the National Front whose presence had come to be felt in the locality. The combination of a critique of the major parties with a denunciation of racist violence was related to local issues:

56

*Keep Robert Montefiore School open
  - no cuts in our services.

*Support the fight to keep Bethnal Green Hospital open
  - fight for a better health service.

*Decent housing for all - build tenants associations for every estate and expand the council's direct works department.

*Stop the racists and organise against racist attacks
  - support for community action to defend ourselves against the Nazis.

*Fight immigration controls.

The borough council was castigated for its failure to improve housing conditions in Spitalfields and in Varden Street, St. Mary's. The theme of housing and racial harassment was related to the criticism of the borough council's attempt to evict Asian families from Varden Street:

> Many of these families had been council tenants who had fled to Varden Street to escape from the harassment they were getting from racist thugs. The council were hitting out at a group of people who had already suffered badly.

More generally, racial violence was set in the context of class by Alocke Biswas, an Indian who had been involved in SWP activities in the locality -

> Racism divides us, makes us all weak. Black and white alike are helpless if we are at each others' throats. How can we improve conditions on our estates if we are divided? The only people who benefit from our weakness are the ruling class. Ordinary people have got to take a stand against racism.

The SWP's election address was in sharp contrast to the defence of the council's record proposed by the Labour Party's circular. The SWP rejected any assumption that the existing council represented local people and their interests. Voters were exhorted to fight against the attack on their rights by all levels of government through 'militant action' as well as through the ballot box. Industrial action, demonstra-

57

tions, carnivals, defence organisations against racial attacks
and tenants associations were probably more important to the
SWP than the election of their one candidate in Tower
Hamlets to the borough council.

Although issues affecting local Bangladeshis were
recognised in the SWP address, no specific mention was made
of the community. Care was taken to refer to black people
and to relate anti-black racism to the class solidarity of all
'ordinary people', both black and white, in opposition to the
country's 'ruling class' whose interests were served by the
existing local and central government.

The Socialist Unity address was far less lavish than the
SWP publication. It also referred to general and local issues.
Generally it attacked Labour government's economic policies
and its stand on Northern Ireland and proposed a freeze on all
prices and rents. Its view on racism was linked to the
defence of gays and those affected by the recently
introduced Prevention of Terrorism Act, viz:

> *Fight Racism. End all discrimination in jobs,
> housing, social life and political affairs. No platform
> for fascists. End immigration laws . . . . .

> *Defence of democratic rights. An end to state inter-
> vention in anti-fascist activities such as the recent
> ban on marches. An end to state attacks on gay
> people, their organisations and press. Repeal of the
> Prevention of Terrorism Act.

Britain was described as an 'imperialist country'
always exploiting other countries for the benefit of the
bosses. Local concerns were recognised in references to the
Robert Montefiore Secondary School and Bethnal Green
Hospital - a 'fightback' on these issues was combined with a
call to 'oppose all immigration controls', to 'stop the transfer
of GLC Housing to the borough' and to support 'free abortion
on demand - a woman's right to choose'.

Again the Bangladeshi residents of Spitalfields were
not appealed to directly and racism was related to a
'socialist' critique of British capitalism and the state. The
specific rights of workers, women, pensioners, children, the
unemployed, one-parent families, the sick, council tenants,
Northern Irish, gays, Left-wing activists and black people
were interpreted by both SWP and Socialist Unity in terms of
a socialist attack on local and central government which
contrasted sharply with the Labour Party's address and its
justification of the borough council's record. Significantly,
the Labour address did not even use the passing reference to

'socialism' which was contained in Geoff White's 1977 publication; the party appeared to be convinced that its achievements and its long-established support in Spitalfields as elsewhere would be sufficent for victory.

(iv) Spitalfields Labour Party address, 1982

The changes within the Spitalfields Labour Party between 1981 and the 1982 council election have already been described. The party's electoral address, not surprisingly, revealed considerable changes in language and style compared with the 1978 election publication.

The address criticised not only the Conservative central government, but also, indirectly, the local council's national government. Indeed, the proposals suggested were closer to those presented by Socialist Unity four years before than to the Majority Group, viz. a rent freeze, opposition to cuts in public services, a refusal to implement sales of talk of a fight back against Tory policies. For the first time there was specific mention of Bangladeshis in the demand for more Bengali-speaking housing officers. Racial discrimination in council lettings was also condemned and other concerns of Bangladeshi groups were discussed in the following passage:

> The Tower Hamlets Labour Party has strongly supported measures to campaign for police accountability. The Council must play a firmer role in the fight against racism, particularly against racial violence on council estates. Anyone threatened with deportation to be defended.

Again, for the first time in the 1977-82 addresses, reference was made to the 'working class' in an attack on the Liberal/SDP alliance which appeared to pose a major threat in the council elections -

> The Liberal/SDP are a new team of Tories, exploiting the grievances without having an alternative. They have already proved this locally and in Liverpool by carrying out anti-working class policies.

The 1982 ward party address still expressed the belief that the main preoccupations of voters concerned housing, unemployment, public services in transport, education, personal and social services. The social categories referred to were council tenants, the unemployed, the old, disabled and sick, women and racial minorities. Electoral support for the party was seen as only the first step in a fight back against the central government -

Vote Labour and prepare to fight for there is no other way to stop the Tories - it must be a fight which unites the new Council, trade unionists, tenants and residents of Tower Hamlets in the struggle to stop the Tories.

The change in tone revealed by the 1982 ward party address must not be overemphasised. Although there was a change to criticism of council policies in the past and a call for a struggle against central government in the immediate future, the central issues were still economic and environmental problems. Racial conflict and the local Bangladeshi population were at last explicitly mentioned, but the address reflected the preoccupation of the Left-wing opponents of the council's political elite - racial minorities were seen as one of a series of social categories experiencing hardship, their plight could only be resolved through 'socialist' struggle within the local working class. The address for the first time expressed Left-wing concerns which had existed in Labour pronouncements at various levels of the party between 1977 and 1982 but had only now found expression in Spitalfields Labour Party statements. Rather than defend past achievements of the Majority Group, the address attacked attempts by all levels of government, whether the Labour borough council or the Conservative central government, to cut public spending and 'wipe out all the gains we have made in the last forty years.'

(v)   SDP address, 1982

The SDP challenge in Spitalfields was ostensibly a serious threat to Labour. The new party entered three experienced men - Geoff White, Bill Kelly and a Bangladeshi community representative, Golam Mustafa. The SDP adress claimed to offer voters 'a New Start and a New Team'. Although the poor state of services in the borough was partly blamed on the Conservative government, the SDP's attack, not surprisingly, concentrated on the borough council. The SDP's alternative was spelt out in the following terms -

The SDP response to the many problems which this Borough faces is not simply to pour more money - your money - into the services. FIRST we must clear up the neglect, the waste and the inefficiency. SECOND we must re-think why the services are so bad and make a new start with a new team. THIRDLY we must make sure that local people have a real say in the way things are run. For these three reasons, the

SDP ALLIANCE. will organise public debate throughout Tower Hamlets so that people can choose their own form of neighbourhood council for democratic local control and make the service work for and be accountable to local people.

The Labour-led council was portrayed as inefficient, uncaring and unaccountable. The SDP and Liberal Focus Team based their appeal to the borough's voters on plans for the decentralisation of local government functions, especially with regard to public housing. The Spitalfields Labour Party's address had reflected the borough party's response to the SDP/Liberal Alliance challenge by proposing a 'borough housing committee', 'more democratic control of the estates' and an 'estate-based' repair service'. The SDP publication discussed reforms involving accommodation in greater detail than Labour's address and supported it with an appeal from the three candidates which concentrated on their local experience, their desire to make a new start in the borough and 'to see Spitalfields transformed into a decent neighbourhood with clean streets - a thriving community of homes, shops and workplaces; somewhere to be proud of!'

Like previous Labour Party statements the SDP public addresses concentrated on physical issues - housing in particular and the environment. Both parties referred to the same categories of people in certain cases, i.e. council tenants, self-help groups and the unemployed, although the 'centrist' and 'neighbourhood' strategies of the SDP/Alliance were revealed in references to young house-buyers, small businesses and neighbourhood councils. Both parties' addresses implied that voters would choose between the various promises and policies concerning 'bread and butter issues'.

The SDP also followed the Labour Party's traditional practice of recognising the importance of personal links between candidates and voters in local government elections. In May 1982, the SDP chose a Spitalfields Bangladeshi community activist, Golam Mustafa, and the former ward councillor, Geoff White, who had established ties with both Bangladeshi and white residents. With the Irish Catholic background and local community experience of Bill Kelly, the third SDP candidate the party seemed to pose a formidable threat to the Labour Party's electoral hopes in the ward.

(vi)   PDA address,1982

The entry of four Independent Bangladeshi candidates, as we have seen, weakened the SDP's prospects. The two most formidable contestants proved to be Nurul Huque and Syed Nurul Islam who were supported by the ad hoc People's Democratic Alliance. The address produced for Huque and Islam concentrated, like other addresses, on practical issues and was similar to the SDP document in its references to 'quick repairs', 'a clean Spitalfields', to local people running their 'own affairs' and to the 'decentralisation of borough council administrative powers'. Although the PDA brought together Bangladeshi community workers, the two candidates appealed to 'black' and 'white' sections of the 'local working class' against uncaring 'bureaucrats and politicians' - at all levels of government presumably.

> We have painfully observed that nobody cares for the local working class people of Spitalfields. We, the working class people, have been exploited too much and for too long both by the bureaucrats and the politicians. The local working class people, whether black or white, have been deprived of any access to the decision making process. In fact we are completely powerless to mould our destiny. Unemployment, housing problems, endless delay in repair works, rubbish, smell etc, have made us sick.
> So we have decided to fight the ensuing Borough Council elections.

The PDA-supported candidates brought out both an English and a Bengali version of their electoral address. The Labour Party had done the same in 1978 and 1982, and the SDP also published a Bengali version in 1982. Yet while the Labour and SDP Bengali addresses were translations of an English language original, the drafters of the PDA leaflet altered the focus of their Bengali language appeal, suggesting a distinction between two audiences. Their Bengali version put the appeal to the electorate before the list of demands and made no mention of the 'local working class', preferring instead to speak of the need for the whole community to support the two candidates -

> Dear Brother and Sister,
> On behalf of our community we are today, supporting Nurul Huque and Syed Nurul Islam. We firmly believe that all brothers and sisters will be united too in their

support for the two candidates at the election on 6 May so that we can overcome all our problems through their efforts.

The list of issues for which the candidates campaigned covered some of the same ground as the English version but there were significant differences in the order of issues to be tackled -

1. Houses and flats
2. Repairs of houses and flats
3. Education and training
4. Anti-racist movement
5. Unemployment benefit
6. Unemployment and job opportunities
7. Rate and rent increases
8. Rubbish clearance and parking facilities
9. Sports and recreational opportunities; Bengali programmes on T.V.

These issues combined general concerns with the particular grievances of the youth groups and their national organisation, the FBYO, whose officers played an important part in the development of the PDA. Education was referred to much earlier in the Bengali version of problems which concerned the two candidates. The 'anti-racist movement' was also given a higher priority, while there was no reference made to local self-management and the de-centralisation of council administrative powers. Those producing the PDA electoral address in English and Bengali appeared to have two slightly different audiences in mind. Their appeal was primarily to the Bangladeshi electorate and the Bengali-language address reflected the priorities of the many community activists supporting the two PDA candidates.

NOTES

[1] Public participation in borough elections was very low - 14.3% of the total electorate voted in 1968, 25.9% in 1971, 18.3% in 1974 and 28.3% in 1978. See Crawley, op. cit., p.69. Some seats were not even contested by Labour's opponents.

[2] Ibid., p.65

[3] See Crawley, op cit., p.69, and London Borough Council Elections, 6 May, 1982 (GLC, 1983). The 1982 turn-out compared with 34.2% in neighbouring Hackney and 31.4% in Newham.

63

[4]   Soon after the election he tried to join the Labour
        Party - see the next chapter for further details of his
        application.
[5]   For election results see Appendix.
[6]   See, for example, Dunleavy, P., 'Voting and the
        Electorate' in Drucker, H., (gen. ed.), Developments in
        British Politics, Macmillan, London, 1983 and
        Whiteley, P., 'Predicting the Labour Vote in 1983:
        Social Backgrounds versus Subjective Evaluations,
        Political Studies, vol.34 no. 1, March 1986.
[7]   See Anwar, M., 'Asian Participation in the 1974
        Autumn Election', New Community vol.2, no.4,
        Autumn 1973 and The Myth of Return, Heinemann
        Educational Books, London, 1979.
[8]   Dearlove (1973); Saunders (1979); Crawley, I., 'The
        London Borough of Tower Hamlets and the Greater
        London Council's Spitalfields Project, Pt. 2, The Case
        Study', M.A. dissertation, City of London Polytechnic,
        1979.
[9]   For a discussion of managerialism and corporatist
        developments encouraged by the Labour government
        during the 1970s, see Dunleavy P., and Rhodes,
        R.A.W., 'Beyond Whitehall' in Drucker, H., (ed.)
        Developments in British Politics, Macmillan, London,
        1983.

3 The Spitalfields Labour Party and Bangladeshi community representation, 1982-86

(A) **INTRODUCTION**

The May 1982 borough elections had apparently demonstrated the strength of the Bangladeshi electorate in the western wards of Tower Hamlets and the key role played there by Bangladeshi community organisers. Between May 1982 and July 1985 Labour ward parties in localities where there were sizeable concentrations of Bangladeshi settlers encouraged the recruitment of Bangladeshi members far more than ever before. Bangladeshi community workers became important intermediaries between white members of the ward parties and the new Bangladeshi members who were not fluent in English.

By July 1985 some of these community workers had risen to positions of responsibility at various levels of the party and one of them, Abbas Uddin, was selected by the Spitalfields ward party to be its first Bangladeshi candidate when the death of the veteran councillor, Annie Elboz, necessitated a by-election. As in 1982 the party was challenged by a Bangladeshi Independent who worked closely with the ward's Independent Bangladeshi councillor, Nurul Huque, and in a very close contest the party's choice, Abbas Uddin, defeated his Bangladeshi opponent by only nine votes. [1]

65

The recruitment of Bangladeshi members became embroiled in conflicts between community organisers which overlapped, to some extent, with intra-party rivalries. Party struggles in the national and local press were explained in terms of political differences between 'Right' and 'Left', with distinctions sometimes being made to the 'hard' and 'soft' Left, for example, as well as references to various Left-wing groups, i.e. London Labour Briefing, Militant Tendency and Socialist Organiser. [2] At borough council level the conflicts centred around the divisions between the Majority Group leadership, nine Left-wing councillors and the eighteen Liberals.[3] In full council meetings Left-wingers could join in temporary alliance with the Liberals (and Nurul Huque, the lone Independent) to defeat Majority Group proposals.

Sue Carlyle's participation with other Left-wingers in such action resulted in great tension between her and her ward councillor colleague, Annie Elboz. Sue Carlyle found ready support for her action from other ward party radicals, who had taken over control of the Spitalfields Labour Party during 1982-83, and Annie Elboz became a virtually isolated figure at ward meetings.

The advance of white Left-wingers at ward party level led to their entry into positions of responsibility at the next level of the General Management Committee (GMC) of the party. By 1981 the GMC of the borough party had a strong Left-wing presence. During 1983 before the July general election the recommendations of the parliamentary Boundary Commission resulted in the creation of two new Constituency Labour Parties (CLPs) with separate GMCs. [4] Instead of the north/south division, the borough was separated by a west/east line. Spitalfields, which had previously belonged to the Bethnal Green and Bow constituency represented by the veteran Tribunite Left-winger, Ian Mikardo, now formed part of the new constituency of Bethnal Green and Stepney with Peter Shore as MP.

Disagreements soon raged between Peter Shore and Left-wingers on the new GMC and the conflict during 1984 and 1985 involved the process of selecting the CLP's candidate for the next general election. Peter Shore faced the danger of de-selection by his constituency's GMC and a challenge from one of the white leaders of the Spitalfields Labour Party, Jill Cove, who applied for selection against him.

The electoral support of Bangladeshi voters became a crucial consideration to Labour Party activists engaged in these intra-party conflicts. Peter Shore was reputed to be a popular figure among Bangladeshi residents and vigorous efforts were made to mobilise Bangladeshi support for Peter Shore and his colleague, Ian Mikardo, during the 1983 general campaign. The electoral success enjoyed by the two MPs in the new constituencies appeared to provide further evidence of the importance of the party of Bangladeshi political support. [5]The strategy of white Left-wing officers in the Spitalfields Labour Party was bound up with the attempt by the various elements of the Left to represent particular communities within the working class in their struggles with Right-wing party opponents. This strategy has to be understood in the context of other claims to representation, both inside and outside the arena of political institutions. Moreover, attention to the strategies of political actors or groups must not be allowed to obscure the operation of practices which constrained those strategies. The following account will consider, therefore, not just the strategies and struggles of party members but also the practices involved in their meetings, membership drives and local campaigns, for example.

(B)   **CAMPAIGNING ON LOCAL AND MORE GLOBAL ISSUES**

The white activists who took control of the ward party, tried to reach out to local residents by campaigning on a number of issues. A series of leaflets and posters were produced between 1982 and 1985 exhorting residents to join party campaigns and become party members.

During 1982 and 1983 the leaflets concentrated on issues set out in the May 1982 electoral address, i.e. measures relating to housing, traffic, social services, police and racism. The first publication, produced after the 1982 council election, indicated the attempt of the new white leaders to campaign over local events affecting Bangladeshis. The leaflet, written in English, criticised the Majority Group leadership in the borough council for failing to stop the sale of National Front literature on Brick Lane. A link was made between the National Front issue and racial harassment and racist attacks on council estates across the borough. The ward party planned to support the rival borough Trades Council stall on Brick Lane and encouraged residents to attend a meeting at the Bangladesh Welfare Association, to join the ward party and to visit the surgeries of the two Labour councillors.

The leaflet explained racism in relation to economic and political processes:

> Racist ideas lead to racist attacks. These ideas breed and take root in people's minds because of the real problems they face - unemployment and poor housing, results of anti-working class policies and neglect by successive councils and now a vicious Tory government.

In the struggle against racism and 'the real problems' local people faced, the ward party leaflet claimed that:

> We need to meet with community groups to discuss these problems. And also how as a community we can organise to stop the attacks. As a ward we welcome and will help organise these meetings.

The campaign against racism was to be undertaken, therefore, through struggles at local and more global levels. The ward party would co-operate with Bangladeshi community organisations, in particular, but it also sought to pressurise the borough council through its 'strongly worded resolution' and, in another leaflet produced in September 1982, it referred to the action by the constituency's Labour MP, Ian Mikardo, at central government level. The anti-racist struggle was intended to be waged across 'the broad Labour movement', bringing together ward party members, ward councillors, parliamentary representatives, trade unionists as well as local residents - the 'Spitalfields people'.

Racism was discussed in both handbills with reference to other issues, i.e. the 'real problems' encountered by people which were caused by local and central government policies in the area of employment, housing, welfare and social services. The ward party leaflets, therefore, criticised both the Labour Majority Group in the borough council and the Conservative government for 'anti-working class policies and neglect'. Although the leaflets referred to the activities of both Labour councillors for the ward, Annie Flboz and Sue Carlyle, the strategy which they outlined was supported at borough council level only by Sue Carlyle, who joined with her 'rebel' Labour councillors in embarrassing the Majority Group leadership on a number of issues including the National Front stall, office development and an increased charge on Meals on Wheels.

68

Pressure was to be applied not only through the various levels of the political structure but also through public demonstrations and the mobilisation of support from various organisations outside the Labour Party. The public protests over the National Front stall during the summer of 1982 were not the sole preserve of the party and its allies, however. A Far Left group, ELWAR, (a local branch of the Revolutionary Communist Party)[6] supported the public demonstration of 29 August, which was attended by Labour Party members, Trades Council representatives and members of local community groups. ELWAR had organised protective vigils for Bangladeshi families on council estates where they were being harassed and attacked. The Spitalfields Labour Party leaflets published during the summer of 1982, were directed at both local residents and Far Left critics outside the party who accused the Labour Party and its representatives in the borough council for failing to defend local, working class interests. The ward party, by linking together local grievances with more general political issues and other levels of the 'broad Labour movement', tried to substantiate its claim that the 'Labour Party is the only Party that is interested in Working People'.

After the general election in June 1983 the ward party activists proposed another campaign which would necessitate co-operation with other organisations and mobilise local support. Reference had already been made to the deleterious effects of office development in the ward with regard to plans concerning the Spitalfields Fruit and Vegetable Market. The ward party now called on local residents to sign a petition against 'further office development in the area' and pledged itself 'to campaign for the land to be used for housing, open spaces and industry which gives jobs to local people'.

The leaflet, distributed during July 1983, came at a time of considerable activity concerning housing and planning development in the ward. As the leaflet noted, a Housing Committee had been established at borough council level. Since 1978 council housing had been administered by a Tower Hamlets/GLC Joint Housing Management Committee, with the borough's representatives on the committee coming from the Majority Group leadership. After the 1982 borough elections the opponents of the Majority Group leadership were in a position to impose their will at full council meetings on certain issues and in November 1982, a temporary alliance of Liberals and nine 'rebel' Labour councillors voted through a proposal to replace the JHMC[7] with a borough Housing Committee [8].

The strategy of mobilising local support for campaigns which overlapped with the activities of non-political, single issue pressure groups gave way to a strategy of encouraging members to join public meetings and demonstrations, held by other units of the party and trades unions to protest against borough council and central government measures. The poor attendance of ward party members and local residents at a campaign conference in November 1983, held at the Montefiore Community Education Centre, East Spitalfields, had revealed a lack of interest in discussing issues which the ward party leaders considered to be crucial. Nevertheless, during 1984, residents were exhorted to support campaigns against NHS cuts and in defence of the striking miners. Public meetings were held in York Hall, Bethnal Green, in February 1984 with national and local speakers to discuss the NHS cuts, while trade union representatives and a Left-wing MP, Dennis Skinner[9]spoke at an October 1984 meeting in a nearby Bethnal Green ward on behalf of the striking miners. During July 1984 ward party members were asked by the ward secretary to help in a public collection for the striking miners in St. Katharine's ward to the south of Spitalfields.

The miners' strike was given pride of place in ward party leaflets distributed from the summer of 1984 until the beginning of 1985. The strike's significance was explained in a passage based on a speech by Tony Benn. A ward party leaflet, publicising the October 1984 meeting, asserted that:

> The Labour Party has been at the forefront of the local campaign to support the miners. The campaign is a battle to change our society. It is a battle to get work for everyone. It is a battle to see our children get a decent education and a good health service. It is a battle to give dignity to retired people. It is a struggle for the democratic control of local government, of our industries, of the police, and the mass media. The Labour Party and the striking miners want a country controlled by the people who produce its wealth.

In another leaflet, produced during 1984, the importance of supporting the strike was argued in the following terms:

> The Miners have taken a stand to resist the Government's policy of destroying communities like ours, by taking up the fight to defend their jobs and their way of life. They are our first line of defence against Thatcher.

A third leaflet, published during 1984, related the miners' strike to the activities of its two councillors concerning housing, the local impact of the central government's proposal to abolish the GLC, property development on behalf of 'the rich, the National Front bookstall campaign and the Police and Criminal Evidence Bill. Local participation in this leaflet was confined to the suggestion that people should take their problems to party surgeries and that they should enter the ward party 'to join us in the fight for Socialism'.

Since the National Front bookstall campaign in the summer of 1982 the ward party had rarely addressed itself to the particular grievances of the Bangladeshi population. Party leaflets discussed issues of housing, welfare and social services, pollution and employment which affected both whites and Bangladeshis, although surveys had revealed the heavier impact of material deprivation on Bangladeshi residents. The ward party tried to appeal to white and Bangladeshi residents by discussing general material problems and political policies and distributing most of its leaflets in English and Bengali. When it considered the Police and Criminal Evidence Bill in the 1984 leaflet under the heading 'Fighting Racism', it spoke of the 'liberty of ordinary people', rather than any racial or ethnic group, and its deleterious effect on relations between the police and 'the community which the police are supposed to serve'.

The campaigns advocated by the ward party between 1982 ands 1985 referred to general issues which were believed to affect local people. The pursuit of local Bangladeshi grievances was mainly directed by the ward party through its councillors' surgeries. Although an anti-racist committee had been established by the ward party during late 1984, little had been achieved by the middle of 1985. Anti-racist campaigns were organised at other levels of the party between 1982 and 1985 while the white radical leadership of the Spitalfields Labour Party grappled with the problems of co-operating with large numbers of new Bangladeshi recruits.

(C)   **THE RECRUITMENT OF NEW MEMBERS**

The leaflets distributed between 1982 and 1985 usually encouraged residents to join the party. The general election campaign during June 1983 was fought with the help of numerous Bangladeshi community workers including the Independent councillor, Nurul Huque, and the July 1983 leaflet referred to the recruitment of twenty four members during June. By the end of 1983 membership had risen to

71

over one hundred and by March 1985 the figure had increased to almost 200. Some of the new recruits were white residents, mostly young and engaged in white collar occupations across the borough and in the City of London. The majority, however, were Bangladeshi residents whose English was poor and who relied upon the mediation of a small minority of Bangladeshi community organisers at party meetings.

The appointment of a Membership Secretary at the 1982 annual general meeting of the ward party was crucial to the strategy of expanding party membership which was advocated by white opponents of Annie Elboz and Bill Harris who had controlled the ward party through their coteries of supporters. The Membership Secretary's validation of members' cards was criticised by Annie Elboz at the 1983 AGM in an abortive challenge to the new ward party leadership which ended in Annie Elboz and her few supporters walking out of the meeting. The Membership Secretary's record of membership had been approved at the higher level of the party structure and the veteran councillor was no longer in a position to pack crucial meetings with her allies.

The rapid expansion of membership, after the June 1983 general election, was mainly due to the recruitment of Bangladeshi residents by certain Bengali members who were deeply involved in Bangladeshi community activities. Applications, which had to be approved at the higher level of the GMC of the Constituency Labour Party, were sometimes the subject of much debate and tactical manoeuvring - as in the case of Bangladeshi community activist, Nurul Huque (the Independent councillor) and Rafique Ullah (an SDP candidate in the 1982 borough elections).

Soon after the borough election Nurul Huque had applied to join the ward party and his application was discussed at several monthly meetings down to November 1983, with Bangladeshi and white members both supporting and opposing the application. At the January 1983 meeting it was agreed to accept his application as long as he 'previously resigned as Independent Councillor for the Ward, thereby causing a by-election'. The offer, if accepted, would have ended Huque's career as a councillor in the short term, because he would not have been eligible as a new member to be selected by the ward party as its candidate. Nurul Huque not surprisingly rejected the offer in a detailed reply and the ward party continued to be dogged by a ward councillor who provided a focus around which other disaffected Bangladeshis could rally.

Rafique Ullah's application had to be accepted, however, despite the ward party's resolution in April 1984 that it did not 'want ex-members of members of the SDP or individuals who have stood against the Labour Party candidates to become members of Spitalfields Labour Party.' Rafique Ullah had become a member of the St. Peter's ward party and the Spitalfields Labour Party was obliged to accept his application with the proviso that the ward secretary was 'to confirm the legitimacy of (his membership) card'. [10]

Opposition to Rafique Ullah's entry into the ward party came from several active white and Bangladeshi members. White radicals claimed that Rafique Ullah was a supporter of Peter Shore and was co-operating in a campaign to ensure the MP's selection as the Constituency Labour Party's candidate for the next general election.[11] Some Bangladeshi party members had also opposed him in conflicts over the control of Bangladeshi community organisations (the FBYO, the Kobi Nazrul Centre and BENTH).[12] It was argued that Peter Shore and his supporters were taking advantage of Bangladeshi community conflicts to fight a political contest within the Constituency Labour Party. When Rafique Ullah helped to submit a list of over forty applications for ward membership in late 1984, ward leaders anticipated an attempt to oust them in the election of party officers at the approaching AGM of February 1985.

As two of the ward party radicals held the positions of chairperson and secretary at the GMC where new applications were ratified, confirmation of the applications could be delayed. The attempt, by Rafique Ullah and another community activist, Abdul Hannan, a Welfare Rights worker for the Bangladesh Welfare Association (BWA), to gain election to ward party offices was defeated, even after a successful appeal against the February meeting by the leadership's opponents had been made to the Regional Labour Party and a second election of officers had been held in April with the Regional Party Secretary in attendance.

The list of applicants submitted by Rafique Ullah to the ward party was eventually approved by the GMC after the vital February 1985 meeting. The party leadership had gained sufficient time to mobilise its own support, especially among Bangladeshi activists who could encourage Bangladeshi residents to attend specific meetings. New members were able to formulate opinions about the respective merits of individuals seeking office at AGMs, even if their views were shaped by community or personal loyalties which were dubbed 'non-political' by white party officers. Most ward party meetings were well attended by a small minority of activists who were well acquainted with the complex procedural rules guiding meetings and the wide array of business covering the many levels of the Labour movement. New members, who came to these meetings unless they were already well versed in political affairs, would find participation very difficult.

The recruitment of many Bangladeshi residents, who were not involved in community organisation, presented the white ward party activists with several problems. The barriers of language prevented white officers from getting to know the Bangladeshi newcomers since white members could not speak Sylheti dialects. Bangladeshi community organisers became vital intermediaries but, as a result, white officers depended on those organisers for information abut the newcomers and were obliged to support their Bangladeshi colleagues in conflicts with other Bangladeshi activists.

Ward party members who fought against Rafique Ullah and Abdul Hannan also claimed that the two Bengali activists were pursuing their own personal ambitions and were not loyal to the party. They justified their claim by pointing to the events which took place between April and July 1985. The death of Annie Elboz during April necessitated the holding of a by-election and after the selection of another second generation community organiser, Abbas Uddin, to represent the ward party in the contest, Abdul Hannan entered the lists as an Independent with Nurul Huque's overt support and, it was contended, also with Rafique Ullah's encouragement.

The dispute over Rafique Ullah's entry into the ward party, the new membership applications and other events leading up to the 1985 by-election could not be understood solely in terms of intra-communal conflicts between Bengali activists, however. Left-wing white leaders and their Bengali allies also argued that competition within the ward party was bound up with their opposition to the constituency's MP, Peter Shore, and his supporters. The socialist campaigning strategy of the ward party leadership was intended to convince Bangladeshi residents that the Left-wing members of the party had their interests at heart rather than Peter Shore and his supporters. Peter Shore was believed to be a popular figure among the Bangladeshi electorate and special efforts were made to appeal to Bangladeshi voters on his behalf. The previous chapter revealed the links which he had established during the 1970s with Bangladeshi entrepreneurs and community activists such as Golam Mustafa, who left the party to fight the 1982 borough election for the SDP with the ex-Labour councillor, Geoff White. Peter Shore maintained links with the BWA and addressed its members during the

1983 general election campaign. By discrediting the role of the BWA and its leadership of businessmen and elders, the ward party radicals were also attacking Peter Shore.

The relationship between Peter Shore and Bangladeshi businessmen was raised in the particular application for ward party membership by a young Sylheti entrepreneur, Abdul Latif, who ran several outlets on Brick Lane. In one of a series of Labour Briefing handbills criticising Peter Shore, the MP was accused of supporting an application by Abdul Latif to the borough council for the establishment of an amusement arcade on Brick Lane.

His application to the Spitalfields Labour Party had been rejected on the grounds that he lived outside the borough. The application was seen by party radicals as yet another sign of the attempt by their Right-wing opponents to challenge their leadership of the ward party in an area where Bangladeshi voters were believed to favour Peter Shore.

(D)   POLITICAL EDUCATION AND BLACK SECTIONS

The leaflets produced between 1982 and 1985 and local campaigns were also intended to educate new members about the political issue over which the ward party should be fighting. The failure of the Labour Party to win the general election was interpreted by Phil Maxwell, the party secretary, as underlining 'the failure of the Party to communicate its policies to the public'. He contended that:

> Labour must become a campaigning party engaged in political action designed to challenge the entrenched interests of capital and big business. Locally the party must fight around the issues of housing, unemployment, racism and the pervading poverty which underpins life in Spitalfields. We need to take our socialist message to the people and develop a broad programme of political education.

He then suggested a proposal which resulted in the campaign conference of November 1983. A ward party sub-committee should be formed, he argued, 'open to all ward members, with a brief to organise a day of political education followed by an evening social within the next 3 months'. The meeting should be 'open to members of the local community and take account of local as well as national issues'. Bangladeshi residents were a prime target for such political education and the meeting should particularly be a response 'to those who speak English as a second language'.

The campaign conference did not attract many new members of Bangladeshi residents. Most participants were white party members from various wards and a few Bangladeshi community organisers. The lack of participation by Bangladeshi residents in party affairs and tenants associations was noted at a conference a year later at the Montefiore Community Education Centre which was held by the GMC to develop a constituency party anti-racism policy. Another member of the ward party who was also secretary of the GMC, Robbie McDuff, reported from a workshop discussing black organisations in Tower Hamlets that:

> There was generally a lack of participation by ethnic groups in the Party and in TAs (Tenants Associations). Even where on paper there were members, few were active. Recruitment material and information packs in Sylheti needed to be distributed.

McDuff proceeded to draw a distinction between party political issues and non-political differences:

> There were fears that the GMC would find it difficult to deal with the contradictory positions taken by some black organisations. What was important were the political arguments, which must be distinguished from non-political differences.

The statement reflected a concern, voiced usually in informal discussions rather than in formal publications, that male Bengali activists were eager to espouse the cause of anti-racism but were not prepared to question their 'sexist' behaviour towards their female colleagues. Another source of contradiction was the loyalty to relatives and friends based upon rural ties in Sylhet. Political support could be mobilised among Bangladeshi residents not in terms of political issues but through social networks and personal loyalties.

Robbie McDuff expressed more clearly the distinction which he and other white Left-wing leaders made between political issues and personal intra-communal loyalties in an article describing the July 1985 by-election. He argued that:

> The campaign . . . has been complicated because voting intentions may not be dictated by loyalty to the Labour Party but by bonds inherent to Bengali culture.

Hannan is claiming the members of the community should vote for him because they must be loyal to the village areas with which they have family ties in Bangladesh.

The Bengali Welfare Association - the community face of businessmen and elders - is also supporting Hannan. In the past the association's tightly controlled advice and welfare work in the area has encouraged loyalty and deference in return.

These traditional and personal ties had been weakened, it was asserted, by the emergence of the ward party as a campaigner for 'the needs of the Bengali community'. The new ward party strategy was presented as developing since 1983 on account of 'significant changes with left-wing control replacing the old guard complacency'.

The distinction which Robbie McDuff made between political and non-political issues highlighted the problem encountered by white activists in approaching the Bangladeshi population. Their lack of knowledge about the population and their inability to speak Sylheti dialects or standard Bengali prevented them from acquiring a deep understanding of those whom they wished to involve in the party. They did not formally consider their limited knowledge to constitute a major problem because all party members were supposed to engage in the mainstream political debates of the Labour Party. The ward party had to engage in anti-racist campaigns and develop multi-racial practices but Bengali members, in their turn, had to engage in ideological debates about socialism and the intra-party conflicts which centred around political policies.

The interpretation of politics employed by white Left-wingers like McDuff excluded, therefore, many of the debates and personal loyalties which involved Bengali activists, both inside and outside the party. Yet in the context of intra-party conflicts Left-wingers needed the support of Bengali activists and those whom the activists could mobilise in the Bangladeshi community. White Left-wingers explained their alliances with certain Bengali party members in terms of ideological debates about socialism and party conflicts between Left and Right but, in making those alliances, white Left-wingers became implicated in the competition between Bengali community organisers and in issues which were excluded by their particular definition of what constituted politics.

White Left-wing concern about the possibility of ambitious Bangladeshi activists exploiting the institutions of the party to further their personal careers was expressed in

77

Robbie McDuff's report to the GMC anti-racism conference concerning 'black sections'. Considerable pressure had been generated in various CLPs across the country by Afro-Caribbean and South Asian members to establish a national system of special sections for black party members which would be affiliated to the party and would be represented through reserved seats on party committees. Approval for such a scheme had been rejected at the autumn 1984 national party conference and renewed pressure was again resisted at the 1985 conference, although black sections campaigners increased their support through the trade unions. [13]

Many fears had been expressed by white party leaders over the establishment of a separate black section structure within the party. White Left-wingers like Robbie McDuff did not want to alienate Bengali allies who supported the formal establishment of black sections but they wished to refer to certain dangers which the introduction of black sections might encounter. Consequently, McDuff's summary of the GMC conference discussion raised the issue of non-representative groups and individuals within ethnic groups exploiting black sections for their own advantage:

> Fears had been expressed that black sections could become the vehicle of non-representative groups. It must be ensured that Bengali comrades organised these groups. If black sections were adopted they must not be forced on the local community, but must depend on local demand. If black sections were not set up it was suggested each ward could be asked to put aside one ward delegate place for black representatives.

In spite of rebuffs at the 1984 and 1985 national conferences certain institutional reforms had been formally approved by the party during late 1985 and early 1986. A Black and Asian Advisory Committee chaired by Left-wing MP for Barking, East London, J. Richardson, was formed at NEC level and one of the members of the Spitalfields ward party, Jan Alam, joined that committee as CLP nominee. Second generation Bangladeshis like Jan Alam and Habib Ullah took the intiative in forming an Ethnic Minorities Group (EMG) within the Bethnal Green and Stepney CLP.

At the EMG's inaugural meeting in April 1986 Jan Alam, Habib Ullah and other relatively young community organisers who had recently joined the Labour Party were elected to positions on the EMG's Executive Committee by a predominantly second and third generation Bangladeshi community activist membership. The only community activist from another ethnic minority who took any significant part in the proceedings was an Afro-Caribbean teacher, who had long been involved in community relations organisations through the Tower Hamlets Commission for Racial Equality (THCRE), the Tower Hamlets Association for Racial Justice (THARJ), and, more recently in collaboration with Habib Ullah, the Tower Hamlets Association for Racial Equality (THARE). [14]

The new group, representing ethnic minority opinion at the formal level of the party structure, was controlled by the second generation Bengali community activists and their collaborators among younger members of Bangladeshi voluntary associations who were emerging from the third generation. The EMG's leaders vigorously competed with each other for the right to articulate the needs of 'their community' but they also found common cause against the representational claims of older Bengali businessmen within the party and young Bangladeshi community activists who left the party to campaign on behalf of the SDP. Two of the young SDP candidates who were contesting the May 1986 borough elections tried to attend the EMG Meeting but were asked to leave. The defeat of Bengali opponents of the Labour Party in the May 1986 elections [15] strengthened the position of the EMG leaders and their supporters as they proceeded to take over from the CLP's Anti-Racist Working Party the role of formally representing ethnic minority members within the locality.

The fears expressed by Robbie McDuff about the formation of black sections within the party appeared to have been allayed by the creation of the Ethnic Minorities Group. Bengali comrades had indeed organised the new institution and their involvement in the numerous Bangladeshi voluntary associations and local community projects was related to their claims to be representative of the largest ethnic minority in the borough. Even so, the Ethnic Minority Group was dominated by a small network of Bangladeshi community activists who were prepared to co-operate with white Left-wingers within the party. The discussion of black sections in terms of representative/non-representative groups and 'local demand' failed to convey the complexity of ethnic minority representation and alliances between white and Bengali party members which were bound up with intra-party and intra-community struggles.

79

(E)   WARD MEETINGS

Community involvement and campaigns on specific issues of local interest was part of the attempt by Left-wing activists in many urban areas of the country to establish links between the party and the local population. White radicals had learned from the community politics of Liberals which had appeared effective in generating electoral support in local government contests. Two of the leading members of the Spitalfields ward party, Robbie McDuff and Phil Maxwell, were well acquainted with the Liberal strategy in Liverpool where Liberals had enjoyed an electoral majority during the 1970s. The two ward members also understood the Left-wing response which partly entailed the production of vivid campaign materials and a 'democratic' transformation of the bureaucratic, formalistic character of the party structure. At ward party level the strategy entailed the involvement of members in activities outside monthly meetings and the greater participation of members other than the officers in ward meetings. One of the Left-wing party publications, London Labour Briefing, encouraged members to follow the example set by the GLC Labour Party's production of well designed pamphlets, its support for various minority groups (i.e. ethnic minorities, gays, women) and its association of politics with enjoyment through its arts and leisure activities. [16]

Ward meetings lasted for no more than two hours once every month. In that time minutes of the previous meeting had to be approved and matters arising from the minutes had to be discussed.   Reports were usually received from the party secretary, councillors and GMC delegates and other business dealt with the various levels of the party structure and affiliated organisations, epecially the trades unions. Sometimes speakers were invited to address members on particular topics and resolutions to the borough council and GMC, for example, had to be debated. An issue of especial interest to party members, such as the application of Nurul Huque and other Bangladeshi individuals, could take up a large period of the time available and could recur at several monthly meetings.

Most monthly meetings were attended by between fifteen and twenty-five members during 1983 and there were repeated criticisms of low attendance in various party records. The November 1984 seminar on an anti-racist policy by the party noted the poor attendance of Bangladeshi and other black members at ward meetings across the borough, and the Spitalfields ward party minutes in the same month recorded criticisms of the lack of members, in general, at the seminar and at the GMC. The minutes also reproved its delegate to SHAPRS for failing to attend SHAPRS meetings 'which meant that the Labour Party was without a voice in opposing local building developments which did not serve the needs of the local community'.

An awareness of the barriers of language between white and Bangladeshi party members led to the proposal that the previous party minutes and current party business be briefly described in Sylheti by one of the Bangladeshi members. Bangladeshi community activists filled that role and were relied on to translate campaign material between 1982 and 1985 into standard literary Bengali. Yet, since debates were held in English, only a few Bangladeshi members were able to contribute to party business and they were usually community workers.

The command of formal procedures had enabled white radicals to gain control of the ward party and they could use the complex rules governing business at all levels of the party structure in their defence. Annie Elboz's challenge at the 1983 AGM had been defeated because the Membership Secretary had kept careful records of people's payments and had ratified ward party membership through the borough party official. When Rafique Ullah's submission of new members raised the prospect of the leadership being ambushed by a block vote of new members at the 1985 AGM, Robbie McDuff held up the validation of the applications in his capacity as GMC secretary. He claimed that approval would be delayed because the electoral register was incomplete and the names submitted could not be checked in time for them to vote in the AGM. These and other tactics could be used to resist presumed attacks from opponents.

White radicals wanted to establish close ties with Bangladeshi community workers because it was they, among the increasing numbers of Bangladeshi members, who were accustomed to complex regulations and formal debates in English. The maintenance of loose alliances with certain Bangladeshi community activists embroiled white radicals in the conflicts between their Bangladeshi allies and other Bangladeshi community organisers. White radical opposition to the entry of Nurul Huque into the ward party and to the activities of Rafique Ullah and Abdul Hannan was partly caused by the hostility of some Bangladeshi activists, already in the ward party, who were engaged in disputes outside the political arena which involved the three men, directly or indirectly.

81

The alliance was a loose one because the white and Bangladeshi leaders of the ward party did not constitute a cohesive faction. They were all too busy in the variety of other activities on which they spent their time outside of ward party meetings, i.e, meetings outside day-time work at other levels of the party and across the trade union movement, the Spitalfields Local Committee, the various community organisations, meetings of school governors and visits from clients. The strategy of local campaigning also entailed designing, writing, translating, printing and distributing party leaflets. The very pressure of political and community activities prevented even the most committed party member from attending every monthly ward meeting.

Competing political ambitions and ideological differences also prevented party activists from forming a cohesive unit. Bangladeshi members were eager to gain ward party nomination for the three seats to be contested at the 1986 borough elections, and they were able to promote their own cause when Annie Elboz's death necessitated the selection of a candidate to fight the July 1985 by-election. Doubts about her chances of being re-elected to contest the 1986 elections for the ward party encouraged Sue Carlyle to accept a nomination in another ward, St. Dunstan's, during 1985. Sometimes tension arose between female white radicals and Bangladeshi male activists over the issue of sexism. Most new Bangladeshi members were males and it was male Bangladeshi community activists who engaged in the disputes described above and acted as intermediaries in ward party meetings. Although the ward party formally debated anti-racist strategies, members also referred to anti-sexist struggles and sexual liberation about which male Bangladeshi community workers had relatively little to say.

The practices of ward party meetings did not change much between 1982 and 1985 because they helped to maintain Left-wing control of the ward party and the ward party had to operate within the constraints of the party structure. The monthly meetings promoted the political education of new members, especially Bangladeshis, while the complex procedural rules and use of English (with brief summaries in Sylheti) favoured the relatively few regular white and Bangladeshi members. The ward party leadership could still be outflanked by block voting at AGMs, but the use of delaying tactics at another level of the party structure enabled that possibility to be forestalled in February 1985. The leadership's opponents also had recourse to another level of the party, the Regional Labour Party, but when the AGM was recalled in April, the leadership had been able to mobilise its own support. After these two lively, well attended meetings, the ward party reverted to the minority of regular members and officers who undertook most of the campaigning work despite their protests about the lack of widespread support from other members.

(F)   APPOINTMENTS TO PARTY OFFICES

The loose alliance between white radicals and certain Bangladeshi community workers found expression in the elections to official positions at ward and more global levels of the party.

During 1982 Bill Harris and Annie Elboz had been replaced as secretary and chairperson by two new white party members who worked closely with the recently appointed Membership Secretary. After the withdrawal of Annie Elboz and her supporters from the 1982 AGM, the twenty-two members remaining were able to elect a mixture of whites and Bangladeshis to various posts in the ward party and other sections of the Labour Party. The two Bangladeshis elected in 1982 were joined a year later by three other Bangladeshi colleagues. The increase of Bangladeshi officers was promoted by the creation of new posts: co-chairperson, assistant secretary and ethnic minorities officer. All the Bangladeshi officers were male except for Begum Khatun who briefly held the position of Ethnic Minorities Officer during 1984.

From 1982 to 1985 Bangladeshi members were elected to positions outside the ward party, i.e. to the GMC and the Executive Committee of the Constituency Labour Party and to the Local Government Committee which linked the two Constituency Labour Parties in the borough. They were also nominated to the Local Government panel from which ward parties could select their candidates for the 1986 borough election and were available for selection in local GLC and ILEA contests. [17] The first electoral success of these Bangladeshi activists, whose political careers had begun at the Spitalfields ward party, was achieved by Abbas Uddin who retained Annie Elboz's old seat in the July 1985 by-election.

Like many of the Bangladeshi activists who were supported by the white party radicals, Abbas Uddin was a second generation settler who had initially been involved in Bangladeshi youth organisations. He gained wider experience of pressure group activities by working with SHAPRS and the Bangladeshi homeless families based in bed and breakfast hotels in Finsbury Park. He had been employed by the Camden borough council as an outreach worker and helped to organise an occupation of the Camden council chamber by Bangladeshi homeless families after a fire had killed the members of one of the families in 1984. His involvement in housing issues largely affecting Bangladeshis in the ward was extended by his role as chairperson of the Spitalfields Housing Co-operative, while his youth links were strengthened by his appointment as an adviser in the City and East London Youth Service.

Abbas Uddin joined the ward party during 1982 and at the 1983 AGM he was elected as a delegate to the GMC. His work in Camden had prevented him from regularly attending ward meetings, but his appointment as a youth adviser in the borough enabled him to spend more time in the ward and during late 1984 he took a prominent part in the organisation of the November seminar on anti-racism arranged by the GMC. His support for Bangladeshi female party members was indicated by his agreement to 'investigate the possibility of booking a nursery for children of ward members to enable more women to attend meetings' in December 1984.

Abbas Uddin's competitor for the ward nomination came from another second generation settler in his thirties. Jan Alam had come to Spitalfields from Birmingham in 1982 and had been appointed as a member of the Ethnic Minorities Unit of the local DHSS office based in the Toynbee Hall premises. During 1984 he began a two year degree course at Ruskin College, Oxford, but he spent his vacation back in Spitalfields with his white wife. At the February ward 1983 AGM he was elected to the GMC and he also became a member of the Executive Committee of the new Bethnal Green and Stepney Constituency Labour Party and the Local Government Committee. He was also nominated to the Local Government Panel from which ward parties could select their candidates. Even though Jan Alam failed to gain selection for the Spitalfields by-election as the ward party's choice, he was invited to contest the St. Dunstan's ward with another Spitalfields colleague and councillor, Sue Carlyle.

The expansion of ward party posts at the 1983 AGM to help the entry of Bangladeshis into positions of responsibility had been criticised by Jan Alam on the grounds of racism. Phil Maxwell, the ward secretary, had argued in his report to the February 1984 AGM that:

> We will only gain the loyalty of the local population if we are seen to be an active campaigning party, opposing racism in an uncompromising way, and fighting for better housing, jobs, decent health care and an education system which meets the needs of the local population.

Jan Alam was absent from the AGM but immediately wrote to the ward secretary complaining about the creation of the new offices and claiming that:

> In the process we have sown the seeds of dividing the Party into two racial lines - more crudely perhaps I ought to say, we are creating once again second class status for the majority of the people of Spitalfields.

He expressed the hope that the new leadership was not repeating the mistake of the ousted party officers in being indifferent to 'the person on the street' and 'making the Party platform available to the pseudo intellectuals of the area only'.

Jan Alam touched on a problem which involved him as well. The radical white party leaders wanted Bangladeshis to gain experience in running the party at ward and more global levels, but those who possessed the requisite skills and were acceptable to white members were the articulate Bangladeshi community workers like Abbas Uddin and Alam himself. The boundaries of language and knowledge, as well as the practices of the party, provided a screen between the white leaders and the Bangladeshi 'people on the street', and Jan Alam's political career was enhanced by the role of intermediary which he and other multi-lingual Bangladeshis were able to play.

The advance of certain Bangladeshi party members was associated withh the emergence of white Left-wing leaders at ward and other levels of the party in the borough. Besides Sue Carlyle, three white members took a prominent part in ward and constituency affairs, co-operating with Left-wingers in other ward parties to develop a campaigning strategy which would involve Bangladeshis and unseat Peter Shore as the constituency MP.

Jill Cove had come to live in the ward during the 1970s and took a leading role in challenging Bill Harris and Annie Elboz, becoming chairperson of the ward party when Annie Elboz resigned during the summer of 1982. She was older than the other two radicals, Phil Maxwell and Robbie McDuff, but like them she lived in rented accommodation and was engaged in white-collar work as a probation officer. When the Bethnal Green and Stepney Constituency Labour Party was formed she was elected to the chair of the GMC and George Roberts, replaced her as ward party chairperson. During 1984 she stepped down from the post of GMC chairperson because of her duties of chairperson of her trade union's National Executive Committee. By 1985 she was confident enough to challenge Peter Shore with four other candidates for the nomination as the Constituency Labour Party's choice for the next general election.

Phil Maxwell and Robbie McDuff, like Abbas Uddin and Jan Alam, were young men engaged in white-collar occupations. They had come to the ward after experience of ward politics in Liverpool, renting a GLC flat together in East Spitalfields. Phil Maxwell replaced George Roberts as ward secretary at the 1983 AGM when Robbie McDuff was elected as ward delegate to the GMC where he came to partner Jill Cove as GMC secretary. Both Phil Maxwell and Robbie McDuff played an important role in trying to ensure that Spitalfields ward members at other levels of the party in the borough attacked the party's Right-wing and Peter Shore as the local MP.

Despite the close political links between Jill Cove, Phil Maxwell and Robbie McDuff and the ties which they maintained with other white activists such as George Roberts and Sue Carlyle, they were held together only in a loose alliance and co-operated again only on certain occasions with Left-wingers from other wards. The so-called 'Left' opposition to Peter Shore and other 'Right-wingers' at GMC level was riven by ideological divisions which helped to create considerable dissension over the correct 'socialist' policies to pursue. Jill Cove, Phil Maxwell and Robbie McDuff may have worked to unite Left-wingers in other wards around the loose party alliance of London Labour Briefing, but despite the problems of ensuring collective action within even that broad alliance, they had also to collaborate with other Left-wingers who owed allegiance to different alliances or groups. Socialist Organiser, Militant Tendency, the Campaign for Labour Party Democracy (CLPD) and the LCC Left-wingers could be mobilised around an electoral slate at the AGMs of the GMC, for example, but Left-wingers elected to party office could then be criticised for their involvement in decisions which other Left-wingers disliked.

Yet the evidence from the Spitalfields ward suggested that other factors had to be borne in mind. Close co-operation among Left-wingers at ward level was hampered by the diverse involvements of activists in a variety of political and community organisations. The burden of work entailed by such activities made it difficult for Left-wingers to meet together outside of certain meetings unless they were linked together by informal ties. All party activists, whether 'Right' or 'Left', were caught up in a variety of levels, organisations and practices which gave the party not only a certain unity but also considerable diversity. Moreover, each level had its

86

own particular practices and business which prevented the local ward party from simply reflecting the will of more global levels culminating in the national centre of party power.

NOTES

[1] See Appendix for the election result. The by-election and other local elections involving Bangladeshi activists between 1982 and 1986 have also been discussed in my article. 'The political representation of a South Asian minority in a working class area: the Bangladeshi community in Tower Hamlets, East London', South Asia Research. vol. 7, no. 1, May 1987.

[2] London Labour Briefing was a loose alliance of Left-wing activists which regularly met at the GLC County Hall while a local Briefing group met in Labour Party rooms at Bethnal Green. Briefing was more influential than Militant Tendency, while the main political protagonist of the Socialist Organiser in the borough council was Sue Carlyle. See Webster, P., 'Why Shore must make a stand - if he is to stand again', The Times, 1 August, 1984, p.12.

[3] The loss of a by-election during 1984 after one of the nine rebel councillors resigned his seat increased Liberal representation to 19. Webster claimed that 'As Labour has raged, the Liberals have profited. From a 10.8 per cent share of the borough election vote in 1978, they achieved 40.1 per cent in 1982, and now hold 18 of the 50 seats to Labour's 30. A Liberal council in 1986 is a distinct possibility'. Ibid.

[4] The Tower Hamlets Labour Party was broken up, therefore, but the two CLPs were linked together by a borough Local Government Committee which became responsible for the panel from which party candidates were chosen to contest the 1986 borough elections.

[5] The main threat from the Liberals was defeated in both new constituencies, although the Liberal share of the vote increased significantly. In the two seats the Labour party's share fell by 6.2% form 56.5% to 50.3%, while the Liberal share rose from 14.9% in 1979 to 30.9%. The Conservative vote fell from 20.3% to 15%. See Bethnal Green and Stepney CLP, Election Agent's Report: General Election, 9 June, 1983.

[6] ELWAR or the East London War Against Racism group contested the 1981 GLC election in Bethnal Green and Bow but its candidate, Fran Eden, gained only 211 votes. The group did not fight the 1983 general election in the borough.

[7]   The GLC representatives were Ken Livingstone, Sir A. Bramall, P. Boateng (Chair of Police Committee) and T. McBrearty (Chair of Housing Committee).

[8]   This Committee was eventually composed of eight Labour and four Liberal councillors.

[9]   MP for Bolsover and closely associated with Militant Tendency according to Forester, T., 'The Labour Party's Militant moles', New Society, 10 Jan. 1980, p.53.

[10]   See Spitalfields Labour Party minutes, Nov. 1984.

[11]   The reselection process was to begin after the March 1985 AGM of the GMC. However, disputes over ward AGMs in Spitalfields and other wards prevented the AGM from taking place and giving both sides time to muster their forces.

[12]   Abbas Uddin, who was nominated to fight the 1985 ward by-election, Riaz, who had also been nominated to the Local Government panel together with Jan Alam, prospective candidate for St. Dunstan's ward, were just three opposed to R. Ullah in those disputes.

[13]   Chris Kamis, a member of the Black Sections National Committee whose establishment had caused considerable controversy within the party leadership, claimed that the conference 'marked a big step forward for the Black Sections movement. We trebled our vote over last year's total to almost 1.2 million. As well as the NUM, two other large unions voted with us: NUPE and NUR'. London Labour Briefing, no.54, Nov. 1985, p.4.

[14]   A discussion of these three borough-level community organisations will be provided in the following chapter.

[15]   See Appendix for the election results.

[16]   See for example, Tate, C., 'Images of Socialism', London Labour Briefing. no.31, July 1983, and no.41, July 1984.

[17]   The ILEA elections were to be held at the same time as the borough council elections in 1986. The borough was split into two ILEA constituencies, each returning two members in 1986 (in subsequent elections only one would be returned from each constituency). During late 1985 competition for selection of party nominees began to develop - selection of a least one Bangladeshi candidate in either constituency appeared likely but in the event this did not occur.

4 The GLC, the borough council and Bangladeshi representation

(A) **INTRODUCTION**

After the 1981 GLC election, Left-wing members of the Labour Party in Tower Hamlets were encouraged in their strategy of appealing to the Bangladeshi community by the initiatives of the new Labour Majority Group leadership at County Hall. The GLC Majority Group leader, Ken Livingstone, was closely associated with the formation of a new council committee, the Ethnic Minorities Committee (EMC), and an administrative support group servicing the new committee called the Ethnic Minorities Unit. The EMC was able to allocate funds directly to local community groups and, in its first year of operation, 1982/83, the FBYO and the BYA were the first Bangladeshi organisations in Tower Hamlets to benefit from the EMC grants. Other GLC committees also gave financial support to Bangladeshi and other ethnic minority groups from 1982 onwards, viz. the Arts and Recreation Committee and Women's Committee. Spitalfields organisations serving a largely Bangladeshi clientele also enjoyed GLC funding - the Spitalfields Small Businesses Association, the Tower Hamlets Training Forum and SHAPRS.

During 1983 the organisational changes and funding of local projects were supplemented by two other GLC initiatives. A Race and Housing Action Team (RHAT) was established in the District Housing Office and included a mixture of white, Bangladeshi and other ethnic minority members. Although the GLC had handed over its housing stock to local boroughs, the transfer of its responsibility to the Tower Hamlets borough council was not to be completed until 1985. Consequently, the GLC still controlled over half the council housing in the borough, while, in Spitalfields, most of the council accommodation was the GLC's responsibility. The Race and Housing Action Team was expected to strive for greater equality and security for ethnic minorities in GLC housing across the borough at a time of swingeing reductions in housing resources and outbreaks of violence on council estates, where Bangladeshi were the principal victims.

The other GLC initiative during 1983, which affected local community groups, was the incorporation of Spitalfields into its Community Areas Policy. The GLC still retained a strategic role in planning and urban development, and its Planning Committee tried to protect various areas in a ring around central London from the perceived adverse effects of office expansion and commercial development. The declaration of Spitalfields as a GLC community area encouraged the resistance of local groups, i.e. the Spitalfields Local Committee and SHAPRS, to office development and to the proposed Tower Hamlets Borough Plan, published and publicly debated during 1983-4. Community groups were also able to apply for funding to the GLC Planning Committee through the Community Areas Policy under certain criteria. [1]

Bangladeshi and other local organisations were encouraged to apply for funding during 1983 from the virtually autonomous Education Committee of ILEA through its Tower Hamlets Initiative, which was originally designed to extend until 1985. The GLC also became involved during 1984, together with the Tower Hamlets borough council and the DoE, in the funding of an Inner Area Programme for the areas including Spitalfields outside the southern wards which had been incorporated within the LDDC area. Approximately £6,000,000 a year was primarily intended to be spent on 'capital' or one-off projects (such as buying land or buildings, buying equipment, furniture or vehicles)' although during the second year of the scheme greater allowance was made for the funding of salaries and community schemes. [2] Once again, local community groups benefitted financially from the Programme, with the FBYO playing a prominent representational role among Bangladeshi community organisations.

These various funding projects were combined by the GLC with organisational changes and publicity initiatives - the conferences with ethnic minority representatives, the 'Anti-Racist Year' campaign of 1984 and the production of extensive written material, for example. They constituted a vital component of a Left-wing political strategy which entailed the establishment of an alliance with ethnic minority community organisations in confrontation with the Conservative central government. The strategy was publicised by contributors to London Labour Briefing and encouraged Briefing supporters in Tower Hamlets and the Spitalfields Labour Party specifically.

Although Ken Livingstone's refusal in 1985 to join with other Labour-controlled councils in defying the central government's restrictions on local government expenditure alienated other Left-wingers and contributors to London Labour Briefing,[3] Left-wing activists in Tower Hamlets, however, were encouraged by GLC initiatives to pursue their struggle with the borough's Majority Group leadership. Despite the borough council's support for local community groups in Spitalfields, for example, through the Spitalfields Urban Programme and the Inner Areas Programme, the borough's Majority Group leadership could be made to look tardy and niggardly in its support for ethnic minorities and other groups represented by local organisations.

The following account will describe the attempts by the Tower Hamlets Majority Group to introduce organisational changes concerning the representation of ethnic minorities at borough level. Its initiatives were related to the GLC's policies since 1981 and to the changes brought about by other boroughs in the metropolis, especially those controlled by the Labour Party. The proposals of the borough's political leaders and senior administrative officials were also affected by the strategies of other councillors and community organisers. The issue of 'race relations' and ethnic minority groups was fought out in conflicts at the level of council committees and administrative units, on the one hand, and at the level of community organisations, on the other. Each level contained certain practices particular to the institutions operating at that level. These practices imposed constraints on attempts to articulate ethnic minority opinion at borough level. They also helped to prevent the establishment of anything more than a tentative alliance between the Left-wing critics of the Majority Group leadership and those representing ethnic minorities through a borough-wide institution.

(B) RACE RELATIONS AND INSTITUTIONAL CHANGES, 1980 - 85

(i) Suggested reforms, 1980-82

A Working Party on Race Relations was established by the central unit of the council political structure, the Policy Committee, during the summer of 1980. The Working Party consisted of administrative officers from the various departments at the borough council, as well as a representative from the borough Trades Council and the Commission for Racial Equality (CRE). In its first report to the Policy Sub-Committee a year later, the Working Party referred to the problem of ethnic minority representation -

> The Working Party agreed that it could not operate effectively without its membership including representatives of ethnic minorities, and therefore, it has made arrangements for ethnic minority groups to nominate four members of the Working Party. Because of present uncertainties affecting certain of the ethnic minority organisations in the Borough, difficulties were experienced in deciding the numbers of minority representatives and which organisations should be invited to nominate them. [4]

The Working Party then turned to the future arrangement of ethnic minority representation at borough level. It suggested the formation of a Joint Consultative Committee (JCC) 'involving members of the Council and representatives of ethnic minority groups, either individually or via the local Community Relations Council'.[5] Descriptions of existing JCCs in five London boroughs were provided, and it was noted that 'three out of the five examples involve ethnic minority representation via the local CRC as well, or instead of, directly from minority organisations'. [6]

References to the local Community Relations Council suggested a preference for the representation of ethnic minority groups at borough level through the Commission of Racial Equality (CRE), whose national representative contributed to the Working Party's first report. However, the borough's CRC office, the Tower Hamlets Commission for Racial Equality (THCRE), based in premises next to the Montefiore Community Education Centre in East Spitalfields, had signally failed to engage the support of Bangladeshi community organisations. During 1979 the Tower Hamlets Association for Racial Justice (THARJ) had been founded to carry out tasks which its leaders believed the local CRC had ignored.

92

In the Working Party's second report the problems caused by this rift were recognised through a paper submitted by the borough Trades Council which the Working Party endorsed. As a result a review of the situation was undertaken by senior officers from the borough council and ILEA. Their findings were submitted in the Stebbings Report, which was sent to the Policy Committee in September 1982. The Report commented on the various divisions in community representation by observing that:

In evidence we have heard the following:

(a) THCRE is an exclusive organisation dominated by Caribbeans with the implication that others, particularly Bangladeshis, may take second place;

(b) THARJ is white dominated and has a bias in favour of Bangladeshis;

(c) The Bangladeshis feel that they can fit in perfectly well without recourse to either the THCRE or THARJ. The Bangladesh Welfare Association claims to be much longer standing than either of the other two bodies and to be more effective at looking after the welfare of Bangladeshis.

With the great weight of numbers of Bangladeshis and Caribbeans the smaller ethnic groups are inclined to be overlooked in discussion. [7]

The writers of the Stebbings Report suggested various ways in which the THCRE and THARJ could proceed, but they also declared in their conclusion that:

. . . the problems they have been asked to consider will not be resolved unless a critical eye is regularly passed over LBTH, ILEA and the CRE. The responsibility for promoting good race relations within the Borough must of necessity be primarily their's, central government is too remote. The many race relations bodies, including THCRE and THARJ, upon whom so much for good race relations must depend, are too diverse to accept primary responsibility. Race relations is, in the opinion of the Review Group, so significant an issue for the well-being of all citizens of the Borough, that they feel LBTH might consider grasping co-ordinating responsibility and appointing a senior officer with the necessary qualifications and experience to be responsible for co-ordination directly to the Chief Executive of the Borough. [8]

By September 1982, four months after the May borough council elections, three major organisational changes had been recommended to the central Policy Committee and its chairman, Paul Beasley. The Working Party on Race Relations had suggested the creation of a Joint Consultative Committee (JCC), while the Stebbings Report had considered the problems of creating a unified race relations body which would represent local ethnic minorities at the JCC. The Stebbings Report had also advocated the appointment of a senior official to co-ordinate the representation of race relations issues within the borough's administrative apparatus.

The three reforms were influenced, to some extent, by changes in other London boroughs, as the references to Haringey, Kensington and Chelsea, Islington, Brent and Lewisham indicated. The closest model appears to be Haringey, since it already possessed an Ethnic Minorities Joint Consultative Committee, which was serviced by a Race Relations and Ethnic Adviser and was composed of council committee chairmen, other councillors, nominees from the local CRC and representatives of ethnic minority groups. [9] The JCC proposed by the Working Party in its Fourth Report (13 October 1981) was designed to fit into the political structure dominated by the Majority Group leadership. The JCC would be chaired by the Leader of the Council and would report to the Policy Committee which the Leader also chaired. Six JCC Members would represent the borough, six would represent ethnic minority groups and three would come from the trades unions 'representing officers, craft and manual employees respectively'. [10] A subsequent report from the Policy Sub-Committee revealed its determination to prevent the possibility of councillors' wishes being over-ruled in the JCC -

> . . . recommendations from the JCC should only go forward for consideration by the Policy Committee where such recommendation is supported by a majority of London Borough of Tower Hamlets representatives. [11]

The Working Party believed that a JCC which fitted into the existing committee structure and Majority Group leadership had two major advantages -

(a)   an improved two way communication between the Council and ethnic minority groups, giving speedier and better identification and articulation of matters of concern and an opportunity to 'sell' solutions which are practical within the Council's financial and other resources.

94

(b)   a better relationship between the Council and
ethnic minorities, arising both from the Council
being seen to consult members of those
minorities, and from the greater responsiveness
of the Council's services to minority needs which
should arise from improved consultation linked
to an effective Race Relations Working Party to
oversee detailed implementation and monitoring.
[12]

The representational and consultative role of the JCC
would be strengthened by its activities as an overseer of the
detailed implementation and monitoring of schemes approved
at the political level of the council committee structure.
The recommendation by the Stebbings Report that a senior
official be appointed to co-ordinate responsibility for race
relations in the borough paved the way for the servicing of
the proposed JCC by an administrative officer with a
particular brief as in Haringey.

(ii)   Political conflict and the creation of the Ethnic
Minorities Committee, 1982-3

After the May 1982 borough elections Left-wing
councillors joined with the Liberal opposition and Nurul
Huque, the Independent member, in a series of disputes which
included the proposals for a JCC. The Left-wingers were
opposed to a plan which gave the Policy Committee direct
control over the political representation of race relations in
the borough. They were encouraged by the example of
another Labour-controlled authority, the GLC, which had
established during 1981-82 a separate Ethnic Minorities
Committee (EMC) supported by an Ethnic Minorities Unit.
Between May 1982 and October 1983 they pressed for the
formation of a borough EMC which would not be dominated
by the Majority Group leadership. Their pressure was part of
an attempt to establish other committees free from Majority
Group leaders' control, i.e. the Housing and Police
Committees, and they allied temporarily with Liberals who
also wanted greater representation on council committees.

After the May 1982 borough election the Majority
Group leadership was obliged to include Liberal councillors on
council committees, although it retained control of the key
committee posts of chairman and vice-chairman. Since the
central unit, the Policy Committee, was composed mainly of
the chairmen of the other committees and was chaired by the
Majority Group leader, the challenge from the leadership's
opponents, both inside and outside the Majority Group, was
strictly limited. Although the creation of the Police Com-

95

mittee under Left-wing pressure ensured the entry of its young radical chairman into the Policy Committee, he was a lone figure and could be compromised in the eyes of his Left-wing colleagues by his participation in Policy Committee decisions.

The Policy Committee had been chaired continuously since 1974 by Paul Beasley. When he resigned as Majority Group leader in 1984 he was replaced as Policy Committee chairman and Group leader by John Riley, who had become a councillor just two years before Beasley, and had been vice-chairman of the Policy Committee between 1974 and 1976 and again from 1978 to 1984. Beasley and Riley were joined in the Policy Committee by a close-knit group of Labour councillors whose average length of service as councillors was over 18 years, while five had served for more than 20 years by the end of 1985.

These Labour councillors worked intimately with senior officers who were similarly long established in borough service. The most senior official, the Chief Executive (Jack Wolkind) also resigned during 1984 after almost 50 years' service in local council posts. Wolkind had been Deputy Town Clerk and Solicitor to the Stepney Borough Council before the creation of Tower Hamlets where he became Town Clerk and later Chief Executive. He was replaced by a man who first worked for the Bethnal Green borough council in 1948 and had headed the Tower Hamlets Directorate of Finance since 1973. Similar long service in the borough was evident among senior officers, whose activities were co-ordinated by the Chief Executive through a Management Team. The Team met regularly to discuss business being handled by the borough's six directorates and the central office of the borough administration, the Secretariat. The Chief Executive and his senior colleagues also consulted senior councillors before committee and full council meetings, while senior councillors of the Majority Group met other members of the Majority Group to co-ordinate policy before full council meetings.

This integrated system of decision-making was threatened by political pressure from both inside and outside the Majority Group between 1982 and 1985. Yet despite the much publicised refusals by Labour 'rebel' councillors to obey Majority Group orders and certain defeats in full council debates, long established councillors in the Majority Group still chaired most council committees and maintained close contact with senior officials. Left-wing Labour and Liberal avoided co-operating too closely for political reasons, and the Majority Group leadership could exploit the political divisions between their opponents. The only way in which the Group leaders could be made to abandon their control of the key

96

institutions at the political level was to force them to retire or to ensure their de-selection at ward party level. During 1985 resignations and de-selections did indeed appear to be ensuring the return of a new leadership at the 1986 borough elections.

During October 1982 the nine Labour 'rebels' joined with Liberal councillors and Nurul Huque in a full council vote to establish a Housing Committee. Three of the Labour councillors indicated, in a letter to the East London Advertiser, that their vote was part of a campaign which included the introduction of an Ethnic Minorities Committee. The establishment of the EMC took almost another year, since it did not hold its first meeting until August 1983. Its membership demonstrated that the Majority Group leadership still retained the initiative, even in a committee which had been campaigned for by Left-wing councillors and which replaced the proposed JCC.

Four members of the Majority Group leadership were ex-officio members of the EMC, as in all other committees. The person who was elected chairman was also a long-standing Majority Group councillor, and he could count on the support of another Labour councillor who had served on the council since 1968. Four of the nine 'rebels' were appointed to the new committee, but one of them, Ashik Ali (the first Labour Bangladeshi councillor), became vice-chairman and worked closely with the chairman in arranging the business of committee meetings and consulting with senior administrative officials. The leader of the Liberal 'Minority Party' was an ex-officio member, three Liberals were ordinary members, and the list was completed by the sole Bangladeshi Independent, Nurul Huque. Spitalfields ward was represented, therefore, by Nurul Huque and another of the 'rebel' Labour councillors, Sue Carlyle.

The possibility of 'rebel' Labour members dominating the committee was made remote by the interweaving of various loyalties between the members. Left-wing domination was also made less likely because of the initiative which the chairmen and vice-chairmen enjoyed through their collaboration with each other and with senior officers and through the chairman's attendance at Policy Committee meetings.

The EMC's powers were restricted to the consultative and representational role outlined in the Working Party on Race Relations' earlier recommendations concerning a JCC. It had a minute budget of its own to administer unlike the big-spending Social Services, Housing, Works, Amenities and Administration Committees. [13] Its Orders of Reference included a clause which outlined its duty -

97

To formulate, promote, implement, co-ordinate, monitor and recommend to other Standing Committees of the Council policies and practices designed to achieve good race relations and racial equality. [14]

However, the EMC had no powers to force other committees to agree with its proposals as well as very little revenue to pursue schemes of its own devising. Its activities under Clause 2 of its Orders of Reference could be interpreted by other committees as an unwelcome intrusion into their afffairs. It soon became clear that race relations and the affairs of ethnic minorities were not the sole preserve of the EMC.

(iii)   Ethnic monitoring

The limited ability of the EMC to pursue its Orders of Rerference was quickly exposed by its advocacy of ethnic monitoring - an issue espoused by Left-wingers in the GLC and other London boroughs. The issue had been touched on right at the beginning of the Working Party on Race Relations' deliberations in 1980. It had been discussed more fully in the Working Party's fourth report in July 1981, where race relations were linked to equal opportunities. In its discussion of the proposed JCC's terms of reference, the Working Party argued that they should be similar to those of the Working Party with the major exception that:

. . . when the Council's Equal Opportunities Policy is implemented the JCC be responsible for monitoring and examination of the Policy, and thus, in addition to its responsibilities for Race Relations in relation to residents and workers in the Borough, have an Equal Opportunities responsibility in relation to the Council's employees. The Working Party recognised that Race Relations and Equal Opportunities represent two distinct areas of work, one mainly with Ethnic Minority representatives and the other mainly with Trade Union representatives of the Council's employees and that a strong case can be made for separate bodies to deal with them. The reasons which the Working Party felt out-weighed these considerations were:

(1)   There are important areas of overlap between the two.

These include -

98

- ethnic record keeping
- recruitment of ethnic minority staff
- positive discrimination towards ethnic minority staff
- recruitment of staff speaking ethnic minority languages
- training for staff dealing with ethnic minorities. [15]

The Working Party's statement on the relationship between race relations and equal opportunities in July 1981 was part of a protracted debate over the advisability of introducing ethnic record keeping, which involved various council committees between 1981 and 1985. The Administration Committee, which was responsible for council staffing matters, staunchly resisted pressure from the Working Party, the Social Services Committee and, later, the EMC to accept the practice, and the issue was handed over to the Policy Committee for lengthy deliberation during 1984. The GLC's advocacy of ethnic record keeping, in its much publicised campaigns over equal opportunities and anti-racism between 1981 and 1985, encouraged Left-wing borough councillors to criticise the Majority Group leadership for failing to commit itself unequivocally to the introduction of the practice.

The Working Party had attempted to include the monitoring of council employment in its terms of reference well before the July 1981 statement. Its first report in November 1980 suggested that it should 'examine and monitor the Council's personnel and management policies vis-a-vis its own staff', [16] but the Policy Committee dismissed the suggestion on the grounds that 'this was already a function of the Chief Executive and the Head of Personnel and Management Services'. [17] When the Working Party reiterated its interest in council employment through its July 1981 statement, the Policy Committee used the delaying tactic of deferring the controversial aspects of the statement 'for further consideration' by its sub-committee. [18]

The Working Party returned to the charge when the Administration Committee adopted an Equal Opportunities in Employment Policy Statement during November 1981 at the same time as the GLC issued a similar statement. The Policy Statement included a commitment to 'the maintenance of ethnic records of the workforce', [19] but the Administration Committee sidestepped the recommendations by asking the Working Party for confirmation 'that ethnic minorities accept the recommendation that ethnic records be created and maintained'.[20] The Working Party replied with the assertion tat 'the Equal Opportunities Policy can only adequately be monitored and its effectiveness gauged if records of ethnic

99

origin are kept'. [21] It advocated the adoption of a system of self-classification recommended by the CRE, but in December 1981 the Administration Committee again rejected the Working Party proposal.

In a confidential report to the Administration Committee during September 1981 the Chief Executive accepted the assertion made by the Working Party. He argued that 'without a system of ethnic record' it would not be possible 'for the Council to demonstrate its commitment to equal opportunities or to identify with precision and authority any area where action may need to be taken'. [22] He also added cautiously:

> Certainly the minority group representatives on the Race Relations Working Party are disappointed at what is, perhaps, interpreted as lack of commitment to the policy. [23]

The Chief Executive also noted the problems other committees were facing through the absence of ethnic monitoring and record keeping:

> On a more practical note, since the publication of the policy, there has been an increase in requests for information dependent on a knowledge of the ethnic composition of the workforce. In particular, the Policy Committee has asked for information on 'the low level of ethnic minority recruitment' and recommendations on what 'measures can be taken to improve matters'. The Committee will appreciate that, at the present time, it is impossible authoritatively to confirm or deny that there is a low level of ethnic minority recruitment. [24]

Despite the Chief Executive's comment the Administration Committee again refused to accept ethnic record keeping in September 1982, and the EMC came into being during August 1983 with the issue still dead-locked.

The EMC's Orders of Reference carried forward the Working Party's concern for council employment and ethnic minority representation. Clauses 3 and 4 committed the EMC -

> 3   To request the Administration Committee to investigate and report on employment practices of the Council or any of its departments, where areas of concern have been identified.

4   To request Service Committees to investigate and report on service delivery by the Council or any of its departments where concern has arisen regarding facilities for ethnic minorities. [25]

The issue of ethnic records came before the EMC in a confidential report from the Chief Executive at its first ordinary meeting in September 1983. The Policy Committee in June had consulted all the other committees about the issue, but all except the Social Services Committee had sidestepped the matter by waiting for the EMC's recommendations.

The Social Services Committee produced a report which noted the duty of local authorities under the 1976 Race Relations Act 'to eliminate unlawful discrimination and to promote equality of opportunity and good race relations'. [26] On the specific issue of ethnic records the report observed the CRE'S support for the maintenance of ethnic records and explained its own need for such information -

Although the Social Services Committee provides services on the basis of need without reference to race or colour, it could not defend itself against accusations of indirect discrimination resulting unintentionally from its policies, or the criteria used in the allocation of services, without maintaining records of the ethnic origin of service users. [27]

The report proceeded to comment more generally that:

The case for monitoring is simply that in a society which subscribes to equal opportunities, and in which services are distributed on the basis of need, it is important to assess the needs of the community and to monitor the working of local authority provision to ensure that need and service correspond. [28]

It also referred to what it considered to be a major obstacle to the adoption of the practice :

The basic fear underlying many objections to record keeping is that information collected for one purpose may be used for another. The scrupulous observation of rules of confidentiality, a clear statement about the purpose of record keeping, prior discussion with representative ethnic organisation and voluntary compliance with record keeping are the necessary conditions which should govern the introduction of records of ethnic origin. [29]

The Social Services Committee's enthusiasm over ethnic record keeping was not shared by other committees besides the Administration Committee, according to the October 1983 confidential report by the Chief Executive to the EMC. The Housing Management, Amenities and Development Committees had deferred consideration of the issue while the EMC formulated an opinion, and the Works and the Health and Consumer Services Committees 'felt unable to express a view on the matter'. [30] The Finance Committee, like the Administration Committee, simply rejected the proposal without any reported justification of its decision.   The only other committee which supported the general principle of ethnic record keeping was the Police Committee. Even so, this committee declared:

> Strong reservations concerning the civil liberty implications which precluded it from endorsing the practice of ethnic record keeping until it had considered the precise form which such a procedure would take and was satisfied that it met the needs of the Police Committee. [31]

Resistance to calls for ethnic record keeping in the borough council could be used by critics of the Majority Group leadership to support their charges of 'racism' against senior Labour councillors, especially those in the Administration and Finance Committees.   However, the cautionary remarks of the Police Committee, which was not popularly associated with the Group leadership, suggested the greater complexity of the issue.   The Social Services Committee's report had recognised the concern about the uses to which information could be put and, in the past, attempts to include questions concerning ethnic background in national surveys had been fiercely opposed by minority pressure groups.

The EMC decided to move carefully over the issue, given the problems raised by the proposal to introduce ethnic record keeping.   It gathered information through administrative officials of existing practice in other London boroughs, while officials also discussed among themselves how ethnic record keeping could be implemented. After the production of reports in late 1983, the matter was again referred to the Policy Committee, which had still not taken a decision by early 1985 when the Chief Executive raised the issue again with the Administration Committee.   The Chief Executive's report to the Administration Committee indicated the increasing difficulty caused for officials and the Policy Committee by the absence of ethnic records, but his appeal fell on deaf ears.

Despite the repeated failure of recommendations by the EMC to other committees, the EMC decided at the beginning of 1985 to continue the momentum established at a Public Sector Employment Workshop with senior officials held in November 1984. It sent recommendations to the Policy Committee on ethnic monitoring, ethnic record keeping and employment targets for ethnic minorities. [32] These recommendations were combined in a submission to the Administration Committee concerning racial discrimination and Section 11 posts, while another submission was made to the Finance Committee concerning contract work arranged by that committee. Once again the EMC linked its efforts on behalf of ethnic minorities with the council's equal opportunity policies, commenting pointedly that 'the adoption and implementation of equal opportunity policies throughout the Council's service areas depended on the political will of Members of the Council'. [33] The appeals to the Policy, Administration and Finance Committees implied a test of that political will by the EMC.

During July 1985 the Policy Sub-Committee finally agreed in principle to introduce ethnic record keeping and monitoring in the areas of social services and housing. The transfer of GLC housing stock during 1985 to the borough council raised the issue of whether the borough would continue the GLC practice of maintaining ethnic records for housing applicants. The borough's Director of Housing had argued forcefully for the continuation of the practice in September 1984, and his argument was supported by a report from the Chief Executive's Management Team in July 1985. The report discussed certain problems, viz. the difficulty 'in determining the extent to which records should be kept' and the evidence that in other boroughs 'attempts to introduce ethnic monitoring have resulted in staff refusal to co-operate'. [34] Yet the advantages were also outlined, for example -

- such record keeping would highlight imbalances in recruitment and training policies.
- record keeping in Social Services Directorate was an essential requirement especially in relation to back up evidence in support of Section 11 funding following recent changes in Government requirements.
- record keeping and monitoring was essential insofar as it enabled the determination of special requirements of individual groups and minorities such as handicapped and disabled as well as meals-on-wheels requirements for different religious groups . . .

103

- ethnic minority recording could improve current information regarding the racial infrastructure of the Borough. [35]

The Management Team rested its case not just on the need to satisfy local ethnic minority groups. It drew attention to the pressure of central government changes in funding regulations, to the needs of handicapped and disabled people and to the provision of meals-on-wheels which serviced the elderly Jewish population for example. The report appeared to present a rational, balanced consideration of the advantages and disadvantages of ethnic monitoring, which looked beyond the borough to other local authorities and central government. It concluded that the Team was 'generally in favour of maintaining ethnic records and felt that this was an inevitable necessity'. [36] The Team sugggested that 'a pilot exercise should be undertaken within the Housing and Social Services Directorates - with a view to determining the extent of record keeping and the problems of such an exercise'. [37]

The Management Team's proposal was approved by the Policy Sub-Committee, and by early 1986 the pilot exercise was well under way. The extension of ethnic record keeping and monitoring to the borough's own employment practices proved more intractable, however. An administrative working party had been formed in February 1984 'to review the Council's personnel procedures in the light of the Equal Opportunities Policy' [38] and the Senior Race Relations Adviser had been included in its deliberations. The working party formally recognised the importance of the Code of Practice published by the CRE during April 1984, as well as the CRE's investigation of the Hackney borough council's provision of housing to ethnic minorities which was published in January 1985. [39]

The working party had still not completed its report by October 1985 when the EMC considered the CRE's annual report. At that EMC meeting reference was made to the desire of certain members 'of the ethnic minority community' to introduce a similar investigation by the CRE of 'Tower Hamlets Council in aspects of service delivery, particularly housing'.[40] The EMC was advised by the Chief Executive, at the end of 1985, that the working party's report was in draft form and would soon be sent to the Council and Staff (Officers) Joint Committee. The EMC, however, had already tried to exert its own pressure by asking senior officers 'for their written comments on the various employment practices adopted throughout the Council's service areas to enable the Committee to consider whether it was acting in accordance with its terms of reference'.[41] Pressure was also to be exerted specifically on the Administration Committee through the Chief Executive's recommendation that the EMC reconsidered 'the implications of the Council adopting the CRE Code of Practice as a means of eliminating racial discrimination in employment and to make appropriate recommendations to the Administration Committee'.[42]

By the beginning of 1986 there had been some change over the issue of ethnic record keeping and monitoring. Unlike the GLC the borough's political leadership had not flung its support behind the introduction of practices intended to combat racial discrimination and to promote equal opportunities in housing, social services and council employment, for example. The changes proposed by the EMC had become the focus of struggle within the Majority Group between senior councillors and Left-wing 'rebels'. The conflict was made more complicated by the role of Liberal councillors and the Independent councillor from Spitalfields, Nurul Huque, who claimed to represent Bangladeshi interests.

These political differences were bound up with the particular concerns of different committees and with the rivalries between them which could not be explained solely in terms of party political conflicts. Despite the central authority of the Policy Committee, the Administration Committee was able to reject repeated appeals to approve ethnic record keeping between 1981 and 1985, even when the inefficiencies caused by the lack of information were pointed out by the Chief Executive.

The agreement, in principle, to introduce ethnic record keeping and monitoring during 1985 and the establishment of pilot projects on social services and housing provision suggested that the Policy Committee had been swayed more by external than internal pressures. The transfer of GLC housing responsibilities to the borough, the changing of central government regulations and the activities of the CRE all helped the Chief Executive to argue that ethnic records were 'an inevitable necessity'.[43] No change had been made over the monitoring of council employment by early 1986, but the lengthy deliberations of the officer working party and the recommendations by the EMC to the Administration Committee were also supported by the influence of external pressures, particularly from the CRE.

(C) **REPRESENTATIONS OF ETHNIC MINORITY GROUPS OUTSIDE THE COUNCIL COMMITTEE SYSTEM**

(i) The creation of the Tower Hamlets Association for Racial Equality (THARE), 1984

During 1983 and 1984 not only was the Ethnic Minorities Committee founded, but also a Senior Race

Relations Adviser was appointed to service the new committee and united race relations organisation was established after lengthy discussions with THCRE and THARJ. The two changes were designed to establish links between the EMC and the council administration, on the one hand, and the local ethnic groups, on the other. The creation of the new representational organisation, the Tower Hamlets Association for Racial Equality (THARE) and its activities will be discussed in detail, so that the relationship can be explored between the levels of the council committee system and local pressure groups.

Conflicts at council level were fought out in terms of committee and administrative practices, but the issues under discussion involved groups outside the political and administrative structure of the borough council. Attempts to reach out to local community groups were partly constrained by the conflicts and the practices particular to those groups. Like the borough council itself, the new borough race relations organisation, THARE, was not a neatly co-ordinated unit with a united voice, even though certain officers held the initiative on many occasions. As a result the image projected in official documents of one body speaking to another was often well wide of the mark.

The Stebbings Report, which was submitted to the Policy Committee during September 1982, had suggested various ways in which the two borough groups, THCRE and THARJ, could operate in the future. Nevertheless, the Report clearly favoured the establishment of a united ethnic minority organisation, which would represent ethnic groups to the borough council. By August 1983 the negotiations between THCRE and THARJ were still continuing, and so the new Ethnic Minorities Committee was drawn into the arena, establishing a working party of councillors to help the proceedings along. By June 1984 THCRE and THARJ agreed to form a new institution, the Tower Hamlets Association for Racial Equality (THARE). THARE's inaugural general meeting was held in July 1984 at the Robert Montefiore Secondary School, East Spitalfields, with between 300 and 350 people in attendance.

The formation of THARE gave the young Bangladeshi community activists the opportunity to gain control of a united borough ethnic minority organisation, and they duly seized the initiative. However, the conflicts between Bangladeshi community organisers, which had erupted within the FBYO, the Kobi Nazrul Centre, the Bangladesh Welfare Association and BENTH, prevented the young activists from presenting a united front themselves. Kashem Ali, who was involved in those conflicts, alluded to the fragmentation of the Bangladeshi community in his comments at the meeting, and it appeared from the speeches of the chairmen of THCRE and THARJ that their own aspirations for office in the new organisation would be swept aside in the competition between young Bangladeshi activists. Indeed, the new chairman, elected by a massive majority, was a young FBYO leader, Habib Ullah, who had also played a prominent role within BENTH and in conflicts with Kashem Ali and other young Bangladeshi community organisers during 1983 and 1984.

The Treasurer of the new organisation was an older Bangladeshi entrepreneur, Hajji Abdul Hamid, with whom Habib Ullah had collaborated during disputes in the BWA and BENTH. Indeed, the alliance of FBYO leaders and their supporters would have taken all the officer positions had not Abdul Malik, another young Bangladeshi activist, agreed to stand down. Eight of the 16 elected to the Executive Committee were Bangladeshi community workers, most of whom co-operated with Habib Ullah in the FYBO.

The election heavily favoured members of the FBYO and THARJ. Only one member of the THCRE was elected to the Executive Committee of the new organisation, THARE, and Habib Ullah had easily defeated the challenge of Simon Ramdin, the chairman of the THCRE Education Sub-Committee in 1983/4. THCRE representation was improved by the co-option of two members on to THARE's Executive Committee in August 1984, but the dissatisfaction of THCRE officials with the THARE election resulted in their refusal for several months to recognise the new organisation. THCRE's prestige was dealt a further blow by the appointment of THARJ's Development Worker as the first Senior Race Relations Adviser servicing the Ethnic Minorities Committee.

By August 1984 the three major reforms suggested by the Working Party on Race Relations and the Stebbings Report had been implemented, although not quite in the form outlined originally. The JCC had been replaced by a full council committee and the union of THCRE and THARJ had become involved in intra-communal rivalries and competition between community organisations. The Bangladeshi community representatives might have finally gained ascendancy over the new organisation, THARE, but in so doing they alienated THCRE community representatives who came from the Afro-Caribbean and Bangladeshi population. Consequently, there was a further danger that those claiming to represent smaller ethnic groups, i.e. Afro-Caribbean, Somali and Chinese settlers, would resent any preoccupation among THARE members with Bangladeshi interests and competition between Bangladeshi activists.

The speeches at the inaugural meeting of THARE had emphasised the need for unity among the borough's ethnic minorities. Dr. Ahmad, the THCRE chairman who contested the validity of the THARE election after the July inaugural meeting, called for unity, warning that 'if the differing ethnic groups remained divided, then there would be no community relations organisation in the borough for the next 10 years, as had been the case in past years'. [44] THARJ's chairman, the Bishop of Stepney, who was not elected to any position at the July meeting but was later co-opted on to the Executive Committee, also contended that:

> . . . during the past 5 years, there had been no improvements in race relations in the borough and in particular to the reaction of the police to the question of racial harassment. Due to the fact that the ethnic minorities had been divided it followed that the local authority and other institutions had often been allowed to ignore their responsibilities. [45]

Kashem Ali developed the theme of unity with regard to the role of the smaller ethnic groups when he claimed that:

> . . . the constitution should reflect a fair representation of the smaller ethnic groups which had not been happening in the past. Due to the fact that the Bangladeshi community was fragmented he requested that these smaller groups ought to unite in order to promote better race relations. [46]

The Executive Committee of THARE, after the August co-options, had a wider spread of THCRE and THARJ members. White, Bangladeshi, Afro-Caribbean, Somali and Chinese activists were brought together in a loose alliance, which tried to make good its claim to be the sole borough-wide representative of ethnic minority opinion. The relationship between THARE and the borough council's Ethnic Minorities Committee remained a matter of dispute and a source of potential conflict between the two organisations.

(ii)   Consultation between THARE and the borough council, 1984-5

The refusal of THCRE officials to recognise THARE ended in failure during late 1984, but a more serious challenge to the pretensions of THARE's leaders appeared to come from the EMC's proposal in September 1984 to establish another consultative organisation known as the Ethnic Minorities Forum. The proposal had stemmed from the EMC's decision of its first meeting in August 1983 to establish a Forum, which would 'enable the local community to participate in discussions about matters of importance to the ethnic minority population'.[47] Because the EMC had replaced the plan to establish a JCC which brought councillors and ethnic minority representatives together, there was no official link between the EMC and ethnic minority groups. The new Senior Race Relations Adviser included the establishment of the Forum in his work programme submitted to the EMC in September 1984 and, in a special report, the Chief Executive suggested that:

> Although the (Ethnic Minorities Committee) does have a substantial number of contacts with local groups, it might be considered to be more satisfactory to obtain a list of interested groups by public advertisement and to hold a meeting of those groups to elect representatives to the Forum. This would ensure that no group was inadvertently overlooked and would demonstrate that the Forum would not be under the Council's control.[48]

The Forum was intended to help the EMC to fulfil its role of liaising between council committees and outside organisations. A Housing Forum had already been established by the borough's Housing Committee during 1983 and both the GLC and ILEA had established similar consultative forums. The Ethnic Minorities Forum would include '20 (?) representatives of local groups and organisations working with and for ethnic minorities' in the borough as well as the EMC chairman and vice-chairman.[49]

During late 1984 the proposal came under attack from representatives of THARE. Habib Ullah, THARE's chairman, argued that the Forum would constitute an 'alternative organisation to THARE', thereby 'challenging the authority and validity of the new Race Relations Body'. He also questioned 'the point of having these committees which many view as "Talking Shops" without any real authority or power to influence the decision-making machinery which is the main obstacle setting back the cause of Race Relations'.[50]

Discussions during late 1984 and early 1985 between THARE and council representatives considered the possibilities for a closer relationship between THARE and the EMC through a consultative body like the Forum. In February 1985 THARE's Executive Committee suggested the creation of a Liaison Group, consisting of EMC and THARE representatives together with three 'representatives from other community groups'.[51] The Executive Committee expressed its unanimous view that 'the important thing is to impress upon the Council's Leadership the need to engage in meaningful consultations' and, hence, 'the desirability of engaging in any such discussions, the Leader of the Council'.[52]

THARE's leaders were determined to resist any institutional reforms which weakened their claim to represent ethnic minorities in Tower Hamlets to councillors and officials. In an Ethnic Minorities Forum, which was recruited from numerous local community groups, THARE's influence would be much weaker than in the Liaison Group where three THARE members would be complemented by only three other community activists. THARE hoped that the Liaison Group would enable community representatives to participate more closely in the decision-making structures of the borough council through the EMC and the Majority Group leader.

The EMC supported THARE in its attempts to pressurise the Majority Leader and the Policy Committee into initiating changes. The EMC had taken up THARE's suggestions about involvement in decision-making by requesting the Policy Committee to allow ethnic minority representatives to be co-opted onto the EMC and other council committees. In February 1985 the Policy Committee rejected the request, and although the EMC repeated its proposal, by June 1985 the Liaison Group appeared to be the only means by which THARE could participate more closely in council business. THARE's Executive agreed to the scheme which would bring together three EMC members, three THARE representatives and three other community activists. Habib Ullah was to represent THARE with an Afro-Caribbean and Chinese colleague. The Executive Committee also suggested that the Bangladesh Welfare Association and a Somali community group be asked to send representatives. Since the Somali group was represented in THARE, the proposal appeared to be designed to offset any major challenge to THARE from other community organisations, such as the Bangladesh Welfare Association.

By the end of 1985 the negotiations over the formation of an Ethnic Forum had led to a proposed Ethnic Minorities Liaison Group with a much smaller membership, The suggested changes indicated the EMC's sensitivity to the views of THARE's leaders. If THARE's suggestions about the composition of the Liaison Group were approved, THARE representatives would enjoy a much stronger position than in the Ethnic Minorities Forum. Although THARE's attempt to gain access to council decision-making through co-options to council committees had been rebuffed by the Policy Committee, it continued its efforts during 1985 by seeking representational changes in the social services area, for example. At its September 1985 conference on the borough's delivery of social services to ethnic minority groups, THARE proposed that:

a proper consultative machinery be established with member level involvement. . . under the auspices of THARE. This group comprising of representatives from all minority communities in Tower Hamlets will monitor and advise the Social Services Department on all aspects of service delivery, employment and training. This Group will be serviced by the Director and senior management of the Social Services Department. [53]

The proposal and other comments on social service provision were formally noted by the borough Director of Social Services, who worked with other officers and members of the Social Services Committee during late 1985 to produce a report for the attention of other committees, particularly the Policy Committee.

The involvement of THARE in the proposed Liaison Group and the consultative body concerned with social services contained the danger of THARE being associated with an exclusive establishment group, which local activists could blame for failing to respond to ethnic minority needs. THARE's Executive Committee expressed its fear about such a danger when it considered the Liaison Group proposal. It noted that the Group 'could be construed a "select club" which would meet to discuss issues of community concern to the exclusion of other influential interest groups'. [54] THARE's advocacy of the representation of the Bangladesh Welfare Association on the Liaison Group was a further sign of its desire to avoid the charge of being exclusive. The BWA was not a group member of THARE and it harboured its own pretensions to represent a specific ethnic minoirity as the oldest Bangladeshi community organisation

The dominance gained by young Bangladeshi activists over THARE at the first election of officers and the Executive Committee in July 1984 had raised the possibility of activists from other ethnic minorities seeking borough council support outside THARE. During 1984 and 1985 the claims of Afro-Caribbean, Somali, Vietnamese and Chinese residents were presented with vigour through THARE and, sometimes, through direct representation to the EMC. THARE's proposal for the Liaison Group membership, as well as the papers presented on different ethnic minorities needs at the social services conference in September 1985, were further signs that Bangladeshi activists appreciated the danger of alienating activists from other ethnic groups.

Just as the EMC could not claim race relations as its own preserve at council committee level and depended upon the support of other committees for the pursuit of its claims, so THARE was unable to act as the sole representative of ethnic minorities in Tower Hamlets. THARE was subject to internal conflicts between Bangladeshi and other ethnic minority activists, who were engaged in competition for funds from the borough council and other statutory bodies. The role of white activists in the representation of ethnic minority grievances had also to be recognised if THARE was not to lose the support of such influential figures as the former chairman of THARJ, the Anglican Bishop of Stepney. Moreover, attempts to gain access to what were seen as the decision-making structures of local government had to be balanced with the strategy of criticising those structures for failing to meet ethnic minority needs.

NOTES

[1]   See GLC Planning Committee, Report by Controller of Transportation and Development, Community Areas Policy Summary of Grant Applications for Community Area Projects - 1983/84. 23 June 1983.

[2]   See LBTH Policy Committee, Tower Hamlets Inner Area Programme 1985/86, 24 June 1985, pt. 2.3 and 5.2.

[3]   See, for example, Wood, D. 'County Hall farce', London Labour Briefing, no.50, June 1985.

[4]   LBTH Policy Sub-Committee, First Report of Tower Hamlets Working Party on Race Relations, (hereafter referred to as the First Report on Race Relations), 13 July 1981, p.2.

[5]   Ibid.

[6]   Ibid.

[7]   See LBTH Policy Committee, Review by Officers' Group of Race Relations in the London Borough of Tower Hamlets, September 1982, pp. 21-22.

[8]   Ibid., p.26.

[9]   See The First Report on Race Relations, 13 July 1981, app. B, p.2.

[10]   See LBTH Policy Sub-Committee, Fourth Report of Tower Hamlets Working Party on Race Relations, (hereafter referred to as The Fourth Report on Race Relations), 13 July 1981, p.2.

[11]   LBTH Policy Sub-Committee, Report of the Policy Sub-Committee - 24.3.81, 30 March 1982.

[12]   First Report on Race Relations, p.2.

[13]   The Social Services Committee was responsible for £20,165,000 in 1984/5 or 30.7% of the council budget. Figures for the other big-spending committees were Housing £16,371,000 or 24.8%, Works £9,354,000 or 14.2%. Amenities £9,233,000 or 14.0%, Administration

112

£4,754,000 or 7.2%. The EMC was allocated £20,000, the lowest sum and well below the £99,000 received by the next low-budget committee, the Police Committee. See LBTH Policy Committee, <u>Revenue Budget 1986/7</u>, 24 June 1985, item 4.28, app. A.

[14] LBTH Ethnic Minorities Committee, <u>Orders of Reference</u>, 3 August 1983.

[15] <u>Fourth Report on Race Relations</u>, p.2.

[16] <u>First Report on Race Relations</u>, app.A.

[17] LBTH Policy Sub-Committee, <u>Report of Policy Sub-Committee - 13 July 1981 - Race Relations Matters</u>, 16 July 1981, item 4 (2).

[18] Ibid., item 7.1.

[19] See LBTH Administration Committee, <u>Equal Opportunities in Employment,</u> 28 September 1982, item 4 (12).

[20] LBTH Ethnic Minorities Committee, <u>Equal Opportunities Policy Statement</u>, 6 February 1985, item 12.2.

[21] Ibid.

[22] Ibid.

[23] Ibid.

[24] Ibid.

[25] LBTH Ethnic Minorities Committee, <u>Orders of Reference</u>, 3 August 1983.

[26] LBTH Ethnic Minorities Committee, <u>The Keeping of Ethnic Records</u>, 5 September 1983, item 3.3, app. A.

[27] Ibid.

[28] Ibid.

[29] Ibid.

[30] LBTH Ethnic Minorities Committee, <u>The Keeping of Ethnic Records</u>, 20 October 1983, item 3.2.

[31] Ibid.

[32] See LBTH Administration Committee, <u>Public Sector Employment Workshop Held On 10 November 1984</u>, 4 February 1985, item 7.3.2.

[33] Ibid.

[34] LBTH Policy Sub-Committee, <u>Ethnic Monitoring</u>, 10 July 1985, item 2.2.

[35] Ibid.

[36] Ibid.

[37] Ibid.

[38] See LBTH Ethnic Minorities Committee, <u>CRE's Code of Practice on Employment Matters</u>, 4 December 1985, item 5.2.3.

[39] See LBTH Ethnic Minorities Committee, <u>Meeting with CRE - The Hackney Report</u>, 6 February 1985, item 6.8.

[40]   LBTH Ethnic Minorities Committee, <u>CRE's Code of Practice on Employment Matters</u>, 4 December 1985, item 5.2.5.
[41]   Ibid., 5.2.7.
[42]   Ibid., 5.4.1.
[43]   LBTH Policy Sub-Committee, <u>Ethnic Monitoring</u>, 10 July 1985, item 3.10, pt. 2.4.
[44]   Ibid., p.1.
[45]   Ibid., p.2.
[46]   Ibid.
[47]   See LBTH Ethnic Minorities Committee, <u>Ethnic Minorities Forum</u>, 5 September 1984, item 5.2.1.
[48]   Ibid., item 5.2.2.
[49]   Ibid., pt.4.
[50]   LBTH Ethnic Minorities Committee, <u>Ethnic Minorities Forum</u>, 24 October 1984, item 5.13.
[51]   LBTH Ethnic Minorities Committee, <u>Ethnic Minorities Forum</u>, 6 February 1985, item 2.4.
[52]   Ibid., item 2.5.
[53]   LBTH Ethnic Minorities Committee, <u>THARE Conference on Social Services - 17/9/85</u>, 16 October 1985, item 6.7.
[54]   LBTH Ethnic Minorities Committee, <u>Ethnic Minorities Forum</u>, 6 February 1985, item 2.5.

5 Housing, the Bangladeshi community and local authorities

(A) **INTRODUCTION**

So far attention has been paid to the representation of the Bangladeshi community at various levels of the political and administrative system. The preceding chapter moved away from political developments taking place largely in Spitalfields ward to consider changes involving community representation at the level of the borough council and the GLC. In the following analysis the relationship between Spitalfields community groups and local authorities will be investigated with reference to a particular issue of local concern - housing.

In Spitalfields, as in other wards of the borough, most residents depended upon public housing administered by the borough council and the GLC. Central government restrictions on public housing expenditure from the late 1970s had increased competition among local residents for council housing and had weakened the ability of local authorities to satisfy local demands for such housing. At the same time, the growth of community organisations in wards like Spitalfields had enabled residents to put pressure on councillors and local government officials in order to satisfy their particular objectives. The following discussion will concentrate upon debates and institutional changes concerning the housing of Bangladeshis on local authority estates, particularly in Spitalfields. The emphasis will be upon the housing allocation practices of the GLC and borough council and upon the attempts to change them between 1981 and 1985.

(B) **THE DISCUSSION OF LOCAL AUTHORITY HOUSING ALLOCATION PRACTICES, 1981-85**

(i)   Criticism by SHAPRS of GLC housing allocations
        In Spitalfields the most vociferous and influential pressure group concerned with housing was the Spitalfields Housing and Planning Rights Services (SHAPRS) which was established during 1979. SHAPRS produced the first major survey of housing in the ward by a local community organisation. The survey criticised both the GLC and borough council for the poor conditions it recorded in Spitalfields. The report also drew attention to the particular plight of the 'Asian community' composed overwhelmingly of Bangladeshis:

> Apart from an overall shortage of accommodation this survey reveals that there are major problems of access to public housing facing the Asian community and that those households who do gain a tenancy are concentrated disproportionately in the least desirable property. Overall, on every possible indicator, Spitalfields' Asian community is facing worse housing conditions than the rest of the population taken as a whole. At the same time they are the group who most want to stay in the area but, perversely, are also the group that has been subjected to the greatest pressure to move out. Housing officials, and senior GLC officials in particular, have argued that conditions for Asians can only be improved if they move away from E1 and that policies should be geared to achieving such a dispersal in order to avoid 'creating ghettoes'. [1]

SHAPRS concentrated its attack upon the GLC since the authority was responsible for most of the public housing in the ward. The Spitalfields Survey aggressively criticised the GLC's housing allocations policies in the following terms:

116

Present allocations policies may not be racist in intent, but they are often racist in effect. In 1978 at a time when predominantly Asian households were being 'decanted' by the GLC from Brunswick Buildings, a Victorian slum tenement, the newly built Granby Estate off Brick Lane was being allocated. Only 1 Asian household was initially granted a tenancy on an estate of over 180 dwellings, despite the fact that many wanted to stay in the area AND were in the GLC's top priority category for rehousing. [2]

This discussion touched on a number of themes which were to recur in later debates between community groups and local authorities over housing - (a) the disproportionately high numbers of Bangladeshis in poor housing, (b) the preponderance of Bangladeshis wanting to stay or move into Spitalfields, (c) the dispersal of Bangladeshis from Spitalfields and other wards in the E1 postal district eastwards across the borough and (d) the implicit racism of GLC housing allocations practices.

(ii)   Official response to SHAPRS criticisms, 1980-81
The borough council and GLC leadership had already been alienated by SHAPRS' criticism of their policies affecting Spitalfields, not only with regard to housing but also office development.   Both local authorities withdrew their financial support of SHAPRS during 1980, but after the 1981 GLC election the new Labour Majority Group restored funding, even though the borough council continued to refuse assistance.
The two local authorities' political and administrative elites had been offended by SHAPRS assertions which they believed to be unsubstantiated and partial. SHAPRS claimed to represent local community groups and residents. The organisation challenged the local authorities' contention that they catered for local needs as far as possible within the wider context of borough or metropolitan management and central government constraints.
A number of official responses were made to the Survey - technical observations by the GLC officers, 16 September 1981, a report by the GLC Co-ordinator of Housing Services, 25 January 1982, and a report by the borough Planning Officer, 22 September 1981.   Guarded approval of certain aspects of the Survey was given in those documents, but many faults were detected on general and technical grounds. The GLC Co-ordinator of Housing Services and the borough Planning Officer were agreed that the

117

Survey would have to be set in the context of a more thoroughly analysed, borough-wide survey. The Co-ordinator's report concluded that:

> Spitalfields is recognised as having severe housing stress. As a ward it probably rates the highest priority in the Borough. But there are other blocks and groups of dwellings with equally severe problems. Until the housing problems of the Borough have been adequately quantified and given some order to priority, and until the supply and demand for housing has been received on an area basis it is not possible to make firm proposals for tackling the problems on a rational basis. The current limitations of finance would to some extent make any firm proposal academic. However the identification and quantification of the housing needs of the Borough, in more detail than hitherto, is seen as essential and urgent if an effective case is to be made for more funds, and also to ensure that funds that are available are used most effectively. [3]

The official emphasis upon objectivity, rationality, quantification and efficiency was well expressed in the letter and appeared again in the Planning Officer's comments. The Survey was welcomed for its 'quantification of population characteristics' but was criticised for its lack of content, biased data and failure to consider non-Bangladeshi citizens.

The official responses to the SHAPRS survey were mainly justifications of local authority practices. However, on the specific issue of housing allocations, the GLC Co-ordinator noted recent changes in its priority points system ad recognised 'the need for further review when more is known about the validity of the waiting list and the availability and demand for dwellings on an area basis'.[4]

(iii) GLC anti-racist statements with reference to housing, 1982-84

In May 1981 a new Labour Majority Group was formed, and its leaders publicly committed themselves to change practices which discriminated against London's ethnic minorities directly or indirectly. The GLC Ethnic Minorities Committee was created to promote the implementation of the GLC's anti-racist strategy, and in late 1982 the committee identified eight targets which included -

118

(iv)   Liaising with tenants associations and other interest groups concerned with the housing equality needs of ethnic minorities in Tower Hamlets and Thamesmead as well as on racial harassment matters.
(v)   Monitoring equal opportunities in housing allocations and lettings. [5]

The committee admitted that its own administrative structure and practices had indirectly discriminated against ethnic minorities -

The (Ethnic Minorities) Committee's central objective is that of tackling institutional and structural racism. To do so fundamentally means changing the way the GLC operates in that it is a large institution that has historically discriminated indirectly against black people and other ethnic minorities. [6]

The GLC committee also made a specific commitment to:

Developing an effective integrated housing and race advisory service in Tower Hamlets including full time Bengali speaking workers. [7]

By late 1983 the Race and Housing Action Team, consisting of eight staff, had been approved by the GLC's various committees. [8] The team was required to examine housing allocations to GLC housing in Tower Hamlets and to 'amend those housing policies, which, for whatever reasons, have led to many estates being either all "white" or all "black" '. [9]

(iv)   <u>Criticism by SHAPRS of GLC housing allocations practices, 1982-84</u>

SHAPRS continued to criticise GLC housing allocations practices throughout the period of 1982-84 in a series of publications, complaints to GLC committees and administrative departments, and at public meetings in Spitalfields. In March 1982 it published another survey, which looked beyond Spitalfields to other wards as well in the E1 postal district. In their introduction the authors repeated their charge that the GLC allocations policy was racist and argued that a non-racist policy should be introduced where 'allocations are made on the basis of housing need'. [10]

The SHAPRS report was considered by the Joint Housing Management Committee (JHMC), consisting of GLC and Tower Hamlets councillors and housing officials. The JHMC was responsible for jointly managing public authority housing in the borough during a period when the GLC was arranging the transfer of its property to the borough. Certain changes were made in the allocations process and one specific new site in E1, Royal Mint Square, was monitored by the JHMC during 1982-83. Nevertheless, a further survey by SHAPRS argued that 'fundamentally the situation on the estates has not changed'. [11] The survey continued with the claim that:

> With 3 new estates, and the empty flats on the other good estates in the E1 area, there have been about a thousand new allocations made by the GLC. Only about 7% of them have gone to Asian households. And this has happened since the GLC accepted the findings of our first report and promised action. [12]

The report laid the blame for this inequitable share of good housing on the shoulders of the GLC housing allocators :

> Somewhere, somehow, deliberate decisions are being taken over which estates people were going to be 'allowed' to live on. Not only have these decisions been taken, but they are still being acted on. Nothing said or done by the GLC administration over the last 3 years has changed this. [13]

(v)   GLC response to SHAPRS criticism of GLC housing allocations practices, 1982-84

The SHAPRS report, Bengalis and GLC allocations in E1, 1982 was considered by the GLC Housing Committee, the JHMC, the Ethnic Minorities Committee and the central Policy Co-ordinating Committee, but no major concessions were granted. The most influential responses appear to have come from the Controller of Housing and Technical Services in the Housing Department and the Chairman of the GLC Housing Committee.

The Controller of Housing and Technical Services again questioned the reliability of SHAPRS' data and asserted SHAPRS' failure to consider the general borough situation and non-Bengali residents. To the charge of racist housing allocations practices the Controller replied:

120

The report, based on outdated information, concentrates on selected estates in the E1 and E2 areas and from this limited platform cannot be taken to prove that the allocation policies are racist.

The argument that the allocation system is racist in effect and biassed against the Bengalis cannot be upheld if it can be shown that those of a particular ethnic minority or race receive more or less than their fair share of allocation of relevant dwellings. What constitutes 'fair share' is a very complicated issue and is not one which the SHAPRS survey attempts to define unless it be concluded that all or nearly all family dwellings in the E1 area should be allocated to this minority group regardless of the JHMC's other commitments. The JHMC last year rejected a suggestion that additional priority be given to Spitalfields residents for Spitalfields vacancies since it was held that all the Borough should be treated alike. [14]

The problems encountered by Spitalfields residents, especially Bengalis, were largely due to overcrowding in a ward with poor resources. The Controller claimed that:

The JHMC has consistently contended that the solution to the housing problems of Spitalfields residents lies in the public rented stock beyond the E1 area and JHMC action to this end appears to be confirmed by The Spitalfields Survey published in June 1981 by SHAPRS and others which indicates that 27% of the households left the ward over a period of two and a half years leading up to the survey, although it is virtually certain that a number of these remained in E1. From the current report, SHAPRS now accept that if the Bengalis are to achieve even quicker access into public sector rented housing they must move beyond the Spitalfields ward but maintain that this still should be into the remainder of the E1 postal district over a number of years, a time-scale which is unacceptable in view of the known housing stress. [15]

Allegations of racism were denied, therefore, and the solution to the problems encountered by Bengalis in Spitalfields was to be found in rapid movement across the borough.

121

The report by the Chairman of the GLC Housing Committee during September 1982, however, did acknowledge that existing allocation policies might play a part in creating marked differences between Bengalis and whites in publicly rented housing. Four practices which might have affected the entry of Bengalis into the GLC accommodation were mentioned - (a) the allocation of 33% of 'lettings of all newly built property to existing tenants who have applied for transfer', (b) the special quota 'for tenants' sons and daughters who marry and wish to remain on the same estate as their parents or one nearby', (c) the ban on letting 'accommodation above fourth floor level to any family with a child over ten years of age' and (d) the effect of Tower Hamlets housing practices concerning homelessness and its waiting list. [16] Certain modifications were suggested for all four practices, and the particular problems of Spitalfields were to be tackled by modifications in current GLC building developments and a campaign to gain funds from the central government for 'new construction and in the modernisation and rehabilitation of the existing (housing) stock'. [17] The demand by SHAPRS and the GLC Housing Committee in July 1982 for an enquiry into GLC housing allocations practices was rejected.

The Chairman's report also included in an appendix the suggestion that an 'independent action team' be established 'to deal with race equality issues within housing management in Tower Hamlets'. [18] During 1983 the suggestion was followed up by the creation of the Race and Housing Action Team but not until pressure had been applied on the GLC leadership by local meetings, according to SHAPRS. [19]

The formation of an Anti-Racist Year Housing Group during late 1983 gave SHAPRS another opportunity to pressurise the GLC Housing Department over its allocations practices. The updated report on the situation in E1 was presented to the group as well as to the Race and Housing Advisory Group, which supported the new Race and Housing Action Team in Tower Hamlets. The response of the GLC Head of Housing Services to the new report was broadly similar to the reply made by the Controller of Housing and Technical Services in 1982. The contradictions, the highly selective, inaccurate evidence and unsubstantiated assertions in the SHAPRS report were again asserted, together with a denial of racial discrimination by GLC housing officers. The new SHAPRS report was to be used, on a more positive note, to suggest certain modifications of official practices involving the Race and Housing Action Team in allocations of Bengalis to unsafe estates. Consideration would also be given to 'the concept of fairness as applied to allocations to Bengalis'. [20]

(vi)   Other criticisms of GLC housing allocations practices, 1983-85

The GLC Housing Department was criticised by other reports which gave a degree of support to the allegations of racial bias by SHAPRS. In March 1984 the GLC Anti-Racist Year Housing Working Group welcomed a report by the CRE on housing allocations by the borough of Hackney. The report contended that the inequitable distribution of housing between whites and blacks in the borough 'could not be attributed to factors other than race' and that 'direct discrimination had taken place'. [21] The Working Group referred to similar inequitable distribution in GLC housing and drew attention to the SHAPRS survey, Bengalis and GLC Housing Allocation in E1, as evidence.

The Working Group then proceeded to suggest how changes could be made in the areas of direct discrimination, accountability of housing staff, grading of housing applicants, the effects of locational preferences by residents, language problems, separated families, instant lettings, research and community development.

Further support came from an independent review of GLC allocation practices between 1983 and 1984 by an academic researcher, Dr. D.A. Phillips. In the second of her two reports Phillips concluded her analysis of the pattern of housing allocation between January 1983 and May 1984 in the following terms:

. . . the pattern of housing offers made to the Asian and non-Asian sub-groups during the January 1983-May 1984 period did not reflect the Council's stated policy of racial equality. Rules and procedures within the allocations system. . .together with the effects of discretionary decisions have presented a different range of housing opportunities to each group, such that minority households have lost out on better quality offers. [22]

Despite recent 'modifications to the allocations scheme and the proposed introduction of rigorous monitoring procedures', [23] other factors affected the implementation of equal opportunities in GLC housing. Unfavourable stereotyping of housing officials responsible for visiting applicants was one possible factor. Communication of the complex procedures to be followed across language barriers was another. The viewing of accommodation on offer to the applicant had also been affected by hostile reception committees of predominantly white residents, and estate officers played 'an important role in determining the social

123

characteristics and ethnic composition of estates'. [24] Other obstacles came from resistance to change within the GLC housing administration, the uneasy relationship between 'central divisions of the Housing Department and the local branch office', and tension between the Race and Housing Action Team and 'some local white officers'.[25] Problems were also produced by the workings of housing management 'which often reflect greater concern for the efficient handling of the housing stock than for the people housed'. [26]

All these obstacles could produce discrimination against ethnic minorities indirectly, but Phillips also claimed that the GLC Tower Hamlets housing officers revealed a lack of concern, suspicion and resentment and overt racism towards Bangladeshis. Phillips concluded her report thus:

> The Council finds itself in an invidious position. Some strategies designed to promote racial equality will provoke a white backlash and housing management can only tackle one facet of deeply rooted racism in our society. Fostering good relationships with the police and other organisations who help to deal with such incidents as harassment is therefore essential. Nevertheless, as a major institution the GLC must be seen to be taking a lead in anti-racist activities (eg. by dealing with rather than giving in to the white backlash) and must also demonstrate a clear commitment to translating policy into practice. As a provider of public services, the GLC and its officers must be accountable. The outcome of practices must therefore be monitored and strategies for policy implementation regularly reviewed if institutional racism is to be eradicated. [27]

(vii)   SHAPRS links with white and Bangladeshi community groups and local residential interests

The criticisms of official housing policies and practices by local pressure groups have to be seen in the context of the links forged between those groups as well as competing residential interests. SHAPRS, for instance, was created at the end of the Spitalfields Project during 1979 through co-operation between white and Bangladeshi activists, and it included on its Management Committee representatives of groups serving local white and Bangladeshi interests. Some white activists expressed at an early stage their misgivings about the involvement of SHAPRS staff (three whites and one Bangladeshi) in Bangladeshi affairs:

Some members of the Committee felt that the Service spent a disproportionate amount of time on the specific problems relating to the housing of members of the Bangladeshi community, while others felt that the time spent was a simple reflection of working with those people in the greatest housing stress in the area, and therefore saw no conflict at all with our stated and agreed priorities. [28]

Given certain differences in housing need between local whites and Bangladeshis, tension over the communication of those perceived needs through community organisations and pressure groups like SHAPRS was always likely to occur. At public meetings in Spitalfields where local authority councillors could be pressurised by local residents, Bangladeshis and their advocates were able to make their opinions known more easily than representatives of local white council tenants. After a meeting in the Brady Centre, East Spitalfields, attended by Ken Livingstone and other senior GLC councillors to discuss 'Racism and Housing in Tower Hamlets' during September 1983, for example, most of the speakers called from the floor were Bangladeshi activists. Resentment at the way in which the meeting proceeded was expressed at a subsequent meeting of white tenants - the Chicksand Estate Tenants Group. The group complained that the allocation of local authority housing was unfairly allocated in favour of 'Asians' and that the 'white community' had not been adequately consulted.

The Chicksand Estate starkly expressed the inequitable share of GLC council housing between whites and Bangladeshis about which SHAPRS and other groups so long debated. 'Old Chicksand', consisting of inter-war LCC red-brick blocks and the dilapidated post-war housing, was predominantly Bangladeshi, unlike housing in the 'New Chicksand' which contained units most highly desired by white residents. Even so, the division between Old and New Chicksand, Bangladeshis and whites, was not absolute. New Chicksand included buildings which were unpopular among white tenants because of poor facilities or because, in the case of Pauline House, they consisted of a dilapidated high rise block. Some tenants were neither Bangladeshis nor whites; some Bangladeshis and other settlers from South Asia and the Caribbean occupied flats which were considered desirable by white residents. Furthermore, 'whites' as a category concealed ethnic distinctions between Greek and Turkish Cypriots, Maltese, Irish Catholics and Jews, for instance.

Pressure on the GLC had apparently been effective during 1983-85 in producing action over GLC sites in the ward. SHAPRS claimed that GLC moves to develop several sites in the ward was partly as a result of local pressure and the GLC's Community Areas Policy which the Service helped to draw up, along with other community groups in central London. [29]

However, the GLC Housing Committee's decision during 1982 to change the building specification for the Davenant Street site in East Spitalfields to include a higher proportion of four to five bedroom flats was greeted with dismay by local white residents who saw themselves losing out to Bangladeshis and their advocates, given the high demand from Bangladeshis for large units. The issue threatened to divide residents into hostile camps as meetings were held during the summer of 1983 by aggrieved white residents in East Spitalfields, who argued for a higher ratio of two and three bedroom units and houses with gardens.

Community activists tried to prevent the Davenant Street development from polarising around an opposition between white and Bangladeshi tenants by encouraging white tenants to campaign for a more equal mix of bedroom sizes in the undeveloped Selby Street site in East Spitalfields. Local discussions in Spitalfields News, for example, focused on the different housing demands of 'local' people, implicitly refusing to acknowlege the tension between Bangladeshi and white tenants caused by their differing housing situations and desires.

Because SHAPRS concentrated its efforts on those in the greatest housing need, it recognised its preoccupation with Bangladeshi clients, and its own report on the Selby Street site gave little encouragement to white residents in less housing need. The report argued that the site should cater for four categories of local residents - (a) those waiting to be decanted from the Brick Lane Clearance Area, (b) waiting list applicants, (c) the homeless and (d) those awaiting transfer. These categories predominantly applied to Bangladeshis and elderly or disabled white residents. [30]

(ix)   The discussion of housing allocations by the FBYO
Although SHAPRS produced the most voluminous literature by a Spitalfields pressure group on housing allocations, it was only one of a number of organisations which sought to speak for local people on the issue of housing. Bangladeshi groups, for example, campaigned with SHAPRS, but they were also eager to organise their own struggles and to make their own assertions about housing allocations.

126

The FBYO, which tried to co-ordinate the energies of the various Bangladeshi youth groups in Spitalfields and elsewhere, claimed in its 1982-83 Annual Report that:

> The housing policy implemented by council officials are directly racist. Generally new housing is provided for white families, whereas the Bangladeshis are still housed in the oldest and the worst accommodation available. [31]

In its reference to the public meeting with GLC senior councillors during September 1983 the report claimed success for its lobbying campaign:

> As part of our campaign against the use of hotel accommodation, we picketed outside the meeting (as featured in our film 'Fighting Back' shown on Channel 4).
> As a result of our campaign, the GLC has agreed to set up an Ethnic Minorities Team (RHAT) in their Housing Department. We hope that they will also fight racism, not only on the estates, but in Housing Departments as well. [32]

The FBYO also co-operated with Bangladeshi and white activists who were involved in a campaign over the housing of Bangladeshi homeless families in bed and breakfast hotels outside the borough. A committee representing the homeless families in the Finsbury hotels was supported by a part-time white activist based at SHAPRS, but links were established with Bangladeshi groups across London, particularly during the occupation of the Camden Town Hall by Bangladeshi homeless families after the death of a Bangladeshi wife and her children in a bed and breakfast hotel during November 1984. The FBYO's broadsheet, New Voice, reported the Tower Hamlets homeless families' demands in its story about the Camden occupation in the following terms:

> LBTH accept its responsibility to rehouse families it is declaring 'intentionally' homeless.
> LBTH prevent homelessness by appointing an officer to co-ordinate this work.
> Take the 80 small families out of the hotels now.
> Give 20% of the new housing to homeless families.
> Confirm homeless families get at least two offers of accommodation, one of the two offers to be in their area of choice.

Adopt minimum space standards (as proposed by the families) below which no-one will be required to accept a flat.
Use some of the thousands of empty LBTH flats to get the two hundred plus families out of the hotels by:
giving higher priority to repairs on these flats: short-lifing units for use as temporary accommodation for the large families.
Account for the expenditure through savings made on hotel bills.
Implement policy and organise a consultation meeting on racial harassment. Institute a regular six weekly meeting on race and housing with community organisations. [33]

(x)   The co-ordination of pressure group activities and direct action
Most of the demands were similar to the arguments put forward in a report commissioned by the Homeless Families Committee and favourably received by the borough's Housing Committee during November 1983. The complicated process of co-ordinating action by Bangladeshi and white activists over the issue of homelessness and housing allocations was well portrayed in the discussion by SHAPRS of the steps taken during 1983:

The Homeless Families Committee's campaign has received much publicity - including features on the Federation of Bangladeshi Youth Organisations Channel 4 programme, Thames News, Capital Radio and local press coverage.
(A white worker) paid for 10 hours a week to work on the report, has been working full time, drawing in other resources of the Service when required. Throughout we have also kept in touch with other organisations concerned with the issues raised, in Islington - including health visitors, educational officers, environmental health inspectors, under 5s workers, who are trying to provide for the families in the hotels. They have been very effective in ensuring that Islington council has maintained its pressure on Tower Hamlets to take action. Contact is now being strengthened with the Finsbury Park Action Group who are worried for the families, but are also anxious at the way the hotels are eating into their area and their services. Hopefully this will lead to more pressure in other directions - particularly on Hackney council.

128

Links are now also being made with people working on the rehousing of the single homeless in the Borough so that homelessness can be dealt with in one overall strategy.[34]

The occupation of Camden Town Hall by Bangladeshi homeless families and the eventual acceptance of the families' demands by the Labour Majority Group in Camden raised the issue of which methods community groups should use in pressurising local authorities. SHAPRS and other organisations engaged in a variety of approaches involving public meetings, demonstrations, lobbying and detailed submissions to the numerous levels of local authority bureaucracy. A discussion of the homeless families' occupation in Tower Hamlets Association for Racial Equality's broadsheet, THARE News, reminded community workers of the need to consider returning to direct action:

. . . for many community groups in London and elsewhere the result of this occupation will certainly be a source of inspiration. In recent years many so-called progressive boroughs have been trying to hypnotise the black struggle with their apparent anti-racist activities. Camden's expenses on such activities is definitely unmatched and what the black people in Camden end up with is that the empty anti-racist propaganda by Camden Council does not mean anything to them. For many community groups this occupation was a return to methods of struggle on which they were founded. One of the lessons of this occupation is that a return to various sorts of direct action is something that all community groups should seriously consider. [35]

Direct action by homeless families themselves appeared to have won what community activists, both white and Bangladeshi, had failed to achieve by working through the political and administration levels of local authorities. Yet during 1985 THARE, as well as other pressure groups like SHAPRS, continued to seek changes through consultation with local authority committees and administrators rather than by direct action. THARE organised a Race and Housing conference and joined other representational groups in formal meetings with GLC and borough officials to consider, for example, racial harassment on council estates in the borough.

Although THARE's 1984 annual report again referred to the occupation of the Camden Town Hall by homeless families, THARE's strategy as a campaigning body had not led, as yet, to such dramatic acts of direct confrontation.

Almost a year after the occupation the issue of homeless families in Tower Hamlets was being pursued through meetings, conferences and lobbying of local authority personnel. THARE had to be content with asserting that the campaigns, such as the one in Camden, 'have been influencing our thinking and are bound to give us inspiration in the future'. [36]

Groups like THARE, FBYO and SHAPRS sought to pressurise the GLC and the borough council into introducing changes in the allocation of public housing which would benefit the most deprived category of local residents, i.e. members of the Bangladeshi community. Because the GLC was mainly responsible for local authority housing in Spitalfields until April 1985, local pressure groups concentrated their campaigns upon the GLC's political representatives and housing administrative personnel. They tried to challenge GLC representatives at public meetings and conferences, but most of their efforts were directed through detailed discussions with housing officers which entailed the presentation and examination of evidence. Despite the attractions of public confrontation with councillors and officials through direct action, local pressure groups mostly confined themselves to seeking change through less dramatic means. The transfer of GLC housing responsibilities to the borough council during 1985, therefore, involved pressure groups like THARE, FBYO and SHAPRS in relatively discreet lobbying of borough council committees to ensure the maintenance of administrative units, such as the Race and Housing Action Team, and administrative practices designed to eliminate racial inequality.

(C) **DISCUSSIONS OF HOUSING STRATEGIES AND REFORMS OF HOUSING ALLOCATIONS PRACTICES, 1982-85**

(i) Housing strategies and Bangladeshi access to local authority housing in the borough

The previous section has described the various discussions surrounding local authority housing and the Bangladeshi community which have involved local pressure groups particularly SHAPRS. Attention will now focus more closely upon the discussions of the housing strategies of local authorities and local residents, both white and Bangladeshi.

GLC and borough council officials had made clear their strategy of encouraging Bangladeshis to seek acommodation outside Spitalfields. They denied the charge levied by SHAPRS, for example, that their strategy entailed the forcible dispersal of the Bangladeshi community. The

GLC Controller of Housing and Technical Services defended the policy of the Joint Housing Management Committee of GLC and borough council representatives on the grounds that:

> the population of Spitalfields is likely to increase by 40% over the next few years as the existing Bangladeshi residents' dependants arrive from Bangladesh. If they are not to live in distressing conditions the JHMC must continue to do all it can to encourage the Bengalis to live beyond Spitalfields where they can be housed more quickly. This is not forcible dispersal, this is the same procedure used in dealing with any applicant black or white, whose housing location demands cannot be met within a reasonable time span. [37]

Tower Hamlets senior officials also perceived certain advantages in encouraging Bangladeshis to enter council housing outside the E1 area. In his discussion of recent attacks on Bangladeshi tenants in new GLC housing on the edge of the E1 area, the Tower Hamlets Director of Housing contended that:

> The experience heightens the need for avoiding any kind of white 'cordon' of estates around E1 where strains created by housing shortages (or by deterioration of the estate fabric and facilities or by a younger generation of families moving in) so easily makes ethnic minority families a scape-goat. The experience points to two kinds of solution:
> (a) to make other areas of the borough more acceptable to Bengali families (by ensuring a sense of security, a provision of community facilities and perhaps local work) on which planning is slowly proceeding;
> (b) to promote proper understanding of allocation proceedings since their obscurity leads to a belief that they can be manipulated. Whether greater local involvement in allocations is possible is a further issue. [38]

The entry of Bangladeshis into council housing outside Spitalfields and other E1 wards was well established by the end of 1985. Significant concentrations had emerged in Weavers, Blackwall, Bromley and Grove wards, for example.[39] Community groups pointed to the preponderance of Bangladeshis, whether in Spitalfields or elsewhere, in the more dilapidated council flats, however, and referred to racial discrimination by housing officers as a cause of such

131

inequality. Although local authority officials strenuously denied charges of direct discrimination, they did appear to recognise implicitly sometimes that their housing strategy for Bangladeshis was constrained by an assessment of what white residents would or would not accept. In his review of housing allocations during September 1984 the borough's Director of Housing claimed that:

> the housing list worked to some extent on a ladder principle whereby tenants could improve their housing opportunities without squeezing out waiting list applicants. The number of homeless families was small enough not to make a serious claim on resources. [40]

Conflict would not have occurred between those applying for transfers to housing which they considered more attractive and those on the waiting list because new housing was being made available by the two authorities:

> transfer applicants would have improved their housing and the resultant vacancy of perhaps less attractive accommodation would be offered to a waiting list applicant. The curtailment of new building (and decline in the quality of accommodation) and the shortage of large accommodation means more competition between transfers and waiting list. Then more favourable treatments for transfers starts to look like housing for the 'deserving' and to create indirect discrimination against ethnic minorities. [41]

The Director of Housing appeared to be suggesting that local authorities could facilitate strategic housing choices by different groups of people in the borough. Long established, predominantly white residents had been pursuing in large numbers a strategy of movement up a housing ladder. They gained transfers to more desirable accommodation which enabled more recent settlers, waiting to enter the local authority housing sector, to occupy dwellings considered less attractive by the more established tenants. The Director argued that if transfer and waiting list applicants were to be treated equally in the allocations process, the 'growing concentration of "need" ' would accentuate 'the drift to "welfare housing"'. [42] People would have to look for better accommodation by leaving the borough - a process which had led to the borough's population decline between 1960 and 1974 but which had virtually halted. Out-migration would eventually have caused 'a "pauperisation" of the Borough,

132

quite contrary to the idea of council housing being an avenue to better homes regardless of circumstances'. The current position was such that:

> It is already virtually impossible to get a transfer just because tenants want better housing or to live somewhere else or to live near parents. If transfers are to get less preference in future the trend will be increased.[43]

The Director of Housing provided a portrait of an allocations system under siege through central government restrictions on housing expenditure, the loss of building land to the LDDC in the south of the borough, a limited supply of new public housing and conflicting demands from different sections of the population, particularly white transfer applicants and Bangladeshis on the waiting list or homeless. Because the GLC and borough council controlled approximately 85% of the housing available in Tower Hamlets, inhabitants looked to the local authorities to satisfy their housing strategies rather than pursue their aspirations through the private, owner-occupant sector. As a result local authorities replaced building societies, estate agents and private landlords as the 'gatekeepers' to various grades of housing. Both local authorities and community activists assumed a consensus about the relative merits of the housing stock in their continual references to 'inferior' and 'better housing' and to the most attractive type of housing for local residents - 'houses with gardens'. Bangladeshi applicants were assumed to share in that consensus, and their disproportionately low representation in better housing was regarded by community activists as the result of racial discrimination.

The general housing strategy of the two local authorities' officials was bound up with the strategies of transfer and waiting list applicants in the borough population, with greater weight being given to transfer applicants from the already established body of council tenants. These three strategies were also related to the practice of the local authorities which encouraged Bangladeshis to look beyond Spitalfields and other 'overcrowded' western wards with relatively poorer housing resources. The operation of a housing ladder system, however, forced Bangladeshis to occupy units in wards outside the E1 area which were less desirable in the opinion of most white council tenants. Bangladeshis came to be associated, for some white residents at least, with inferior housing and even with the creation of 'slum' conditions.

133

A letter by one white council tenant which was published in the local newspaper, East London Advertiser, gave an indication of the approach towards public housing and the Bangladeshi settlement by some white residents. The letter was published as a contribution to an exchange between the GLC Director of Housing and a member of ELWAR, Lindsay Finch, during 1982 over the 'racist' character of GLC housing policies. The author claimed that:

> Over the years and with a growing family, we have gone from one estate to another, a little better each time until five years ago when we moved to the Glamis Estate. It took me 27 years to achieve the best but I appreciate it because I've also had the worse.
> Would the Asians from Shadwell Gardens appreciate a place like mine if they had one? I don't see any of the racial harassment Lindsay Finch complains about. These people seem to be quite happy living in their own environment: after all, it's what they have made it . . .
> Please try and remember there are still English people living in the East End and we have always been here. So fair's fair. Let everyone work their way up the housing ladder and prove they deserve the Glamis and Exmouth estates before listening to any more rubbish from ELWAR. [44]

The letter argued that the process of moving up the housing ladder was not racist but fair. The 'best' housing had to be earned and 'Asians' who did not work their way gradually up the ladder, would not appreciate good accommodation. The Glamis and Exmouth estates were contrasted with the inferior Shadwell Gardens area which contained high concentrations of Bangladeshis, who were held responsible for creating these inferior conditions.

Official references to local housing administrators' appreciation of white residential hostility towards Bangladeshi settlement were scanty. The Phillips Report published an internal memorandum which gave some indication of officer support for white tenants' sensitivities in the context of Bangladeshi occupation of the 'best' estates such as the Exmouth:

. . . I would wish to mention the problem associated
with other estates in the Stepney area, in particular
the Exmouth Estate, where in the past criticism has
been levelled by various agencies that Bengali families
have been excluded from consideration. I mention this
matter, not to be controversial, but to highlight the
difficulties which result from housing families who
enjoy a different social and culinary style in blocks
with internal access and where the aroma of more
savoury cooking tends to permeate the immediate
area. Many tenants find this situation unacceptable
and their objections are certainly not racist but
merely traditional. [45]

Statements from officers at County Hall and the GLC
district offices in Tower Hamlets reflected a consistent
strategy, which was supported by local employees at the
estate officer level. Phillips referred to the desire of estate
officers to maintain a harmonious, smoothly running system,
which the arrival of Bangladeshi tenants on all-white estates
was seen as disturbing. Estate officers acted as 'gatekeepers' to council housing at the local level, but their low
pay and unattractive working conditions led to a high
turnover in staff hindering the establishment of community
links to combat racial harassment. As a recent report
noticed:

such work has proceeded very slowly because of the
high vacancy rate among housing estate officers who
are the heart of this community relations work. [46]

Anti-racist training programmes designed to tackle
racial prejudice among junior housing officers of the GLC
management in Tower Hamlets only appeared to encourage
resistance amongst some employees, at least, according to
the trainers in their letter to the head of the GLC Race and
Housing Action Team. They described seven instances of
concern and concluded with the assertion that:

There is some evidence that the Race and Housing
Action Team, the recently appointed black District
Housing Manager, and the training programme are
being deliberately undermined. [47]

135

Yet the statements of certain senior housing officers indicated stern resistance to the charge that housing practices were intentionally racist or that white hostility to Bangladeshi settlement was necessarily racist. Official conduct was referred to in terms of fairness, sensitivity to the different cultural traditions of tenants, the prevention of overcrowding and the exigencies of a housing ladder system, for example. The letter published in the East London Advertiser also repudiated the charge of racism, although the author blamed Bangladeshi tenants for the deterioration of council properties.

The complex interplay of practices and ideological principles called for a more sophisticated analysis than that advanced by most discussions of racism. There was a tendency among those involved in anti-racist struggles to see racism as a unitary phenomenon, in which racist causes are related to racist effects. The concentration of Bangladeshi settlers in the most inferior public housing was caused by a 'knot of practices' which tied together a variety of racist and non-racist practices.[48] The elimination of direct or indirect racial discrimination in the public housing system, just as in the labour market, would not in itself overcome the unequal distribution of resources between Bangladeshis and whites.

The operation of various administrative regulations concerning the entry into public housing, the division of council properties into different sizes of accommodation, the rules of transfer from one type of flat to another and from one area of London to another, were examples of non-racial practices which were part of the knot of practices causing the concentration of certain categories of people in the most dilapidated council housing. These practices in themselves could have created the situation confronting Bangladeshi settlers in Spitalfields and elsewhere. The elimination of racial discrimination by housing officers and white tenants would have to be accompanied by reform of the other practices which caused Bangladeshis and certain categories of white people to be concentrated in the worst council housing. An example of attempts to change these non-racialist practices will now be considered with reference to the GLC housing allocations system.

(iii)   The GLC's housing allocations system and Bangladeshis
Before the review undertaken by Phillips during 1984 of the racist effects of GLC allocations practices, the authority operated a complex computerised points system based on eight categories in a descending order of priority (see Appendix).

The disadvantages faced by Bangladeshis in the allocations system were largely due, according to Phillips' two reports, to the ways in which the allocations system was operated by housing officials and the inflexibility and complexity of the priority points system. The reports also referred to the possibility that Bangladeshis' lack of knowledge about different estates and about the allocations procedures themselves also contributed to the current situation. [49] The imminent transfer of GLC housing responsibilities to the borough council during 1985 encouraged local pressure groups, such as SHAPRS, to use the Phillips' report to press for changes in the allocations priority system which would ovecome some, at least, of the problems described in the report.

In early 1985 the Tower Hamlets Directorate of Housing proposed a revised system of priority categories after consultation with borough and GLC housing officers and other interested parties (see Appendix). The new priority group system attempted to provide fairer treatment for waiting list applicants and homeless people. The first priority group was to be restricted to only residents occupying housing due for redevelopment. The second priority group included those who occupied housing which needed major repairs or who lived in statutorily overcrowded conditions. The group also covered those who needed accommodation for urgent health reasons, who faced serious social problems including racial harassment, or who were unintentionally homeless. Although accommodation continued to be graded in terms of quality, the three main categories of applicant (transfer, waiting list snd homeless people) in each priority group were to be given access to all grades of housing. The intention was to ensure that 'every group could be given access to new accommodation and unpopular accommodation would not become stereotyped'. [50]

The changes referred to various categories of housing applicant, but a major consideration was the introduction of greater equality for Bangladeshis and other ethnic minorities through such reforms. The new system was to be buttressed by the adoption of the GLC's practice of keeping ethnic records and monitoring allocations. The borough Director of Housing raised the issue of suppressing GLC ethnic records after the transfer of GLC housing stock to the borough but commented that:

Any suggestion of suppression would be highly sensitive at a time when ethnic records become universal in the Greater London Mobility Scheme. It would follow findings from the GLC's own ethnic monitoring that Asian households, have been disadvantaged in housing allocations, even if the process has been neither direct nor conscious. [51]

He noted that ethnic monitoring of housing allocations could be related to another GLC policy of applying ethnic monitoring to staff employment which the borough had not adopted:

There has also been some criticism about the lack of ethnic monitoring in staff recruitment, in view of the lack of ethnic minority staff in the housing offices, in contrast to the local population and the GLC's success in attracting such staff. This is a matter for the Administration Committee. [52]

As has been shown in a previous chapter, the borough council did at last agree to introduce ethnic monitoring of staff employment in both the Housing and Social Services Directorates during 1985.

One of the contentious aspects of the new system concerned the regulations over residence time points. The borough Housing Management Committee was eager to retain the practice of allocating points for length of residence in the borough, 'one for each year of residence up to the present maximum of 20'. [53] Residents frequently assumed that length of residence gave them priority over more recent arrivals, and protests were sometimes publicly voiced against Bangladeshis in particular 'jumping the queue'. [54] However, the old GLC system and the new arrangements were intended to give priority mainly to those in various degrees of housing need rather than benefit those who had simply been in the borough a long time. Although points were awarded on the basis of length of residence, most of the points were allocated according to the housing, social and health conditions confronting applicants.

Another popular misconception concerned the length of time an applicant was on the transfer or waiting lists. Contrary to some assumptions, length of time on those lists was not rewarded with any points at all. The effect of the two misunderstandings about how the points system worked was to exacerbate feelings between white and Bangladeshi residents, as white tenants assumed that Bangladeshis were gaining an unfair advantage over longer established residents.

138

Residence time points was a source of resentment for Bangladeshis since they could only be awarded on the basis of 'continuous residence'. Because of periodic visits to Bangladesh, which often lasted for over thirteen weeks, Bangladeshis automatically lost their residence points. The borough's Director of Housing recognised the effect of the regulation on Bangladeshi applications, but argued that under the new system the rule's 'harshness was softened by the proposal to remove one year's residential requirement (they will not have to wait a year before being re-considered)'. [55] No indication, however, was given as to whether the applicant would have to start again or would retain the points gained before leaving the country.

The new priority points system introduced just before the transfer of GLC housing to the borough council during 1985 had tried to overcome some of the deficiencies outlined by Phillips, whose report supported many of the criticisms levied by SHAPRS against the GLC housing system. The modifications in previous GLC and borough council priority grouping and in matching people to accommodation were intended to benefit those on the waiting list and the unintentionally homeless. Bangladeshis could be indirectly helped thereby, given their large numbers on the waiting list and in the unintentionally homeless category. However, the Phillips report had indicated that a variety of non-racial administrative practices combined with other factors, including racial stereotyping and hostility, to prevent Bangladeshis from benefitting through the old GLC system, whose priority points system was not radically different from the new arrangement. It remained to be seen whether the inflexibility and complexity of the old system had been overcome, as well as the problems of stated preferences, housing staff discretion, Bangladeshi lack of knowledge, estate management and the filling of accommodation.

After the transfer of GLC properties to the borough council in 1985, the energies of housing staff and local pressure groups were directed mainly into drawing up a new tenancy agreement which would contribute to the campaign against racial harassment of Bangladeshi tenants. The formal changes of the priority points system and the tenancy agreement were intended to combat discrimination against Bangladeshis and other disadvantaged groups, but they were a small part of a complex pattern of practices which brought together manifold differentiations based on housing needs and social allegiances. The anti-racist struggles of local pressure groups and the anti-racist strategies of political representatives had contributed to changes in certain non-racial practices, at least, which disadvantaged Bangladeshis in particular.

Changes had to be made in other areas for the situation to be greatly transformed, however, and the resistance of certain white tenants to Bangladeshi occupation of some estates indicated one of the obstacles to providing a wider choice of location and accommodation for Bangladeshis. The declining opportunities of white tenants for transfers to housing which they desired came at a time when the local authority was formally attempting to improve the prospects of waiting list and unintentionally homeless applicants, many of whom were Bangladeshis. The competition between categories of housing applicant tended to overlap with social distinctions between whites and Bangladeshis. The variety of housing needs, the diverse types of housing unit and the complexity of official regulations were reduced to a simple opposition between two social categories in certain situations of conflict.

NOTES

[1]   Spitalfields Housing and Planning Rights Service and the Catholic Housing Aid Society, The Spitalfields Survey, Housing and Social Conditions in 1980, 1981, p.57.
[2]   Ibid.
[3]   GLC Housing Committee, Report of the Co-ordinator of Housing Services, 25 January 1982.
[4]   Ibid.
[5]   GLC Ethnic Minorities Committee, Race Equality and Ethnic Minorities in London, Future Strategy Report 1983-85, December 1982, p.7.
[6]   Ibid.
[7]   Ibid.
[8]   Tower Hamlets News, February 1984, p.5, col.2.
[9]   Ibid.
[10]   SHAPRS, Bengalis and GLC Housing Allocations in E.1, March 1982, p.1.
[11]   SHAPRS, Bengalis and GLC Housing Allocations in E.1. An Update - March 1984.
[12]   Ibid.
[13]   Ibid.
[14]   GLC Housing Committee, Report of the Controller of Housing and Technical Services, 13 July 1982, HG 350.
[15]   Ibid.
[16]   GLC Housing Committee, Report of the Chairman, September 1982.
[17]   Ibid.

[18]   JHMC, <u>Report by the Acting Co-ordinator</u>, 29 March 1983.

[19]   See SHAPRS, <u>Annual Report, December 1983</u>, pp.4-5.

[20]   GLC Housing Committee, <u>Report by the Head of Housing Services</u>, 31 May 1984.

[21]   GLC Race and Housing Advisory Group, <u>Race and the Allocation of Council Housing: A Response to the CRE Investigation in Hackney</u>, 8 March 1984, p.3.

[22]   Phillips, D.A., <u>Race and Housing: GLC Policy and Practice in Tower Hamlets</u>, p.8. The first report was called <u>Monitoring of the Experimental Housing Allocation Scheme for GLC Properties in Tower Hamlets</u>, Report by Dr. D.A. Phillips, 23 November 1984. See also Phillips, D.A., <u>What Price Equality?</u>, GLC, 1986.

[23]   Ibid., p.9.

[24]   Ibid., p.13.

[25]   Ibid., p.16.

[26]   Ibid.

[27]   Ibid., p.23.

[28]   SHAPRS, <u>Annual Report, August 1980</u>, p.4.

[29]   SHAPRS, <u>Annual Report, December 1983</u>. p.2.

[30]   SHAPRS, <u>Selby Street: Make it 200 Council Homes</u>, September 1984.

[31]   FBYO, <u>Annual Report 1982-83</u>, p.4.

[32]   Ibid.

[33]   <u>New Voice</u>, 14 December 1984, p.7, col.2.

[34]   Tower Hamlets Homeless Families Committee, <u>Hotels for the Homeless - Our Way Out</u>. 1983.

[35]   <u>THARE News</u>, January 1985, p.7.

[36]   <u>THARE, Annual Report 1984-85</u>, p.31.

[37]   JHMC, <u>Report of GLC Controller of Housing and Technical Services</u>, 6 June 1982.

[38]   JHMC, <u>Housing Management - Progress Report</u>, 13 September 1983, item 2.8.

[39]   See LBTH Development Committee, <u>A Short Report on the Asian Population of Tower Hamlets</u>, February 1984, table v, p.7.

[40]   Tower Hamlets Housing Management Committee, <u>Report of Director of Housing, Housing Allocations - Review</u>, 11/12 September 1984.

[41]   Ibid.

[42]   Ibid.

[43]   Ibid.

[44]   <u>East London Advertiser</u>, 20 August 1982.

[45]   See Phillips' report, op. cit., p.9.

[46]   LBTH, Multi-Committee Report, <u>Joint Report of Chief Executive and Director of Housing</u>, 6-26 February 1985, section 10.12.

[47]   See the second Phillips report, op. cit., and What Price Equality?, op. cit. p.64.

[48]   Feuchtwang, S., 'Occupational Ghettos', Economy and Society, vol. 11, no. 3, August 1982, p. 279.

[49]   See Phillips' second report, Race and Housing: GLC Policy and Practice in Tower Hamlets, para.26.

[50]   LBTH Housing Management Special Transfer Sub-Committee, Report from Director of Housing, 12 September 1984, para. 3.12.

[51]   Ibid., para. 5.2.

[52]   Ibid., para. 5.4.

[53]   Report from Director of Housing, 12 September 1984, op. cit., para. 4.7.

[54]   J Snooks, a former Labour Party councillor and the representative of the Tenants Forum, a group formed by tenants dissatisfied with the Tower Hamlets Tenants Federation, claimed at a public consultation meeting on racial harassment on council estates, 30 May 1985, that 'Bangladeshi families jumped the housing queue by making themselves homeless'. Racism 'had happened to everyone i.e. Irish, Jews, and that the Bangladeshis will also have to wait'. LBTH Note of Public Consultation Meeting, Thursday 30 May 1985.

[55]   Report from Director of Housing, op. cit., para. 4.9.

6 ILEA and Bangladeshi educational needs in Tower Hamlets

(A) **INTRODUCTION**

Between 1982 and 1985 Bangladeshi community workers became involved in the formal representation of their community's educational needs to the ILEA. Once again Bengali activists claimed to be the authentic voice of their community as negotiations took place with members of ILEA's Education Committee and administrative hierarchy over the distribution of Section II funding to improve groups across the borough. A consultative organisation called BENTH (Bangladeshi Educational Needs in Tower Hamlets) was formed in early 1983 and a variety of demands were expressed through its publication, the BENTH Bulletin, during 1983 and 1984. BENTH leaders became regular visitors to ILEA's district and central offices, while ILEA officers attended meetings at community centres in Spitalfields particularly. The co-operation resulted in a number of community group projects being founded through ILEA's Tower Hamlets Initiative. At the same time the creation of BENTH and Bangladeshi representation on ILEA institutions became embroiled in struggles between Bengali activists which were played out in other arenas, i.e. the Spitalfields Labour Party, the FBYO and the BWA.

The Tower Hamlets Intiative was part of an attempt to combat racial inequality within London's inner city areas. Like the GLC, the Education Committee of ILEA outlined an anti-racist strategy during 1982 and 1983 which involved closer consultation with ethnic minority representatives. The strategy, in turn, was related to a more general campaign against educational disadvantage which was caused, according to ILEA analyses published in 1983, by class and gender as well as racial divisions. [1] The strategy was implemented during 1984 and 1985 not only by increased expenditure for ILEA and ethnic community institutions but also through the introduction of such new practices as ethnic monitoring and new consultative institutions within ILEA, i.e. an Equal Opportunities Sub-Committee and at the level of Tower Hamlets, for example, a Steering Group followed by a Divisional Committee.

This chapter will explore, therefore, the inter-locking of different strategies and practices as ILEA Education Committee members, officials and Bangladeshi comnmunity representatives engaged in the delivery of the Tower Hamlets Iniatitive during 1983 to 1985.

(B)   **ILEA's ANTI-RACIST STRATEGY**

(i)   Public consultation
Although ILEA and the GLC co-operated closely at both political and administrative levels, ILEA was a virtually autonomous institution.   It had its own structure of committees co-ordinated by the Education Committee which consisted of 38 GLC Councilors, 13 members appointed by Inner London borough councils and the City of London, as well as 17 people chosen by ILEA from those experienced in the educational field. [2] Until May 1981 Sir Ashley Bramall, one of Tower Hamlets GLC representatives, had been ILEA leader but he had been replaced by Bryn Davies, who lost the leadership to Frances Morrell during April 1983 in a struggle where Ken Livingstone unsuccessfully intervened in support of Bryn Davies. [3]

Between May 1981 and April 1983 ILEA's committees were engaged in public consultation with ILEA staff, ethnic group and women's representatives, parents and governors concerning the formulation of strategies to combat educational inequalities caused by racial, gender and class divisions. The outcome of such meetings was a series of public statements during 1983 beginning with the publication of four documents in April 1983 which were to form the basis for the eight analyses of educational inequality under the title Race, Sex and Class later in the year.

144

(ii)   ILEA's consultation with Bangladeshi representatives
   During the period of public consultation, 1981-83,
young Bangladeshi activists in the FBYO established a
relationship wth ILEA's political and administrative leaders
which gave them an advantage over their Bangladeshi rivals.
   In July 1982 FBYO representatives met ILEA's Chief
Education Officer at County Hall to explain the educational
needs of their community. The meeting was followed in
February 1983 by a conference at the Asian Studies Centre,
St. Mary's ward, organised by FBYO members in conjunction
with ILEA staff at the Montefiore Community Education
Centre where the FBYO had its offices. The conference was
attended by ILEA's Chief Education Officer, ILEA oficials
and teaching staff, Sir A. Bramall, Bangladeshi community
organisers and Bangladeshi parents. The conference discussed
Bangladeshi educational needs in the light of the planned
Tower Hamlets Initiative which was to allocate
approximately £500,000 in the 1983/84 budget to improve
Bangladeshi and other ethnic minorities' educational
resources.   The conference was followed by the formal
creation of an 'umbrella' organisation, BENTH, which was to
co-operate with ILEA in the negotiation of funding under the
Initiative.
   ILEA established a Tower Hamlets Initiative Steering
Group after April 1983, 'to co-ordinate the work of the
Initiative, make recommendations to sub-committee on the
allocation of resources, and liaise with local community
groups'.[4] The Group was chaired by Sir Ashley Bramall and
included the ILEA Leader and Deputy-Leader as ex-officio
members, representatives from all ILEA's sub-committees,
GLC and borough members from Tower Hamlets, authorised
members for multi-ethnic education and two Minority Party
members. Significantly, from the Bangladeshi organiser's
viewpoint, BENTH also supplied three members while the
Tower Hamlets Afro-Caribbean Association (THACA)
provided one member. BENTH was brought into the decision-
making machinery of ILEA and its representatives
participated in making recommendations concerning the
funding of projects submitted by the numerous Bangladeshi
organisations across the borough. (The Steering Group was
later replaced by the Tower Hamlets Initiative Divisional
Committee).
   The process of reforming ILEA's institutional structure
to allow ethnic minority representation also led to the
agreement by the Education Committee in July 1983 to
introduce a new Equal Opportunities Sub-Committee, with an
Ethnic Minorities Section which would advise the new sub-
committee. Representatives from Tower Hamlets ethnic

145

minority organisations met in October and elected two Bangladeshis - the chairman of BENTH and the President of the BWA.

The consultation between ILEA and BENTH did not go unchallenged by opponents of the BENTH leadership during 1983, while a bitter split within BENTH's ranks in 1984 prompted ILEA to dispense with the Tower Hamlets Initiative Divisional Committee in the summer of 1985. Although both ILEA and BENTH spoke as though they were unitary subjects, the process of consultation was bound up with varying strategies and practices among Bangladeshi community groups and ILEA's diverse institutions.

(C) **THE   REPRESENTATION   OF   BANGLADESHI INTERESTS**

(i) BENTH Bulletin - the authentic voice of the community, May 1983 - February 1984

Between May 1983 and October 1984 BENTH presented the community's needs partly through the BENTH Bulletin which was supported by ILEA funding. The Bulletin repeatedly claimed to be the authentic voice of the community. In its first publication the Bulletin professed its determination 'to be the consistent voice of a commanding educational voice inside the Bangladeshi community'. [5] BENTH was described as an organisation 'mandated by the community to carry on the fight to secure the educational rights of the community', [6] a struggle which began with the emergence of the Bangladeshi community in the borough during the early 1960s. Notice was taken of the narrow origins of BENTH which had, as some commented, 'an orchestrated origin' but the organisation had received the 'overwhelming backing from people inside the Bangladeshi community as soon as the 5 February 1983 conference was successfully concluded'. [7] Eighty-three organisations and individuals were then named in support of BENTH's claim to represent the community.

The May 1983 Bulletin outlined demands which largely matched the changes suggested by ILEA's own declarations during April. The demands were juxtaposed on the central pages with an historical account of the community's struggle which emphasised the role of young Bangladeshis since the murder of Altab Ali in 1978 -

The story since 1978 is a continuing one and education, like housing and employment, is very much a concern of the rising force of Bangladeshi youths. BENTH as an organisation owes considerable amount of clout to the stand taken by the united voice of Bangladeshi youths'. [8]

146

Young Bangladeshis were fighting for their educational rights in a 'professional' manner -

> For the youths, like their more experienced colleagues on the BENTH steering committee, do acknowledge the need for a disciplined and scientific approach to securing demands as are involved in the field of education. [9]

Both the Tower Hamlets Initiative Steering Group and the Ethnic Minorities Section of the Equal Opportunities Sub-Committee met at County Hall. The completion of the detailed administrative work involved in the allocation of funds for 1983/84 enabled ILEA to close down the Steering Group and to devolve its work to the Tower Hamlets Initiative Divisional Committee. The new committee was again chaired by Sir Ashley Bramall but it only contained six ILEA representatives, three of whom came from Tower Hamlets, the three BENTH members and one THACA representative and the two Bangladeshis on the Ethnic Minorities Section of the Equal Opportunities Committee. The committee took part in the assessment of new bids for 1984/85 and 'the evaluation and monitoring of projects already agreed'.[10] It met in ILEA's district offices in Tower Hamlets rather than at County Hall and received advice from local ILEA staff including the Director of the Montefiore Community Education Centre, East Spitalfields, where the FBYO was based.

The references to professionalism, discipline and scientific approach appeared to reflect the willingness of BENTH leaders to organise along lines familiar to community workers and to ILEA members. A steering committee was formed and six representatives to ILEA were chosen (five young Bangladeshis and one of the highly experienced older representatives, Muhammad Reza). Groups were 'affiliated to BENTH on an ad hoc basis strictly on the ground that a formal constitution for BENTH was undergoing adoption as BENTH Bulletin went to press'. [11]

During 1983 the BENTH Bulletins pursued a number of specific issues concerning education, viz. language teaching, ILEA's anti-racist policy and the media, Asian school meals, bi-lingual headteachers, Asian governors in schools and colleges, Bangladeshi under-achievement in local schools library provision of multi-cultural books, audio-visual materials, ethnic minority under-representation in higher education and the ILEA Youth Service. Although the professed desire of ILEA leaders to attack racism and promote greater equality was welcomed, BENTH Bulletin articles questioned the sensitivity of local ILEA institutions

147

to Bangladeshi needs. The third BENTH Bulletin in July 1983 commented on the application of local ILEA centres for funding through the Tower Hamlets Initiative in the following terms -

> Not only had they not sought the views of the local relevant community before rushing in their 'bids', these institutions appeared to be actively trying to exclude from their calculations even those groups inside the community who were already working to improve the standard of educational provisions here. BENTH is duty bound to monitor the progress of these institutions as they go on spending vast sums of money given them in the name of the people in Tower Hamlets. [12]

As the authentic voice of the Bangladeshi community BENTH knew what the community wanted unlike local ILEA institutions which refused to listen to BENTH and other 'groups inside the community'.

In an article 'What about the "proficient" many?' in the fourth BENTH Bulletin the attempt to improve the proficiency of ethnic minority children by 'mainly inner city education authorities like ILEA' was related to the 'continued existence of racism' which was -

> the real obstruction that is erected by policy makers at all levels of society, thus making sure that people of certain groups are discriminated against no matter how properly educated, how thoroughly well versed and proficient they are in their respective art, skill and, of course, the English language. [13]

White teachers were benefitting from the new courses being introduced to improve proficiency in English, even though they lacked the necessary level of commitment and headteacher support 'to match the needs of a community like say, the Bangladeshis in Tower Hamlets'. [14] Ethnic minority 'education workers', on the other hand, were being ignored while 'educational policy makers' considered 'the implications of an initiative or two relating, apparently, to the expressed educational needs of the given community'. [15] The article concluded with the assertion that:

> . . . no progressive educationist and education worker should let the trendy theories about 'proficiency in English' to be used in de facto defense of the status quo in education based on racism. [16]

Anonymous articles like 'What about the "proficient" many?' expressed the beliefs of the young community activists who supplied six of the seven officer posts in the first BENTH election during June 1983. BENTH's chairman, Abdul Motin, brought considerable journalistic experience to the Bulletin as well as radical political beliefs. Muhammad Reza's journalistic expertise and less outspoken views had been made available between the February conference and the second BENTH Bulletin but for the rest of the year he had to retire from community activities. The references to professionalism, discipline and science in the first Bulletin article on the history of Bangladeshi community activism, which bore the hallmarks of Muhammad Reza's style, were replaced by an extensive critique of ILEA institutions and of British society in general. Although BENTH representatives co-operated with ILEA in a limited programme of improving Bangladeshi educational resources through ILEA institutions and community projects, the BENTH Bulletin kept up the pressure on ILEA to look more critically at its own educational service and its involvement in the racism which permeated British society in general.

The fifth BENTH Bulletin in September 1983 again expressed the contributors' determination to look beyond educational reforms to more general issues and to show the relationship between education and other services. A report on physical assaults on young 'Asians' was set beside an article by a female contributor who came from an 'East African Asian' background. Her article continued the theme of white educationists' insensitivity to Asian students, which was established in 'What about the "proficient" many?', although the writer moved on to discuss the experience of 'Asian women' at various levels of the educational system. The problems confronting Asian youths and women were discussed in a Bulletin whose front page brought together information on educational matters with the issue of housing. The GLC's opposition to central government policies was commended but in a reference to the meeting between GLC representatives, local activists and residents at the Brady Centre, East Spitalfields, on 14 September, the article asserted that:

> Quite apart from the Tower Hamlets people's support for the GLC in its campaign to escape Mrs Thatcher's revivalist axe, the GLC or its politicians like Mr Livingstone would lose the support of the people whose grievances are answered by clever . . . shallow words that point to 'a worse enemy than us'. Education is bound to remain beyond the reach of people who are

denied a house! What the GLC and the ILEA should be doing is to start a building programme in Tower Hamlets together with the local council which could do with a bit of initiative from the GLC. The people, of all colours, would back them then. [17]

Housing and education, the GLC and ILEA were seen to be inextricably linked and the pressure had to be maintained on both public authorities so that they could not shuffle off their responsibilities to local 'people' by blaming the central government for not satisfying local demands. At the same time the borough council could be led into showing initiative.

Local struggles were related to international conflicts in several BENTH Bulletins, with references to the Indian sub-continent, Zimbabwe, Cuba, Libya and Iran. The February 1984 front page article, 'The right to speak our language', used the international dimension to establish an even more familiar link for its readers - the Bengali language struggle between 1952 and 1971 against Pakistani state oppression was set beside the demand for mother-tongue teaching within ILEA. The two issues appeared to be explained in terms of a conflict between democracy and bureaucracy -

> Conflict between democracy, the people's wish and bureaucracy which is there to frustrate that wish, may not be new. But it has to be looked at anew every time it appears to be offered as the justification for the stifling of the process which is otherwise well disposed towards delivering the goods to the people who have a right to them. One such right is rooted in the Inner London children of 'non-English' speaking language groups to be taught their own mother tongue. As part of the mainstream curriculum and as a fully recognised academic and life subject. This is a right which has already been recognised by the ILEA. But problems remain. Wherever bureaucracy is seen to be delaying, marginalising or frustrating that recognition the people would resist. The Bangladesh history is a very good example of that prospect. [18]

The front page article was followed by Muhammad Reza's discussion of standard Bengali and regional dialects including Sylheti and an article by Abdul Motin on the Bangladeshi national celebration of 21 February which brought together the Bengali language movement and Bangladeshi nationalism.

150

Although the BENTH Bulletins spoke of the community as a united entity, articles did periodically address themselves to specific categories within the community - school children, those in higher education and women, for instance. There was very little reference to the needs of older Bangladeshis nor were the views of 'traditional' Islamic teachers and fundamentalists aired in the Bulletins between May 1983 and February 1984. The third clause of BENTH's Constitution had committed the organisation to 'promote religious education of Bangladeshis living or working in LBTH'. However, the young activists who provided most of the leadership of BENTH during 1983 had avoided close contact with local religious teachers and mosques. Only five of the 58 groups affiliated to BENTH in May 1983 were organisations involved in religious teaching or youth work with an Islamic orientation. The election in June 1983 of Hajji Abdul Hamid as BENTH's Treasurer brought into the leadership an older businessman who had undertaken the pilgrimage to Mecca and Medinah (the hajj) and thereby claimed the traditionally respected title of Hajji. Even so, the BENTH Bulletins concentrated on gaining reforms within the existing state educational system and public authority funding for local secular community organisations outside ILEA. The BENTH leadership did not provide a forum where demands could be made for the separate education of Muslim children under Islamic principles.

The issue of religious education in the second BENTH Bulletin, June 1983, for example, was related to the need for a bilingual headteacher of a local ILEA primary school in Spitalfields. Canon Barnett school's intake was 'now 100% Bangladeshi in origin' and one of the justifications for 'a bilingual Bengali head' was that only such a person could 'foster close links with the parents and the community at large', could possess a 'real understanding of Bangladeshi culture and customs' and 'be prepared to work in co-operation with local Bengali leaders'. [19]

In the July 1983 Bulletin religious education was discussed with reference to the teaching of Christianity in state schools but, as in the June article, care was taken to link religion to Bangladeshi 'culture' and 'tradition', An interviewer involved in a survey of parental 'interest in their children's schooling' told the Bulletin -

> that many parents were astounded when it was revealed to them that their children, many of whom were girls, had been learning about Christian religion and nothing about Islam and were getting trained to dance and perform music while nothing about their own culture or tradition was being even mentioned let alone being taught. [20]

(ii)   BENTH - divisions and collapse, February 1983 - June 1985

The pretensions of BENTH leaders to be the educational voice of the Bangladeshi community by virtue of the support of numerous local organisations and their election as BENTH officers did not go unchallenged. Young community activists opposed to the FBYO leadership, older businessman holding office in the BWA, the Spitalfields councillor, Nurul Huque, who ran his own voluntary school, religious teachers, Islamic fundamentalists and Bangladeshi women activists claimed to represent particular interests which were not adequately catered for by the BENTH leadership. The election of Walid Ali as a member of the Ethnic Minorities Section of ILEA's Equal Opportunities Sub-Committee, for instance, was bound up with the conflict between Walid Ali and BENTH's Treasurer, Hajji Abdul Hamid, within the BWA as first generation businessmen tried to maintain their claim to speak for the community.

Other activists could plead their own cases directly to ILEA and the GLC. Joganari, a women's group, for example, received funding from the GLC Women's Committee and applied for support through ILEA's Tower Hamlets Initiative Steering Group in order to establish a women's centre:

> where women can meet and learn on their own terms. It should build on community networks. For this reason it should be staffed by local women, in order to facilitate the use of these networks . . . The Centre would be used as a central reserve from which classes could be organised in local neighbourhoods, in community flats, tenant halls, or even small groups of women meeting in each other's flats, as appropriate. [21]

The BENTH Bulletin had discussed a number of issues concerning Bangladeshi women during 1983 and a female activist was included in BENTH's list of officers. Nevertheless, the members of Joganari wanted to operate outside the existing community and public authority institutions and emphasised the role of local women as opposed to activists from outside the borough:

> At the present time many local women feel a deep sense of distrust in existing established institutions in the Borough. While important developmental work may have been done in the past by educationalists from outside Tower Hamlets, the new-found sense of autonomy by women living within the community is

152

strongly felt, as is the need to develop the newly released abilities of self-organisation. The Centre must, therefore, be on separate premises, not attached to any existing institution. These premises must be solely for the use of women. The Centre workers must be responsible to the users. Local control is essential. [22]

Nurul Huque, in his capacity as a borough councillor for Spitalfields and head of his own Bengali-medium school, was also not prepared to recognise BENTH's claim to be the authentic voice of the Bangladeshi community concerning education. He campaigned for his own school outside BENTH fighting, for example, during 1983 for his school to be relocated near the site which it occupied in West Spitalfields and which was to be redeveloped by the GLC. Despite BENTH's discussion of many local developments, Nurul Huque's campaign received no support in the BENTH Bulletins. Indeed, at least one of the BENTH's officers had worked to frustrate Nurul Huque's plans in another context, speaking against Huque's application to join the Spitalfields Labour Party during 1982 and 1983.

BENTH's claim to be the voice of the Bangladeshi community were also hampered by its leaders' involvement in various intra-communal conflicts which were also fought out in political arenas across the borough as previous chapters have made clear. Opposition soon appeared from among the ranks of community activists who felt excluded by the leadership which emerged after the February 1983 conference. A split emerged among prominent youth organisers within the FBYO which resulted in the departure from the FBYO's Executive Committee of Syed Nurul Islam, who had contested the Spitalfields ward election with Nurul Huque in May 1982, and Rafique Ullah who had also entered the May 1982 election as an SDP candidate. The rift emerged during April 1983, so that when Nurul Huque's letter was published two months later in the periodical of the Bangladesh Youth Front where Rafique Ullah was General Secretary, there was an implicit alignment between two activists whose interests were opposed to BENTH and FBYO leaders.

Syed Nurul Islam was a senior member of another youth group based in St. Dunstan's ward. The other two signatories of the handbill which attacked the leadership of BENTH were not directly involved in youth work. Kashem Ali had met numerous Bangladeshi clients through his employment at the Tower Hamlets Law Centre, which was located on the borders of St. Katharine's ward where the fourth signatory, Ashik Ali, had been elected as a Labour councillor in May 1982.

The challenge, however, was successfully defeated by the BENTH leadership between April and June 1983. The support of first generation Bangladeshis was recruited by taking advantage of a dispute between older businessmen in the oldest community organisation, the BWA, whose own pretensions to lead the community had been countered by the creation of the FBYO in 1980. The election of Hajji Abdul Hamid as BENTH Treasurer in June 1983 signalled the BENTH leadership's acceptance of an older businessman who had questioned the constitutional propriety of the election of Walid Ali in 1982 as the BWA President. When Abdul Motin was elected to the Ethnic Minorities Section of ILEA's Equal Opportunities Sub-Committee in October 1983, the strength of BENTH's following was indicated by the 'overwhelming support' he received. Even so, Walid Ali was the other candidate to be elected from Tower Hamlets to the Ethnic Minorities Section - the youth leaders' opponents were still a force to be reckoned with and Walid Ali was supported by Bangladeshi businessmen who were determined to resist exclusion from the new consultative bodies formed between 1983 and 1985.

The conflict between Syed Nurul Islam, Rafique Ullah, Nurul Huque and Kashem Ali, on the one hand, and their FBYO opponents on the other was fought out in other community arenas after June 1983. The leadership of the Kobi Nazrul Centre, which had been opened in October 1982, became a matter of dispute at the October 1983 AGM. Kashem Ali and Rafique Ullah, who held respectively the posts of chairman and general secretary in the Centre's first management committee were opposed by other committee members led by an old colleague of Muhammad Reza and a veteran community organiser, Abdus Samad, and a young FBYO activist, Aziz. Despite attempts by Bangladeshi and white members which involved the Spitalfields Local Committee, the Spitalfields Project and the borough council, the split remained unresolved by April 1984 when the borough council's Policy Committee decided to close the Centre temporarily while its future management and use could be decided.

The repeated eruption of bitter disputes during the preparations for and the holding of AGMs had involved the BWA in 1982 and now the Kobi Nazrul Centre during 1983. BENTH, too, was caught up in the conflict between the supporters of the FBYO leadership and their opponents during

154

the summer of 1984. A split developed between BENTH's chairman, Abdul Motin, and his colleagues over the preparations for the organisation's AGM, although a number of other issues were embroiled in the conflict judging by the allegations made by the disputants. Abdul Motin called upon ILEA to recognise the election of officers at an AGM held on 2 September 1984, while on the same day Huque's colleagues held a special general meeting which denounced his action and expelled him from the 'official' BENTH. Faced with competing claims for recognition and funding, ILEA decided in April 1985 to wind up the Tower Hamlets Initiative Divisional Committee with its BENTH representatives and to withdraw funding for BENTH.

The dispute within BENTH in the summer of 1984 also spilled over into the election of officers for the borough's new race relations organisation, THARE. Officers had been elected at THARE's inaugural meeting in July 1984 and the BENTH/FBYO leadership gained most of the positions for themselves and their supporters. Habib Ullah was elected chairman, Hajji Abdul Hamid became treasurer and six executive committee members were also prominent figures within the FBYO. After the 2 September 1984 split within BENTH Abdul Motin supported the attempt by opponents of the new THARE leadership to challenge the election at the July meeting. According to an article in a 'Naz' BENTH Bulletin brought out by Abdul Motin in September, the opposition of the former THCRE chairman, Dr. Ahmad, to THARE had received the backing of '16 Tower Hamlets groups led by the Bangladesh Welfare Association' whose secretary, Kashem Ali, who had been elected to THARE's executive committee, claimed that 'a group of unrepresentative persons had effectively hijacked what could otherwise be a fairly positive body'. 23

Abdul Motin found support from other opponents of the FBYO leadership besides Kashem Ali. Among the officers elected at the September 1984 meeting called by Abdul Motin, were Syed Nurul Islam, Rafique Ullah and also Abdul Hannan who taught at Nurul Huque's school and later joined Rafique Ullah in challenging the Spitalfields Labour Party leadership at the ward party's AGM in February 1985.

The overlap between disputes in community and political institutions could be seen in the activities of Abdul Motin's opponents. The chairman of the 'Brady' BENTH, Riaz, was also a member of the FBYO's executive committee and a a prominent member of the Spitalfields Labour Party. Riaz had spoken against Nurul Huque's admission to the Labour Party during 1982 and 1983. He had also helped to organise the ward party leadership's response to the challenge by Rafique Ullah and Abdul Hannan and had campaigned vigorously on behalf of his friend and fellow ILEA employee, Abbas Uddin, during the by-election campaign of June 1985, where Abdul Hannan, with the assistance of Nurul Huque, posed such a formidable threat.

Riaz was one of several BENTH leaders who were moving from youth organisational work into local authority jobs and party politics. BENTH's general secretary until July 1984 was Habib Ullah who resigned after taking up an ILEA appointment. Habib's wife had joined the GLC's Race and Housing Action Team during 1983 and took a prominent role in the new women's group, Joganari, which received funding from the GLC Women's Committee. Habib had been a member of the FBYO's executive committee and its general secretary, while Asrob Ullah, who became BENTH's acting general secretary after Habib's resignation in July 1984, was appointed FBYO chairman for 1983/84. A fifth BENTH officer, Sunahwar Ali, was FBYO treasurer for 1983/84, an outreach worker for ILEA's Montefiore Community Education Centre and a prospective Labour candidate in the 1986 borough elections. Another BENTH member who played a key role in the special general meeting on 2 September 1984, when Abdul Motin was expelled, was Jan Alam, a member of the Spitalfields Labour Party who was later to begin a course at Ruskin College, Oxford, and to join the ranks of Bangladeshis chosen as Labour Party candidates for the 1986 borough election.

Some older Bangladeshi leaders were involved in BENTH from the outset. Muhammad Reza and Abdus Samad had established close links with white activists in Spitalfields particularly during the 1970s and co-operated with the youth leadership which emerged in the late 1970s. Muhammad Reza was the only first generation Bangladeshi among the six representatives who met ILEA officials before the formal organisation of BENTH. After a serious operation he returned to play a controversial role in BENTH and became more involved than ever before in Spitalfields community activities through his appointment, under the Tower Hamlets Initiative, to an educational outreach scheme at the Montefiore Community Education Centre. He had long co-operated with another first generation community organiser, Abdus Samad, whose part in the Kobi Nazrul Centre dispute has already been mentioned. Abdus had opposed Nurul Huque's entry into the Labour Party during 1982 and 1983 and was closely associated with the white Left-wing leaders of the Spitalfields Labour Party in his capacity as ward co-chairman during 1984.

The attempt by the BENTH leadership to present a united front to those outside the Bangladeshi community and to speak for the community in educational matters was beset from the beginning by rivalries between community organisations and their leaders. The intra-communal disputes became embroiled in party political conflicts involving white activists. Councillors in the borough, together with their administrative colleagues, posed as neutral arbiters during intra-communal disputes which affected the management of publicly funded community organisations and centres. However, Bangladeshis questioned the lack of involvement by local authorities in community disputes. While there may not have been any deliberate manipulation of community activists and their rivalries, the operation of official practices appeared to contribute to intra-communal conflict.

(D)   **ILEA AND BANGLADESHI EXPLANATIONS OF INTRA - COMMUNAL CONFLICT**

(i)   ILEA's discussion of the BENTH dispute
During April 1985 ILEA's Policy Co-Ordinating Sub-Committee received a lengthy report by its Chief Education Officer on various aspects of the dispute. With regard to ILEA's response to the competing claims of the rival BENTH organisations, the Education Officer relied on the advice of the Head of ILEA's Legal Branch, who took 'the view that the Authority's decision on which, if either, of the two organisations should be supported, would be better taken on pragmatic and policy grounds than on legal grounds'. He added that:

> Although it may appear that 'Brady' BENTH may be considered to have acted with the greater degree of constitutional propriety, much more detailed investigation will be needed to form any sort of con-clusive judgement, and as the issues appear to relate very much to matters and personalities within the Bangladeshi community, the Head of the Legal Branch advises the Authority against attempting to make a decision on the basis of legal niceties which are themselves uncertain. [24]

The problems were caused largely by intra-communal disputes and personality clashes, pre-empting the need for a decision to be taken by ILEA on legal grounds, especially given the unreliable nature of current evidence concerning the particular dispute in question. The Education Officer proceeded to note that the split had led to the suspension of the Tower Hamlets Initiative Divisional Committee and an-

157

other new ILEA organisation, the Tower Hamlets Ethnic Minorities Consultative Committee. The suspension of the Divisional Committee had 'prevented further applications from being submitted for Sub-Committee approval this financial year' but the Education Officer also drew attention to the weakness of the committee when it had been in operation -

> . . . the lengthy, often prolonged consultative processes of the THIDC has meant that many disadvantaged groups have not benefitted from the Initiative. This has caused bad feeling within the community at large and led many people to believe that the Authority is unwilling to honour its intention to increase the educational provision for ethnic minority groups to an acceptable level. [25]

ILEA's Education Officer appeared to be suggesting that ILEA's traditional practice of dealing with the demands of local community groups through its administrative channels and committee structure was more efficient than the consultative organisations established since 1982. He concluded that:

> . . . in the unusual circumstances the interests of the local community would best be served by disbanding the Tower Hamlets Initiative Divisional Committee and instead make use of existing administrative machinery for processing the work of the Initiative. As in many other areas of work involving support to voluntary and statutory organisations, major decisions, including the allocation of resources would be the subject of reports to the relevant Sub-Committee and would include the views of the local community. If members agree to this proposal this would mean that grant-aid to BENTH would cease from a date to be determined by Sub-Committees. [26]

The solution to the problem caused by the BENTH split would be resolved, therefore, by reverting to customary official practice which would deal more efficiently with community groups' demands than the THIDC. ILEA would be relieved of the responsibility for funding BENTH and of having to decide which BENTH it should officially recognise. The recommended decision was also justified on the grounds that 'the interests of the local community would best be served' thereby and ILEA's reputation would no longer be harmed by a consultative committee whose dilatory activities had exacerbated relations between ILEA and the local community. The withdrawal of official support and recognition of BENTH would also affect the other consultative committee on which BENTH was represented -the Tower Hamlets Ethnic Minorities Committee. Abdul Motin's membership of the Ethnic Minorities Section of ILEA's central Equal Opportunities Sub-Committee would not necessarily have been affected by the measures taken concerning ILEA's consultative committees in Tower Hamlets.

(ii) Bangladeshi criticisms of ILEA during 1984

Since the inception of BENTH Bangladeshi representatives had expressed their dissatisfaction with ILEA. They criticised the inadequacy of the amount allocated to the Tower Hamlets Initiative for 1983-5 and the bids made by local ILEA institutions which had failed the community in the past. This insensitivity of ILEA's institutions was explained by some BENTH Bulletin articles in terms of racist beliefs and practices evident throughout British society. Furthermore, education was sometimes presented as a weapon used by the state to control colonial and other oppressed peoples. Even to talk about oppression within Britain's ethnic communities gave racists ammunition to use against those communities -

> Would you go so far as to say that indeed oppression does exist in our community, but the way to combat it, to weaken it and free ourselves from this oppression we need to stop mentioning it as if its existence justifies racists to oppress us even more. . ? [27]

The discussions of the educational situation confronting local Bangladeshis by Abdul Motin's rivals within BENTH also referred to 'racist conspiracies' and the impact of institutionalised racism 'that continues to vitiate all sectors of the British socio-political life including the education establishment.[28]Their BENTH Bulletin published during October 1984 detected the addition of a new element to the 'old tasks of identifying the educational needs and campaigning for remedial measures'. There needed to be:

> positive but critical co-operation with the Educational Authorities to make the best use of the resources that we may be able to wrench from them. Rhetoric and demogogy will have to be supplemented by positive demonstration of the community's willingness and capacity to make creative and constructive contributions towards implementation of the anti-racist policies of the ILEA.[29]

The October 1984 Bulletin emphasised specific projects through which community organisers could develop greater 'professionalism' and exercise their creativity, i.e. Bengali mother-tongue teaching, parental involvement, supplementary schools, curricular materials and teacher training.

In another report by Abdul Motin's rivals a number of problems concerned with ILEA's handling of the Tower Hamlets Initiative were outlined. Only half of the amount promised by ILEA had been allocated and the funds made available were 'Section 11 responsibility' so that 'the funding may be withdrawn by the Home Office whenever they like. [30] Although the Initiative included all ethnic minorities in the borough, the limited allocation prevented their needs from being adequately catered for. The report added:

> Indeed, it will not be wrong to mention that different communities fighting over scarce resources necessarily divide people. The last meeting of the THIDC reached a 'deadlock' due to shortage of funds. [31]

Dissatisfaction with the limited brief of the THIDC was also expressed. The Committee's duty to decide on 'grant-giving' made it difficult to raise policy issues and revealed 'a lack of commitment from the Politicians'. The Committee's ability to discuss policy issues such as 'Mother-Tongue, Halal meals etc' would give it 'more credit than the other so-called powerless "Ethnic Consultative Committees", that can easily be by-passed'.[32]

Bangladeshi community organisers, therefore, were also dissatisfied with the Tower Hamlets Initiative and the Divisional Committee but for different reasons than ILEA's Chief Educational Officer. They wanted a much greater allocation of funds from the mainstream ILEA budget and a discussion of policy issues rather than solely deciding on the distribution of limited resources. The attitude of BENTH representatives opposed to Abdul Motin was similar to that adopted by THARE representatives and the similarity reflected the extensive overlap in the leadership of the two pressure groups. New consultative organisations established by ILEA and the borough council were viewed with scepticism by Bangladeshi activists who wanted to represent their community at the centre of power and decision-making. 'Ethnic Consultative Committees', whether in the form of the borough council's Ethnic Minorities Consultative Committee, were described as 'talking-shops' or 'powerless'.

ILEA's decision during 1985 to terminate the Divisional and Ethnic Minorities Consultative committees brought several advantages for Bangladeshi representatives. The blame for ending these committees and BENTH could be placed on ILEA's shoulders. Bangladeshi representatives would no longer be compromised by participation in committees which attracted much antagonism from activists in local ethnic minority groups. The responsibility for refusing community projects could now be laid at the door of the political and administrative leaders of ILEA. Abdul Motin's opponents within BENTH still retained major advantages over other activists through their participation in projects supported through the Tower Hamlets Initiative, their leadership of other pressure groups, i.e. the FBYO and THARE, and their links with ILEA through the Montefiore Community Education Centre in Spitalfields and, in some cases, as ILEA employees.

The anti-racist strategy outlined by ILEA during 1983 appeared to have become embroiled in Tower Hamlets in a complex set of administrative and community practices during the Initiative of 1983-5. Although the Initiative was presented by ILEA as a practical demonstration of its commitment to an anti-racist strategy, the Initiative involved an administrative and educational hierarchy as well as a plethora of community organisations whose demands could not be co-ordinated to their mutual satisfaction. ILEA officials wanted to implement a programme with limited resources over two years which relied on existing ILEA institutions in the borough. Consultation and co-operation was sought from representatives of a unified 'umbrella' organisation, BENTH, through new committees. Community representatives wanted much greater resources on a longer term or permanent basis and participation in policy decisions. Both ILEA official and BENTH representatives were dissatisfied with the new institutions in which they met together and both found fault with the other for the inadequacies of these institutions. The abolition of the consultative committees and a return to previous methods of negotiation held advantages for both ILEA and Bangladeshi representatives given their different strategies and practices. The failure of the new committees and BENTH was due, therefore, to more than just the clash of personalities and factional conflicts within the Bangladeshi community.

(E)   **PRACTICE AND THE IMPLEMENTATION OF THE TOWER HAMLETS INITIATIVE**

ILEA's decision to allocate money to the improvement of educational resources for ethnic minorities in Tower Hamlets was implemented by bids from interested parties and then deciding as to which bids should be accepted and how much grant each should receive.

The amount demanded by bids which was submitted during 1983 far exceeded the funds allocated to the Initiative. The proposal to the Education Committee to approve certain projects during June 1983 indicated the kind of problems which quickly began to bedevil the Initiative.

The June 1983 proposal earmarked £305,843 of the £525,000 to be spent during the 1983/84 financial year. £77,510 had already been allocated so that only £141,647 remained to be distributed if the June 1983 proposal was accepted. Approximately one-third of the £305,843 was to be spent on the appointment of full-time youth workers to six Bangladeshi voluntary projects, albeit through ILEA's Area Youth Office. Over another one-third was allocated to statutory projects by local ILEA institutions so that less than one-third of the total submission consisted of community schemes outside the direct control of ILEA. The Bangladeshi voluntary groups which were recommended for financial assistance in the June 1983 proposal reflected the pre-eminence of Spitalfields organisations and the youth leadership. Seven of the twelve groups were based in Spitalfields and all of them employed second generation community workers. Five were youth groups whose founders had usually been involved in the first youth activities of the late 1970s and the protests following Altab Ali's death during 1978. These young community organisers regularly met at ILEA's Montefiore Community Education Centre in Spitalfields since the FBYO and several other Bangladeshi community projects operated from the Centre. Under the Initiative the Centre's importance was further increased by the employment of extra staff to 'respond more to the needs identified by existing users of the Centre and local community organisations'. [33]

The June 1983 proposal alienated a variety of activists both inside and outside the Bangladeshi community. Over two-thirds of the total went to projects under ILEA's direct control so that very few Bangladeshi voluntary groups received support for projects run by themselves. Although the community projects which were approved were located in more than just Spitalfields, i.e. Weavers, St. Katharine's, St. Dunstan's and Poplar, groups in other localities were not catered for. Moreover, the June 1983 proposal concentrated on the needs of Bangladeshi organisations - only one other ethnic minority group was to receive assistance, the Tower Hamlets Afro-Caribbean Association. Somali organisations in St. Katharine's ward, for example, were not included.

Most of the revenue to be allocated by the June 1983 proposal to Bangladeshi groups entailed the employment of staff. For two years at least young Bangladeshi activists could gain experience of working full-time for a community project in the area of education and under the direct or indirect control of ILEA. The selection of the particular groups for funding became an issue of great significance to Bangladeshi first and second generation activists, as the previous discussion of events has already indicated. The conflict between Bangladeshi representatives before the June recommendations were submitted may well have affected the distribution of grants. Some of the youth groups which received funds were closely associated with the FBYO and BENTH leadership. Although the Bangladeshi Youth Front was granted £1,000 the amount was derisory compared with its application for £19,335.14. Its acting general secretary was Rafique Ullah who was one of the four who challenged the BENTH leadership during April 1983. The grant of £1,000 to help the BYF's running costs indicated the Initiative's willingness to help its operations but no money was forthcoming to employ staff for the three schemes outlined in the BYF's submission.

The difficulties encountered by the Initiative during 1983-5, therefore, were bound up with the practices pursued by ILEA and the representational umbrella group, BENTH. To show its openness to community groups, ILEA, through its Initiative Co-ordinator, invited bids from any interested parties and then involved BENTH representatives in determining which bids should be recommended for approval. Once the BENTH leadership had been challenged by other Bangladeshi community organisers, the allocation of funds to community groups became a test of strength between community leaders which implicated ILEA and its support for the BENTH leadership. Having decided to co-operate initially with the second generation youth leaders, ILEA found itself caught up in the various struggles of the Bangladeshi community organisers. The June 1983 proposal provided new opportunities for young supporters of the FBYO and BENTH leadership but it also expanded the role of local ILEA institutions, i.e. the Youth Office, the Montefiore CEC, the Tower Hamlets Adult Education Institute and the Divisional Office.

Many of the Bangladeshi groups which applied for Tower Hamlets Initiative grants already received public funding from other resources. From origins in autonomous, self-help activities, community groups had become dependent on the very public authorities which they tried to pressurise and they had to observe a number of conditions on receipt of

163

public funds. ILEA made clear that all voluntary organisations receiving aid under the Initiative were required to observe certain organisational guidelines. Groups were also required to offer equal opportunities to women, to allow trade union membership, to avoid the promotion of opposition to any political party and try to get money from alternative sources. They were expected to make maximum use of voluntary support, acknowledge ILEA's support in any publicity information and, where appropriate, offer ILEA a seat on the group's management board. [34]

Reliance on public funding by the borough council, GLC and central government since the late 1970s had made community workers well aware of the organisational practices required by public authorities. They were adept at framing constitutions, setting up general management committees, arranging elections and lobbying for support. Their experience ensured the speedy erection of a formal structure, BENTH, with which ILEA could deal, involving by June 1983 an Executive Committee, a list of affiliated community groups and individual members, a constitution and regular meetings. Leadership of BENTH which became such a controversial issue in early 1983 was, therefore, 'regularised' by the election of an Executive Committee in June 1983 which ensured the continuing control of BENTH negotiations with ILEA by certain young Bangladeshi community activists and their supporters among the older generation of local Bangladeshis.

ILEA wanted the young community workers to concentrate on certain aspects of the educational service. In a report during January 1983 two objectives were established for the Tower Hamlets Initiative. The Initiative would be designed:

(a)   To link the process of education to the needs of families and young children, providing increased opportunities for learning English language skills, developing mother-tongue teaching, and involving the parents in the education of their children.

(b)   To provide increased opportunities for young people and adults, through in-service training and curriculum development support for work in ESL and mother-tongue teaching, piloting skill-based courses in mother-tongue, developing general access courses, and, in partnership with local youth organisations, making a significant extension of youth provisions. [35]

164

These two objectives were set within a wider context of a high proportion of Bangladeshi children aged four years and below, overcrowding, heavy unemployment and large numbers of people beginning to learn English.

The grants to Bangladeshi youth groups under the June 1983 proposal were an outcome of ILEA's commitment to 'a significant extension of youth provision'. The youth group had become involved in a variety of welfare activities as well as providing recreational facilities. The June 1983 proposal was designed to help certain youth groups' operations by making available full-time staff through ILEA's Youth Office in the borough. Educational facilities were to be extended mainly through ILEA's existing institutions such as the Adult Education Institute, the Montefiore CEC and the Divisional Office, while youth groups, the Asian Unemployment Outreach Project and the Asian Educational Advisory Service would be helped to extend their service to the community outside the field of professional teaching. In the process the community groups could help to establish closer links between Bangladeshi residents and ILEA's local schools and colleges during a period of considerable strain on educational resources caused, according to ILEA's officers, by the combination of Bangladeshi settlement and general socio-economic conditions in Tower Hamlets.

The BENTH Bulletins expressed the desire of BENTH representatives to intervene in the arena of local public education. Rather than confining themselves to extending existing community services and acting as a non-professional support to ILEA, contributors to BENTH Bulletins offered their opinions on various educational issues and criticised local ILEA institutions for their ignorance of Bangladeshi needs. ILEA introduced several courses designed to train young community workers in the professional expertise required by the Authority in the educational area. Young activists such as Habib Ullah, Riaz and Abbas Uddin were employed by the Youth Service and the Adult Education Institute to liaise between ILEA and community organisations and Bangladeshi residents during 1984. At the same time changes in the arena of professional teaching concentrated on the introduction of new courses, curriculum material, mother-tongue and ESL classes. Moreover, grants after the June 1983 proposal encouraged the provision of mother-tongue teaching by supplementary schools outside ILEA's educational structure. Some of these schools run by Bangladeshi parents used ILEA premises outside school hours such as the only mother-tongue project recommended for funding in the June 1983 proposal. Others were based in community schools such as Nurul Huque's East End Comm-

165

unity School in West Spitalfields and the Boundary Community School in the nearby Weavers ward. The October 1984 'Brady' BENTH Bulletin claimed that the Initiative had 'resulted in the increase of Bengali mother-tongue teaching voluntary schools from a mere three or four in 1982 to nearly 39 in 1984'. [36]

ILEA officers were prepared to encourage Bangladeshi community workers to provide educational resources outside the state system through mother-tongue teaching in supplementary schools. Such teaching could be assisted by the children's parents, thereby promoting one of the aims of the Initiative during 1983-5 and appeared to have enabled ILEA to cover all the areas outlined in the two objectives described in its January 1983 paper. The changes wrought by the Initiative between 1983 and 1984 had a number of consequences for BENTH representatives. Some community groups were funded by the Initiative and were brought into closer contact with ILEA. They were accountable to the Authority for the management of their affairs and, in return, they received official assistance with activities which, in some cases, entailed mother-tongue teaching. The professional careers of some activists were promoted by the introduction of courses and new jobs. BENTH representatives became involved in negotiations with ILEA officers and councillors over the distribution of funds to community groups.

At the same time BENTH leaders wanted to pressurise ILEA into making further innovations which would give community activists like themselves a greater influence over decision-making in general and educational resources in particular. Their participation in decision-making through the Tower Hamlets Initiative Steering Group during 1983 and the Divisional Committee in 1984, however, involved them in disappointing numerous community groups given the relatively few projects which could be funded by the Initiative. A large part of the money available for 1984/5 was already taken up by projects approved during the 1983/4 financial year so that there was only limited scope for the validation of new schemes by the Divisional Committee during 1984. The BENTH 1984 annual report also claimed that 'many schemes funded by the THI during the 1983/4 financial year couldn't start operating, very simply due to the lack of proper accommodation' and blamed ILEA for being 'extremely slow in dealing with accommodation cases'. [37] Through their participation in 'grant-giving' BENTH representatives could themselves be blamed for inadequacies which they believed to be created by ILEA's own practices. Membership of official decision-making and consultative institutions enabled BENTH representatives to help in the direction of resources

166

within the Bangladeshi community but BENTH's credentials as a pressure group were impaired in the process. BENTH's leaders could be presented as self-seeking careerists who were using their position as community representatives to further their own careers.

Bangladeshi activists sometimes referred to the problems of intra-communal conflict and careerism. One article in the Spitalfields Youth Magazine spoke of a need for 'the correct leadership, the right type of organisation and effective mobilisation of the masses along non-partisan lines'.[38]The writer, who concentrated on the role of the Bangladeshi youth in Spitalfields, contended that:

> If all of us in Spitalfields can do a good job posterity will remember us. If we let the chance go unheeded and eat up all our energies in factional fightings, petty personal bickerings or for advancing personal career prospects then we will be charged by posterity for failing them. [39]

References to intra-communal struggles in the BENTH Bulletins were explained in terms of manipulation by outsiders and selfish ambition among community leaders. However, references by BENTH representatives to constraints involved in the operation of the Initiative indicated other causes of discontent and conflict among community workers. Moreover, behind the scenes of struggle and pressure group representation, Bangladeshi community organisations were being drawn into a closer relationship with ILEA which entailed accountability to the Authority and the creation of a small number of professionally trained students and ILEA employees. The relationship between ILEA and Bangladeshi representatives had to be understood not just in terms of different strategies and articulated demands. A variety of official and community group practices were also involved which, in their operation and inter-relationship, contributed to the problems encountered by ILEA officials and community representatives during the Tower Hamlets Initiative. Explanations in terms of some unitary phenomenon such as racism, communal factionalism or external manipulation failed to uncover the workings of these practices.

Although ILEA withdrew its financial support for BENTH and abolished the Tower Hamlets Initiative Divisional Committee, it still attempted to involve both BENTH groups in the discussion of Tower Hamlets Initiative proceedings through its Consultative Committee. The 'Brady' BENTH leadership decided, however, to dissociate itself from collaboration wth ILEA and chose to pursue a strategy of public confrontation with ILEA's political and administrative representatives. They joined the FBYO, a Bangladeshi parents' association, the borough's Trades Council and local branches of the National Union of Teachers to form the Campaign against Racism in Schools. The campaign concentrated on racism and racial violence in schools, especially those in the locality.

During the winter term of 1985 the new group organised a demonstration outside ILEA's district offices in the borough at which several demonstrators were arrested. During a subsequent rally outside County Hall criticisms were levelled against the 'failure' of ILEA's anti-racist policies and attempts were made to lobby Frances Morrell, the leader of the Labour Majority Group within ILEA. The dispute quickly embroiled the borough's two Labour councillors in the Majority Group - Sir A. Bramall and P. Aylmer, who were publicly seen as representing the two wings of the party. Aylmer found himself in the position of defending ILEA against Bangladeshi activists to whom he looked for support in conflicts with 'Right-wing' members of the Labour Party. The aftermath of ILEA's decision to withdraw financial support for BENTH revealed the tenuous nature of the alliance between white radicals within the Labour party and Bangladeshi activists noted elsewhere in this study.

NOTES

[1]   See, for example, ILEA, Race, Sex and Class, 1. Achievement in Schools, 1983. Several other statements were published between 1983 and 1985 under the title Race, Sex and Class and were distributed to ILEA institutions and interested parties.
[2]   See ILEA Governors Handbook (1977), Chapter 2.
[3]   See Carvel, J., Citizen Ken, Chatto and Windus, London, 1984, pp.195-6.
[4]   ILEA Policy Co-ordinating Committee, Memorandum to Head of Legal Branch, 15 Nov., 1984, p.1.
[5]   BENTH Bulletin, no.1, May 1983, p.1.
[6]   Ibid., p.2.
[7]   Ibid., p.2.
[8]   Ibid., p.4.
[9]   Ibid., p.2.
[10]   Ibid.
[11]   Ibid., p.4.
[12]   BENTH Bulletin, no.3, July 1983, p.1.
[13]   BENTH Bulletin, no.4, Aug. 1983, p.2.
[14]   Ibid., p.3.
[15]   Ibid.
[16]   Ibid.

[17]   BENTH Bulletin, no.5, Sept. 1983, p.1.
[18]   BENTH Bulletin, no.7, Feb. 1984, p.1.
[19]   BENTH Bulletin, no.2, June 1983, p.6.
[20]   BENTH Bulletin, no.3, July 1983, p.2.
[21]   ILEA Development Sub-Committee, Advisory Section
        on Inner City Programmes - Tower Hamlets, ILEA
        3526, app.1, (b).
[22]   Ibid.
[23]   'Naz' BENTH Bulletin, nos.13-14, Sept.-Oct. 1984, p.3.
[24]   ILEA Policy Co-Ordinating Sub-Committee, Report by
        Education Officer, ILEA P228, item 5, 7 April, 1985,
        p.2.
[25]   Ibid., p.5.
[26]   Ibid.
[27]   BENTH Bulletin, no.6, Jan. 1984, p.3.
[28]   'Brady' BENTH Bulletin, Oct.1984, p.7.
[29]   Ibid.
[30]   'Brady' BENTH Annual Report 1984, p.19.
[31]   Ibid.
[32]   Ibid.
[33]   Report by Education Officer, Tower Hamlets Initiative
        - Community Education Project, ILEA 3296, 14 June
        1983.
[34]   Report by Education Officer, Tower Hamlets Initiative
        Arrangements   for   Financial   Administration   and
        Monitoring Grants, ILEA 3296, 16 June 1983.
[35]   Report by Education Officer and Chief Finance
        Officer, Revenue Estimates 1983-84, ILEA 3007, item
        5, 13 January 1983. A detailed description of the
        relationship between the Bangladeshi population and
        ILEA's school resources was provided in ILEA
        Development Sub-Committee, Review of Primary and
        Secondary Accommodation Needs in Tower Hamlets,
        ILEA 5147, item 3, 3 March 1985.
[36]   'Brady' BENTH Bulletin, October 1984, p.7.
[37]   'Brady' BENTH Annual Report 1984, p.19.
[38]   Spitalfields Youth Magazine, no.6, 1984, p.17.
[39]   Ibid., pp.3 and 17.

Conclusion

(A) **SUMMARY OF THE CHAPTERS**

The substantive account above began with an introduction to the borough of Tower Hamlets and the Spitalfields ward in particular. Although the borough generally experienced a number of economic, environmental and social problems popularly associated with 'inner city' areas, Spitalfields was one of the worst affected wards and contained the highest proportion of Bangladeshi settlers. A description of three broad areas of the ward served not only to give an impression of the economic and environmental character of Spitalfields, but also to outline some of the material differences between Bangladeshi and white residents. Bangladeshis were disproportionately affected by poor material conditions in the ward and the differences between Bengalis and whites were highlighted in the housing sector where Bangladeshis were largely confined to the sector of dilapidated, privately rented accommodation or to the older council blocks.

170

Despite broad differences between Bangladeshis and whites in the context of employment, housing and age, for example, which were supported by cultural distinctions, other social differentiations existed to divide Bangladeshis and whites and to make possible a variety of cross-cutting alliances. The development of community organisations in Spitalfields during the 1970s down to the present day was affected by these numerous social divisions as Bengali and white activists sought to pressurise public authorities over the grievances of local residents, who relied heavily on the distribution of social consumption resources. Although many Spitalfields pressure groups came to be funded by public authorities themselves, they frequently campaigned against official policies, especially those implemented by the borough council and the GLC.

Both white and Bangladeshi activists were involved in the articulation of local Bangladeshi grievances, but as the number of Bangladeshi organisations and activists increased so differences between Bangladehis based upon occupation, generation, kinship and village loyalties, for example, came to be associated with factional conflicts among community organisers. Competition to represent the 'Bangladeshi community' involved not just the first generation settlers, especially the business leaders, but also, more and more, the second generation, younger activists (predominantly males) who worked in white collar occupations, often in the local government sector itself, or in community work jobs funded by public authorities.

The role of Bengali community activists in the arena of Spitalfields ward politics was examined in the second chapter. The ward, like the borough generally, had long been dominated by the Labour Party. A discussion of political developments during the 1970s and leading up to the 1982 borough election recorded the pressure which built up against the Labour Majority Group leadership from both inside and outside the party.

Attention was focused on political events involving the ward Labour Party between 1977 and 1982 which resulted in the selection of only one experienced councillor, flanked by two new, Left-wing candidates, for the 1982 election. These developments were set beside the complicated manoeuvrings of Bangladeshi community activists as they considered their involvement in ward politics. Eventually five Bengalis contested the 1982 ward election on different political platforms and one of them became Spitalfields' first Bangladeshi Independent councillor by defeating one of the two Left-wing Labour candidates.

These political events were related to political statements made by the Spitalfields Labour Party and a number of its opponents between 1977 and 1982. The issues discussed in those statements were considered in relation both to the various communities which the parties claimed to represent and to certain constituencies. viz. socialism, multi-racialism and localism. The various political parties had been engaged in the construction of objects of representation which included such categories as council tenants, the elderly, the working class, the local community and the Bangladeshi community. These objects of representation were discussed mainly in terms of material conditions and needs.

Although, at the national level, the Bangladeshi community had been embraced by the Labour Party as an object of representation with reference to the constituencies of socialism and multi-racialism, the party, at ward and borough level, had directed its attention to other sections of the population and had discussed their needs in localist terms. The increasing influence of Left-wing members during the late 1970s led to the introduction of socialist and anti-racist themes in party statements. Nevertheless, the Spitalfields ward party's appeal to the Bangladeshi community was weakened by its failure to recruit more than a handful of Bangladeshi community activists and its preoccupation with a struggle between 'Right' and 'Left' members.

The victory of the Bangladeshi Independent at the 1982 election indicated the attraction of claims by people outside the Spitalfields Labour Party to represent the Bangladeshi community. As in the other local elections, political support was generated by community loyalties and Bangladeshi activists outside the Labour Party could call upon a variety of ties linking them to local voters. They based their claims to represent their community partly on their understanding of their community's needs - an understanding which was not shared by white representatives. The boundary of knowledge dividing Bangladeshi and white activists had been reinforced during the 1970s by the virtual exclusion of Bangladeshis from the ward Labour Party. As white Left-wing members attempted to build alliances with Bangladeshi activists and involve them in party affairs, so the problems of mutual understanding between Bangladeshi and white activists affected the incorporation of Bangladeshis into the party. White Left-wing members wanted to educate Bangladeshis into the socialist policies and practices which they wished the ward party to pursue. They did not want the party to be involved in the 'non-political' practices evident in conflicts between Bangladeshi organisations.

172

Although the objects of representation were discussed as if they were organic unities speaking through their political representatives, the variety of social differentiations which cut across distinctions between Bangladeshi and white residents belied those discussions. The political events leading up to the 1982 borough election did not reveal a united Bangladeshi community speaking through its political representatives. Moreover, the relationship between white and Bangladeshi activists in Spitalfields demonstrated the widespread distribution of power across various levels of the political system and beyond the system of political institutions and practices.

The third chapter explored political developments involving the Spitalfields Labour Party and Bangladeshi community representatives between 1982 and 1985. The leadership of the ward party after the 1982 borough election was taken over by white Left-wing members who pursued a strategy of campaigning on local and more global issues and recruiting new members. Residents were exhorted by numerous leaflets to join campaigns over local National Front activity, office development, National Health Service cuts and the miners' strike of 1984-5, for example. The issue of racism and the particular interests of Bangladeshi residents were subsumed within a general appeal to local people. Moreover, local concerns were shown to be an aspect of a wider struggle against local and central government policies.

Yet most of the new recruits to the ward party were Bangladeshis and disputes between Bengali activists became embroiled with conflicts between white members of the party. A loose alliance was formed between white ward party leaders and certain Bangladeshi community organisers, who also moved up to more global levels of the party and struggles were fought out between long-established party leaders and their Left-wing opponents. This alliance was subject to extensive strains as party members competed with one another in pursuit of their political ambitions and argued over political beliefs. The pressures of party business and the wide range of activities in which party leaders were involved, prevented them from collaborating closely together and forming a cohesive unit. Although the views of Bangladeshi party members, who were not involved in community work, became a crucial factor in ward party conflicts but white party leaders knew little about these new recruits and feared the influence of 'non-political' community loyalties among them.

The strategy of opening up the ward party to local residents, especially Bangladeshis, was constrained by a number of factors. Party statements between 1982 and 1985 spoke of the Bangladeshi community as an object of representation with reference to socialism and working class struggle against local and central government policies. The complexity and specific character of local social differentiation and associated interests were not encompassed in ward party statements which tried to link socialism, multi-culturalism and anti-racism and related local issues to more global levels of struggle. The ward party did not speak for a united working class and the Bangladeshi community as part of that class.

White party leaders recognised the limitations of their rhetorical appeal to local people by seeking to establish links with the numerous pressure groups in Spitalfields which dealt with the variety of specific interests and demands. White Left-wing activists sought the support of local groups in their assault on the Majority Group leadership at borough level and other long established party leaders, such as the local MP, Peter Shore. However, the basis for unity was a narrow one, given the different interests and practices of political parties and pressure groups. Even Left-wing councillors were associated by community activists with the Labour Majority Group and its policies which affected local residents. Alliances with local organisations could be established by the party's opponents and the large amount of electoral support for the Bangladeshi Independent revealed the continuing attraction of political appeals by those outside the party 'in power'.

Although Left-wing, white activists sought to involve Bangladeshi recruits, especially community organisers, in their campaigns against party leaders at local and more global levels, a variety of political and non-political differences were involved, making broad distinctions between 'Right' and 'Left' of limited value. Even alliances between ward party leaders, who espoused Left-wing views, were riven by competing interests which could lead to frequent breakdown of co-operation between them and the departure of ward members to other wards.

The ward party itself was composed of only a handful of active members, who did not frequently know what the majority of the irregular attenders wanted or what those outside the party politically desired. Campaigns were

174

determined by party considerations, and party business was constrained by internal regulations which did not engage the interest of many members. The language of representation, which presented the party as the voice of the local people and the party leaders as the representatives of the party's will, was belied by the practice of party business and electoral politics. The local people spoke only equivocally through elections so that ward party success in electoral contests did not vindicate claims to represent the will of Spitalfields inhabitants.

Furthermore, despite the links between the ward party and more global levels of the Labour Party structure, the ward party did not express the will of a united political institution. Its members were caught up in local issues which bore little or no relevance to other levels of the party. They also looked beyond the boundaries of institutional politics to local pressure groups and communal solidarities. A distinction has to be made, therefore, between the ideological constituencies, which were used by activists when considering the question of community or class unity, and the various political practices through which the representation of local groups including Bangladeshis was pursued. Activists recognised that in political institutions the needs of particular social collectivities would be variously defined by competing individuals and organisations.

The relationship of local pressure groups to the Labour Party at more global levels of the political structure was examined in the fourth chapter, largely in the context of the borough council and the representation of Bangladeshi and other ethnic minorities. Between 1980 and 1985 steps were taken by the Labour Majority Group leadership to establish a particular unit within the council committee system concerned with the borough's ethnic minorities. The proposal to set up a Joint Consultative Committee chaired by the Majority Group leader was replaced by the establishment of a full council committee, the Ethnic Minorities Committee. The issue of ethnic minority representation became embroiled in conflicts between the Majority Group leaders and their Left-wing opponents, which were influenced by the political strategies and anti-racist reforms pursued by the Labour Majority Group in the GLC.

Left-wing councillors, united with Liberals and Spitalfields' Bangladeshi Independent councillor in challenging the Majority Group leadership on certain occasions, defying the dominance exercised by the political leadership in conjunction with senior officials. The formation of the EMC indicated the ability of the leadership's opponents to impose their will. Even so, the Majority Group leaders retained a number of advantages through the appointment of EMC chairman, the political differences among committee members, the collaboration between the chairman and administrative officials, and the pivotal role of the Policy Committee which gave final approval to the recommendations of all other committees.

The limited capacity of the new committee to press for changes was demonstrated in the lengthy debate over the practice of ethnic monitoring and record-keeping. The practice was associated with Left-wing, anti-racist strategies within the Labour Party and became another focus of struggle between the Majority Group leadership and its Left-wing opponents. The introduction of the practice was considered by various committees and the Policy Committee failed to resolve the issue until 1985 as opposition to the practice emerged, especially from the Administration Committee, which was responsible for implementing an equal opportunities policy in the employment of council staff.

Political pressure to introduce ethnic monitoring and record-keeping was supported during 1984 and 1985 by administrative officials. Detailed research was undertaken into the implementation of the practice by other London authorities. Senior officers pointed to the inconsistencies and inefficiencies created by a failure to introduce the practice as the GLC prepared to transfer its housing responsibilities to the borough during late 1984. Pressure was also exerted by a change in central government regulations and further inconsistency was caused by the Administration Committee's adoption of an equal opportunities policy whose effectiveness could not be demonstrated.

The Policy Committee finally agreed to a pilot scheme which would consider the problems of introducing ethnic record-keeping and monitoring in the Social Services and Housing departments. Yet, by early 1986, the Administration Committee had still not agreed to the practice despite the model set by the national Commission for Racial Equality's code of practice and the threat of a CRE investigation into the borough's administrative practices. As the May 1986 borough elections drew closer and the political futures of most senior Labour councillors were threatened by ward party refusals to nominate them, the Majority Group leadership would in any case, play little part in the actual implementation of a practice popularly advocated by their party opponents.

The co-ordination of race relations matters at administrative level was formally attempted by the appointment of a Senior Race Relations Adviser, who came from one of the two groups claiming to represent ethnic minorities outside the council. The formation of a united race relations organisation, the Tower Hamlets Association for Racial Equality (THARE), had been encouraged by an official investigation and by members of the borough's Ethnic Minorities Committee (EMC). The leadership of the new organisation, THARE, reflected the preponderance of Bangladeshi community groups in Spitalfields and elsewhere. THARE's leadership also revealed the influence of the second generation Bangladeshi activists, who led the resistance to the introduction of another representative body, the Ethnic Minorities Forum, which was intended to act as a consultative link between ethnic minority representatives and the EMC. Although THARE was the local branch of the national CRE, its leaders wanted to maintain close links with the EMC and to gain greater access to the council's decision-making institutions. The Forum would undermine THARE's claim to represent race relations outside the council and it would lack any power to influence council decisions.

A compromise was arranged during 1985 which established a Liaison Group including THARE and other ethnic minority group representatives and maintaining the principle that the EMC should be linked to its own particular consultative body which spoke for ethnic minorities. The Liaison Group modified the predominance gained by second generation Bengalis within THARE and recognised the claims of other Bangladeshi and non-Bangladeshi activists to speak on behalf of their communities.

The developments concerning the representation of ethnic minorities at borough level indicated a considerable lack of integration between council committees and adminstrative practices. Committees jealously defended their particular interests and yet an issue like race relations could not be confined to one committee. Inconsistency was encouraged by external events which impinged upon the borough council as the GLC transferred its housing responsibilities, for example, and the Majority Group leadership considered whether it should adopt practices pursued by the GLC, i.e. ethnic record-keeping and monitoring. Without a clear lead from the Policy Committee the conflict between different committees continued and the inconsistency between administrative practices remained unresolved.

Both the EMC and THARE claimed to speak authoritatively, in different contexts, on the subject of race relations and both established formal links with the numerous ethnic minority groups in Spitalfields and elsewhere. However, neither race relations nor the borough's ethnic minorities were unitary subjects which could be institutionally represented in any clear-cut way. Both the EMC and THARE were composed of people who were swayed by different political or community interests. A degree of unity was maintained within both institutions, but behind the image of unified groups speaking on behalf of race relations and ethnic minorities in the borough there lay a variety of conflicting loyalties and practices involving councillors, administrative officials and community activists.

Even though community organisers tried to gain access to the decision-making institutions where they assumed that power was concentrated, it was evident that power was more widely distributed than activists assumed and involved activists themselves through the organised representation of ethnic minorities at local ward and borough levels. Despite references to united struggle of black and white workers in the context of anti-racism and socialism, ethnic minority representatives had become involved in pressure group practices and links with local authorities which invalidated any claim to be simply engaged in struggle with those who held power.

The representation of ethnic minority grievances at local and more global levels of the political system was examined in the fifth chapter with reference to housing. Attention concentrated again on the Spitalfields ward where the Spitalfields Housing and Planning Rights Services (SHAPRS), in particular, engaged in detailed disputes with public authorities over housing developments in the ward. SHAPRS' campaigns were directed at the GLC as the main provider of council housing in the ward until 1985. SHAPRS focused particularly upon the needs of Bangladeshis who were most adversely affected by housing problems.

The debates between SHAPRS and the GLC housing officers (as well as other local authority representatives), entailed the discussion of housing allocation practices between 1981 and 1985. The allegations of racial discrimination made by SHAPRS were firmly rejected by senior housing officers, who urged the movement of

Bangladeshis away from Spitalfields and the E1 postal district in general as a solution to the problems encountered by members of the community. Modifications were made to allocations practices and the GLC Majority Group leadership encouraged various institutional changes in order to implement their anti-racist strategy outlined after the Labour councillors had won the 1981 metropolitan election. SHAPRS continued its criticisms despite these reforms and found support from various other sources, particularly two reports produced during 1984-85 by an independent researcher, Dr. Phillips, and commissioned by the GLC. The two reports drew attention to practices at various levels of the housing institutional system which indirectly discriminated against 'Asians', who were principally Bangladeshis. These practices involved GLC staff who also revealed considerable racial hostility towards Bangladeshis.

SHAPRS worked with other Spitalfields organisations to put pressure upon the GLC and borough council over housing. The building of new council blocks between 1983 and 1985 threatened to divide residents along racial lines as whites saw themselves losing out to Bangladeshis in the allocation of the new accommodation. SHAPRS' emphasis upon satisfying those in greatest housing need would help primarily Bangladeshis and elderly or disabled white inhabitants. The new buildings did not satisfy the demands of younger white families who were encouraged to campaign for the development of other unused space in the ward.

Other organisations claimed to speak for local residents besides SHAPRS. The Federation of Bangladeshi Youth Organisations (FBYO) also put forward demands, and when FBYO leaders came to dominate the new race relations body, THARE, in 1984 they were able to apply pressure from another source in collaboration with white activists. Although these campaigners professed their support for the homeless families' occupation of Camden Town Hall, they concentrated on less dramatic methods by trying to exert pressure through public meetings, lobbying and detailed discussions of housing practices with administrative officials.

The focus upon housing allocations practices extended to include a closer examination of housing strategies. The GLC's strategy of encouraging Bangladeshis to live outside Spitalfields was part of its stated intention to satisfy the demands of different categories of housing applicant, especially those on the waiting list and those seeking

179

transfers. The housing ladder system enabled everyone's desires to be satisfied in due course. Council housing would provide a range of accommodation and would not be confined to those in greatest housing need.

Central government restrictions on housing expenditure undermined the GLC's housing strategy, increasing competition between waiting list and transfer applicants. The distinction between the two housing categories overlapped with the social differentiation between long established white tenants and Bangladeshi settlers to some extent. Moreover, a number of council estates contained almost exclusively white and Bangladeshi tenants. Because Bangladeshis were disproportionately concentrated on the most dilapidated estates, they were sometimes blamed by white residents for the condition of those estates.

Allegations that the housing ladder system or white tenants' dislike of Bangladeshi traditions were racist met with firm denial from certain white tenants and housing officers. The maintenance of all-white estates was encouraged, according to the Phillips' report, by the desire of estate officers to avoid possible complications by the arrival of Bangladeshi tenants. Official conduct was justified in terms of fairness, objectivity and efficiency but Phillips also drew attention to claims that junior officials, at least, were influenced by racist beliefs and had strenuously resisted anti-racist initiatives.

Attempts to combat racial discrimination within the GLC housing department had to be combined with changes in allocations practices which were not racist in intention. The investigation by Phillips revealed the ways in which Bangladeshis were disadvantaged through the operation of a complicated, priority points system. The revision of the system by the borough council in early 1985 attempted to ensure fairer treatment to waiting list applicants and homeless people. The reforms were to be supported by the adoption of the GLC practice of ethnic record-keeping and monitoring to which the borough council Majority Group leadership agreed in principle during 1985.

The new priority points system for the allocation of all council housing after the GLC transfer in April 1985 formally confirmed the priority of those in greatest housing need and the declining opportunities of those seeking transfers across or beyond the borough. The resentment of white residents, fuelled by misconceptions about how the points sytem worked, was directed against Bangladeshis who were intended to benefit mostly by official reforms and the pressures exerted by local organisations. Greater equality depended, however, on the way in which the new points system was operated and upon a variety of practices involving housing officers, whites and Bangladeshis and extending across different levels of housing administration and the council estates themselves. Racist practices were bound up with non-racist practices to produce discriminatory effects which disadvantaged Bangladeshis in particular.

Local pressure groups, such as SHAPRS, claimed to represent those in greatest housing need on the basis of their knowledge about local conditions. They also tried to apply pressure on local authorities by building alliances among themselves. Unity among local groups was easily undermined on account of differing definitions of housing need and competition between various organisations and their clientele. Competition could frequently polarise around a social distinction between whites and Bangladeshis which belied the variety of categories used in the housing allocations sytem and which cut across the white/Bangladeshi distinction.

Local pressure groups also found support from the GLC Majority Group leadership after the 1981 metropolitan election. The anti-racist strategy of the GLC was part of an attempt to mobilise popular support for the GLC in its confrontation with central government. The alliance between GLC's political leadership and local organisations was limited, however, by their differing interests and practices. Moreover, the political campaign against racism in specific contexts, such as housing, involved more than initiatives at council committee or senior administrative level. The allocation of council housing had to be understood in terms of the relationship between power and resistance at all levels of the administrative system.

The disadvantages experienced by Bangladeshis and the tension between whites and Bangladeshis had also to be examined with reference to the limitations imposed upon knowledge of the housing allocations system. Bangladeshi access to council housing was hampered by limited knowledge about the system and accommodation across the borough. Housing officers made assumptions which affected Bangladeshi housing choices, while tension was heightened by misconceptions among white tenants about how the allocations systems operated. The relationship between power and resistance had, therefore, to be understood also in the context of limitations imposed upon the knowledge of various groups of people.

The sixth and final chapter considered the representation of Bangladeshi needs at local and more global levels in the context of education. Between 1982 and 1985 ILEA also committed itself to an anti-racist strategy in a number of public statements during 1983. ILEA's political leadership, composed again of Labour councillors, engaged in a process of consultation with representatives of ethnic minorities which, in Spitalfields, enabled second generation Bangladeshi activists within the Federation of Bangladesh Youth Organisations (FBYO) to dominate negotiations to improve ILEA's educational resources to the borough's ethnic minorities, particularly Bengalis. These activists provided most of the leaders of a new umbrella group, Bangladeshi Educational Needs in Tower Hamlets (BENTH), which sent representatives to the Tower Hamlets Initiative Steering Group whose task was to assess the claims for funding under the scheme from numerous local groups in Spitalfields and other wards.

BENTH leaders were able to publicise their demands in a BENTH Bulletin funded by the scheme between 1983 and 1984. The Bulletin claimed to be the authentic voice of the Bangladeshi community and the young leaders were portrayed as disciplined and professional representatives of their community. Participation in the allocation of funding under the Tower Hamlets Initiative did not prevent the Bulletin from launching a series of attacks which related the educational deficiencies of ILEA's service to the Bangladeshi community to other issues, such as housing and racism, and to national and international developments. The benevolent intentions of ILEA in devising the Tower Hamlets Initiative were questioned and appeals were made to solidarity among Bangladeshis in the face of insensitive public authorities. Most of the articles dealing with particular educational concerns, such as mother-tongue teaching, were concerned with secular matters. BENTH Bulletins sometimes considered religious affairs but its articles reflected the preoccupations of an umbrella organisation in which religious leaders and the first generation community activists played little part.

BENTH's claim to speak for the Bangladeshi community was challenged at an early stage by first generation activists, and BENTH's young leaders soon became involved in conflicts within the most senior community organisation, the Bangladesh Welfare Association (BWA). The two major contestants within the BWA gained access to the new representational bodies advising ILEA but other local activists, such as Spitalfields' Independent councillor, Nurul Huque, who ran a community school, and women organisers relied upon their own links with ILEA and the GLC to attain their particular objectives.

The leadership of the second generation activists within BENTH was also challenged by other young community organisers in a series of conflicts which involved other community centres, such as the Kobi Nazrul Centre, in Spitalfields. During the summer of 1984 divisions appeared within the BENTH leadership itself resulting in the emergence of two rival BENTH organisatitons. The dispute affected the inaugural elections of the new race relations organisation, THARE, and internal struggles within the Spitalfields Labour Party.

The competition between BENTH leaders also hampered the work of the Tower Hamlets Initiative Divisional Committee and another representational body established at borough level by ILEA - the Tower Hamlets Ethnic Minorities Consultative Committee. During 1985 ILEA disbanded the Divisional Committee and withdrew its funding of BENTH operations which included the BENTH Bulletin. ILEA reverted to its customary practice of dealing with individual applications through its administrative machinery and committee system in order to satisfy the demands of Bangladeshi and other ethnic minority organisations which had been hindered by the BENTH dispute.

Criticisms of ILEA continued in the BENTH Bulletins published during the dispute, and the divisions among Bangladeshis and between different ethnic minorities were blamed upon ILEA and the competition for scarce resources. Fault was found with the various committees set up to consider the allocation of funding and to act as a link between ILEA and local communities. BENTH leaders wanted the allocation of much greater resources and far more influence over ILEA decision-making.

Over two-thirds of the Tower Hamlets Initiative revenue went to local ILEA institutions while the remainder went to a relatively small number of projects which were concentrated in only certain wards, such as Spitalfields, and run mainly by Bangladeshis. Groups which received funding had to observe a number of administrative practices, and the Tower Hamlets Initiative encouraged the development of community organisers who were adept at practices observed by officials whom they wished to pressurise but upon whom they had come to rely for funding. The second generation activists benefitted mainly from these developments as ILEA concentrated upon improving resources for the rapidly expanding third generation of Bangladeshi settlers. Grants to voluntary organisations were accompanied by training courses for young activists who, in some cases, became ILEA employees. The non-professional skills of community organisers were harnessed, together with the support of Bangladeshi parents, to extend the number of Bengali-medium supplementary schools and to encourage changes within ILEA's local educational institutions.

Although the Tower Hamlets Initiative encouraged the greater involvement of Bangladeshis in ILEA affairs, the withdrawal of official support for BENTH after the split in 1984 led one of the groups, the 'Brady' BENTH, to engage in more dramatic, pressure group tactics. During the second half of 1985 its members joined with other pressure groups to challenge ILEA over racism and racial violence in local schools. The campaign had political implications since it involved local white ILEA councillors who would have to seek election in the May 1986 elections.

The events which involved Spitalfields community organisers in the area of education between 1982 and 1985 had to be understood in terms of competing strategies and diverse practices. The implementation of ILEA's anti-racist strategy was expressed in the context of the Tower Hamlets Initiative through a limited programme of funding in consultation between officials and local activists. The political considerations of ILEA Labour councillors were not necessarily shared by ILEA's hierarchy of officials who were concerned with the detailed examination of projects. Most of the revenue was distributed to ILEA's professional staff and the remainder was allocated to organisations which pursued practices approved by ILEA. The general political issues raised by BENTH leaders contrasted sharply with the much more limited administrative task of allocating funds to specific educational ventures for a limited period of time.

184

BENTH, too, was caught up in different strategies and practices. Its claim to represent the Bangladeshi community was belied by the competing strategies of activists inside and outside the organisation. Co-operation with ILEA weakened its claims to pressurise the authority and involved its leaders in decisions which disappointed unsuccessful applicants for funding. The practice of assessing each individual application encouraged competition among Bangladeshi organisations and, as young Bangladeshi leaders of BENTH also discovered in the context of THARE and borough race relations representation, co-operation was further weakened by the ability of organisations to apply directly to public bodies.

(B)   GENERAL DISCUSSION

The substantive account developed in the preceeding six chapters has attempted to provide an original contribution to the understanding of the politics of community. While there are a number of investigations into local politics, state institutions and ethnic minority communities, there appear to be none which analyse those areas from the perspective adopted above. Against the influential tendency to present political institutions, strategies and debates as shaped by such pre-given social solidarities as ethnic minority communities or classes, it has been argued that such terms as the 'Bangladeshi community' or the 'working class' have to be understood in the context of particular debates and practices operating within the political arena. The constitution of political forces on the basis of community or class is a political process which involves political struggles over the distribution of scarce resources. Consequently, the foregoing account has examined local political institutions, Bangladeshi community organisations and more global political, community and administrative institutions in terms of the political construction of community and class through particular statements and practices.

At first sight my study could be seen as providing further support for the pluralist accounts of ethnic groups which were discussed in the Introduction [1] Bangladeshi activists, for example, could be presented as representing the needs of their community to the 'host society' and as operating most effectively at the margins of their community. Yet this pluralist approach explains political represenation as a process whereby the interests of social collectivities, such as ethnic minorities, are directly expressed by their representatives in the political arena. It is

185

my contention, on the other hand, that the plurality of social groups in the political arena is constructed through strategies, statements and practices particular to that arena. Definitions of the needs of those described as members of the 'Bangladeshi community' or the 'working class' were located in political debates about anti-racism and socialism or in specific regulations concerning housing and education, for example. Political representation cannot, therefore, be understood simply in terms of the mobilisation of social groups outside the political system.

My examination of the relationship between community activists, politicians and bureaucrats certainly supported the pluralist case for studying not only formal political institutions and procedures but also the numerous pressure groups outside the formal structure of local government. However, pluralist analyses of urban politics have failed to expose sufficiently the limitations of local 'democratic' political processes. As Dearlove and Saunders, for example, have demonstrated[2]attention must be paid to the way in which local decision-making structures responded to certain pressure groups but not to others. Spitalfields pressure groups were largely kept at a distance by the borough's senior councillors and officials through the rules of access which Dearlove and Saunders have shown to be powerful barriers to groups which were considered 'unhelpful' by the council leadership. Spitalfields groups were not privy to the informal deliberations between senior councillors and officials which played a crucial role in determining the decisions formally made by the council committees and administrative departments. Although the Labour Majority Group's leadership's political base was challenged between 1982 and 1986 by the emergence of Left-wing rivals and, just before the 1986 council election, by de-selection, senior Labour councillors were able to resist such demands as ethnic record keeping and monitoring in spite of pressure from local groups, institutions outside the borough and even the borough's own Chief Executive.

The local borough council, however, was not the only organisation to which local activists could appeal. The GLC and ILEA were also responsible for the provision of resources to local inhabitants. The emergence of Left-wing leaders in those two institutions during the early 1980s helped white and Bangladeshi activists to pursue their demands and several initiatives were undertaken to improve the delivery of resources to Bangladeshis and other minority groups. Nevertheless, as the struggles over housing allocation and the Tower Hamlets Initiative revealed, the implementation of radical policies was hampered by blockages and resistances within the administrative institutions of the GLC and ILEA as well as by conflicts between white and Bangladeshi residents.

This evidence points to the danger of locating power at the centre of local political and administrative institutions. Although Dearlove and Saunders have provided a valuable insight into the power of urban elites it is clear that power and resistance to the power of others operates at all levels of political and administrative systems and extends beyond those institutions to local pressure groups and residents. Consequently, local activists are not engaged simply in struggles of pure resistance to those 'in power'.

Saunders, in his critique of Marxist explanations of urban politics and the local state, [3] has also pointed to the absence of any necessary correspondence between the strategies and practices pursued by local pressure groups, political representatives and administrative officials. This lack of correspondence can be used to explain the failure of local struggles over scarce resources to develop into a wider political class struggle. My study has shown that disjunctions within political and administrative structures also act as barriers to the pursuit of radical strategies. Structures were not neatly integrated systems where decisions made at the centre were implemented at the lower levels of the institution. Each level enjoyed an important degree of autonomy and this limited what an alliance between certain local activists and radical political leaders, for instance, could achieve.

The development of a certain degree of co-operation between local pressure groups, politicians and administrative officials during 1982-6 further challenged the popular assumption of local activists that they were engaged in struggle with those 'in power' at the borough Town Hall, County Hall and Whitehall. Many local organisations came to depend on central and local government funds and were required by funding agencies to observe standard administrative practices. While local campaigns sometimes entailed public confrontation with authorities, pressure groups in Spitalfields usually conformed to the rules of access and tried to influence official decisions through more discreet and 'responsible' procedures. They presented carefully argued evidence, attended formal meetings with

187

officers and councillors and tried to gain the confidence of specific individuals. Furthermore, many community workers were engaged in everyday contact with local clients which involved the explanation of government procedures concerning the allocation of welfare benefits or council housing, for example. Rather than challenging the power of the state the activities of local activists appeared to be facilitating the implementation of state practices, particularly among Bangladeshi residents.

Hence it could be argued that local community organisations were being incorporated into a hierarchical, co-optive state. Community workers emerged as significant mediators in the process of distributing of social consumption resources at the local level at the same time as they tried to pressurise politicians and officials over the provision of those scarce resources. A number of white and Bangladeshi activists even gained access to posts within the very political and administrative institutions which local community groups sought to pressurise. Local activists occupied a highly ambiguous position, therefore, between local residents and the various levels of the state.

The lack of integration frustrated attempts by radical politicians to reform administrative practices in alliance with certain senior officers and local pressure groups. As the analysis of GLC housing reforms showed, the implementation of anti-racist strategies which were agreed at the senior level of the political and administrative system was hampered by the lack of integration between the different levels of the administrative structure. Estate officers on specific GLC estates, for example, exercised considerable power in the process of allocating accommodation to white and Bangladeshi applicants. Furthermore, estate officers' management of GLC housing stock was influenced, in turn, by the opinions of local white residents about 'their' estates.

Power was not simply located at some political and administrative centre, therefore, nor were local activists engaged in pure resistance to those in power. Senior councillors and officials in the borough council, the GLC and ILEA, for instance, still exercised a great deal of control and used the rules of access to keep 'irresponsible' pressure groups at bay. At the same time they could not rely on a beatly integrated chain of command where decisions made at the centre were passed down for implementation by lower levels of the structure. Power and resistance operated together at all levels of state and extended beyond the state to involve local pressure groups in Spitalfields and elsewhere.

The statements made by community and political activists in Spitalfields raised another issue of general interest - the perception of group unity. The Bangladeshi community, as an object of representation, was presented by those activists as a distinctive, united community whose needs they were articulating in the political arena. Feuchtwang has exposed the inadequacies of such assumptions about the cohesion and singularity of social groups. [4] The diversity of local sectoral interests belied any claim to speak on behalf of a united community or local working class in the struggle against singular and coherent racial or class oppressions. Local pressure groups dealt with a variety of demands which cut across Bangladeshi/white distinctions, and local political competition depended upon appeals to numerous social categories which were not directly related to the constituencies of anti-racism and socialism. Indeed, appeals by senior councillors and their Left-wing opponents within the Labour Party at ward and borough level were more frequently located within the constituency of localism which posited another category, 'local people', whose cohesion overlaid the differences between ethnic groups and classes, for example.

The Bangladeshi community, the working class or local people did not speak as subjects through their community or political representatives. Electoral contests at the ward and more global levels of the political system did not provide an unequivocal mandate by cohesive social groups to successful candidates. The knowledge which political and community activists gained about the needs and interests of the Bangladeshi community was, in actuality, based upon contact with individual residents. Although representatives spoke as though they understood the wishes of whole communities, they tried to advance the claims of specific individuals or particular preessure groups. Consultative organisations were established to improve the delivery of local authority services to Bangladeshis and other ethnic minority communities, but the discussion and implementation of reforms involved administrative practices and categories of people which could not be directly related to unitary concepts of communities or classes. Anti-racist strategies, for example, assumed a unity of racist practices which was not in evidence when detailed examinations of particular practices were made in the area of housing, for instance.

189

The difference, set out above, between the ideological constructions of community and class, on the one hand, and the practices of political, community and administrative institutions, on the other, related to two separate issues. It was noted how representatives were often eager to establish as wide a platform as possible on which they could collaborate with each other and local residents. Consequently, they appealed to the unity of various groups and employed several constituencies, i.e. socialism, anti-racism, multi-racialism and localism to achieve that strategy. However, within the arena of representation they were also involved in practices through which individuals and alliances competed to represent differing interests and policies.

My study has described the complex inter-relationship of strategies and institutions as the needs of various social collectivities were defined and campaigned for within political, community and administrative arenas. Its focus is closest to the analysis of the local politics of race by Ben-Tovim and his colleagues [5] in its concentration upon the relationship between local community representatives and various levels of the Labour Party and local and central government institutions. My study also shares their concern with a consideration of the positive aspects of anti-racist struggles and the ways in which local pressure groups could make use of local and central government initiatives.

However, my account takes the analysis further by providing the detailed examination of processes and practices which is lacking in their discussion. What has been offered in this book is an investigation of developments taking place between 1982 and 1986 which led to definite, if limited, improvements in the delivery of scarce resources to Bangladeshi residents in Spitalfields. These developments have been located within the political process of constructing as social collectivities, such an ethnic minority community or the working class, in an attempt to provide an original contribution to the understanding of the politics of community.

NOTES

[1]   See pp. 2-3 above
[2]   See p.7 above.
[3]   See p.13 above
[4]   See p.14 above
[5]   See p.13 above

APPENDIX 1

Spitalfields Ward Election Results

1982

N. Huque (Indep)	638	Elected
A. Elboz (Lab)	560	Elected
S. Carlyle (Lab)	556	Elected
S. Islam (Indep)	530	
S. Corbishley (Lab)	496	
W. Kelly (SDP)	417	
G. Mustafa (SDP)	407	
G. White (SDP)	401	
A. Gofur (Indep)	173	
S. Huque (Indep)	157	

Turnout: 35.8%

By-Election, 1985

A. Uddin (Lab)	784	Elected
A. Hannan (Indep)	775	
P. Ainsworth (Con)	174	

Turnout: 34.6%

1986

A. Uddin (Lab)	1246	Elected
G. Mortuza (Lab)	1019	Elected
P. Maxwell (Lab)	988	Elected
N. Huque (Indep)	837	
A. Rahman (SDP)	590	
W. Kelly (SDP)	444	
G. Mustafa (SDP)	387	
J. Emerson (Con)	215	
B. Wright (Indep)	199	
A. Chapman (Con)	189	

APPENDIX 2

GLC Priority System, January 1984

First Priority   —   Decant families and retiring resident staff (GLC and GLMS) nominees.
Reciprocal requests to aid Decant work.

Second Priority   —   Tenants and GLMS Nominees with the most urgent health or social preference, or living in statutorily overcrowded conditions or tenants of GLC or nominating authorities where their move is required by their landlord. Tenants in the vicinity of Spitalfields, E1, occupying large accommodation, who wish to move to new small dwellings.

Third Priority   —   Homeless Families Nominees.

Fourth Priority   —   Special quota applicants and GLMS nominees. Reciprocal Housing to repay a debt. Moves to promote a particular Council policy, including GLC tenants with children under 10 years living above the fourth floor, who wish to move lower and did not specifically request a high floor within the previous two years.

Fifth Priority   —   Tenants and GLMS Nominees with a less urgent health or social preference, those lacking two or more bed spaces, or those having three rooms in excess of requirements. Reciprocal requests, National Mobility nominees for social reasons.

192

Sixth Priority	—	Tenants and GLMS Nominees with a low health or social preference, those lacking one bed space, those having two rooms in excess of requirements, those needing to move for employment reasons, those lacking adequate facilities and those having five or more years' registration.
Seventh Priority	—	Tenants and GLMS Nominees with less than five years' registration and either one room in excess of requirements or no recognised housing need.
Eighth Priority	—	Approved applicants for Ex-Londoners wishing to return, divorced or separated spouses of GLC tenants, and households without young children, nominated within the Greater London Mobility Scheme. All must be willing to accept low demand accommodation in a wide area.

Source: GLC Housing Department, GLC Lettings, 3 January 1984.

APPENDIX 3

Tower Hamlets Revised Allocations System, 1985

First   Clearance cases and rehabilitation of estates: closing orders and dangerous structure notices.

Second   Transfers for major repairs; important social reasons (threats of violence, racial harassment, re-uniting families etc.); tenants and waiting list cases who are statutorily overcrowded: tenants and waiting list cases who have "urgent" health priority; unintentionally homeless people.

Third   Transfer for people with children under 10 above 4th floor; transfers and waiting list cases with a medical priority; transfers and waiting list cases lacking 2 or more bedrooms; transfers with 3 or more spare rooms.

Fourth   Transfers and waiting list cases with 'B' health priority; transfers with 2 spare rooms; less serious social reasons; transfers and waiting list cases lacking one bedroom.

Fifth   Transfers and waiting list cases with 'C' health priority; transfers and waiting list cases lacking one bedspace; transfers and waiting list cases with shared or lacking facilities; tenants who have lived in less desirable property 5 years or more.

Sixth   Special quotas for key workers, scarcity staff, residential children moving out of homes.

Seventh   Transfers with one room spare.

Eighth   Intra-estate transfers; transfers and waiting list cases for low demand hosing i.e. 'difficult to let'.

Source: SHAPRS, Training on Housing Allocations, 1985.

194

Bibliography

(A)   **PUBLISHED WORKS**

Anwar, M., 'Pakistani participation in the Rochdale by-
    election', <u>New Community,</u> vol. 2, no. 4, 1973.
Anwar, M., 'Asian participation in the 1974 Autumn
    election',<u>New Community,</u> vol. 4, no. 3, 1975.

Anwar, M., <u>The Myth of Return</u>, Heinemann, London, 1979.
Anwar, M., <u>Race and Politics</u>, Tavistock, London, 1986.
Ben Tovim, G., et al., <u>The Local Politics of Race</u>, Macmillan,
    London, 1986.
Bermant, C., <u>Point of Arrival</u>, Eyre Methuen, London, 1975.
Bloomfield, J., (ed.), <u>Class, Hegemony, Party</u>, Lawrence and
    Wishart, London, 1977.
Carey, S., and Shukur, A., 'A profile of the Bangladeshi
    community in East London', <u>New Community</u>, vol. 12,
    no. 3, Winter 1985-6.
Carvel, J., <u>Citizen Ken</u>, Chatto and Windus, London, 1984.
Castells, M., 'Theoretical Propositions for an Experimental
    Study of Urban Social Movements', in Pickvance, C.,
    (ed.), <u>Urban Sociology: Critical Essays</u>, E. Arnold,
    London, 1976.
Castells, M., <u>The City and the Grassroots</u>, E. Arnold,
    London, 1983.

Castells, M., The Urban Question, E. Arnold, London, 1977.
Castells, M., 'Towards a Political Urban Sociology', in
        Harloe, M.,(ed.), Captive Cities, J. Wiley, London,
        1977.
Cater, J., and Jones, T., 'English residential space: the case
        of Asians in Bradford', Tijdschrift vor Economische
        Sociale Geografie, vol. 70, no. 2, 1979.
Cohen, A., 'Introduction' in Cohen, A., (ed.), Urban Ethnicity,
        Tavistock, London, 1974.
Coleman, A., 'The death of the inner city: cause and cure',
        The London Journal, vol. 6, no. 1, 1980.
Damesick, P., 'The inner city economy in industrial and post-
        industrial London', The London Journal, vol. 6, no. 1,
        1980.
Dearlove, J., 'Councillors and Interest Groups in Kensington
        and Chelsea', in Kimber, R., and Richardson, J.J.,
        (eds.), Pressure Groups in Britain, J. M. Dent, London,
        1974.
Drucker, H., (gen. ed.), Developments in British Politics,
        Macmillan, London, 1983.
Duncan, S.S., and Goodwin, M., 'The local state: functional-
        ism, autonomy and class relations in Cockburn and
        Saunders', Political Geography Quarterly, vol. 1, no.
        1, Jan. 1982.
Dunleavy, P., and Rhodes, R.A.W., 'Beyond Whitehall', in
        Drucker (1983).
Eade, J., 'The political representation of a South Asian
        minority in a working class area: the Bangladeshi
        community in Tower Hamlets', South Asia Research,
        vol. 7, no.1, May 1987.
Feuchtwang, S., 'Socialist, feminist- and anti-racist
        struggles', M/F, no. 4, 1980.
Feuchtwang, S., 'Occupational ghettos', Economy and Society,
        vol. 11, no. 3, Aug. 1983.
Fishman, W., The Streets of East London, Duckworth,
        London, 1981.
Forester, T., 'The Labour Party's Militant moles', New
        Society, 10 Jan., 1980.
Gilroy, P.,'There Ain't No Black in The Union Jack',
        Hutchinson, London, 1987.
Gordon, C., (ed.), Power/Knowledge: Selected Interviews and
        Other Writings 1972-1977, Harvester Press, Brighton,
        1980.
Hall, S., et al., Policing The Crisis, Macmillan, London, 1978.
Harloe, M., (ed.), Captive Cities, J. Wiley, London, 1977.
Harloe, M., New Perspectives in Urban Change and Conflict,
        Heinemann, London, 1981.
Herbert, D., and Smith, D., (eds.), Social Problems and the
        City, O U P, London, 1979.

Hindess, B., 'The Concept of Class in Marxist Theory and
    Politics', in Bloomfield (1977).

Hirst, P., 'Economic Classes and Politics', in Hunt (1977).

Howick, C., and Kay, T., The Local Economy of Tower
    Hamlets. An Inner City Profile. Centre for
    Environmental Studies, Research Series, 26, 1978.

Hunt, A., Class and Class Structure, Lawrence and Wishart,
    London, 1977.

Husband, C., (ed.), 'Race' in Britain: Continuity and Change,
    Hutchinson, London, 1982.

Khan, V. Saifullah, 'Pakistanis in Britain: perceptions of a
    population', New Community, vol. 5, no. 3, Autumn
    1976.

Khan, V. Saifullah, 'The Role of the Culture of Dominance in
    Structuring the Experience of Ethnic Minorities', in
    Husband (1982).

Kimber, R., and Richardson, J.J., (eds.)., Pressure Groups in
    Britain, J.M. Dent, London, 1974.

Lojkine, J., 'Big Firm's Strategies, Urban Policy and Urban
    Social Movements' in Harloe (1977).

Lowe, S., Urban Social Movements : The City After Castells,
    Macmillan, London, 1986.

Miles, R., and Phizacklea, A., White Man's Country: Racism
    in British Politics, Pluto, London, 1984.

Miliband, R., Marxism and Politics, O U P, London, 1977.

Pahl, R.E., Whose City?, Penguin, London, 1975.

Pahl, R.E., 'Socio-Political Factors in Resource Allocation',
    in Herbert and Smith (1979).

Peggie, A.C.W., 'Minority youth politics in Southall', New
    Community, vol. 8, no. 2, Summer 1979.

Phillips, D.A., What Price Equality?,G L C, London, 1986.

Rex, J., and Moore, R.,　Race, Community and Conflict,
    O U P, London, 1969.

Rex, J., and Tomlinson, S., Coloured Immigrants in a British
    City, Hutchinson, London, 1979.

Saunders, P., Urban Politics : A Sociological Interpretation,
    Hutchinson, London, 1979.

Saunders, P., Social Theory and the Urban Question,
    Hutchinson, London, 1981.

Saunders, P., 'Community Power, Managerialism and the
    "Local State" ', in Harloe (1981).

Sharma, S., 'The perception of political institutions among
    Asian and English adolescents in Britain', New
    Community, vol. 8, no. 3, Winter 1980.

Sivanandan, A., 'Race, class and the state', Race and Class,
    vol. 17, no. 4, 1976.

Tate, C., 'Images of Socialism', London Labour Briefing, no. 13, July 1983.

Wallman, S., 'Foreword', in Wallman, S., (ed.), Ethnicity at Work, Macmillan, London, 1979.

Whiteley, P., 'Predicting the Labour vote in 1983: Social background versus subjective evaluations', Political Studies, vol. 34, no.1, March 1986.

Webster, P., 'Why Shore must make a stand if he is to stand again', The Times, 1 Aug. 1984.

Werbner, P., 'The organizing of giving and ethnic elites: voluntary associations amongst Manchester Pakistanis', Ethnic and Racial Studies, vol. 8, no. 3, July 1985.

Wood, D., 'County Hall farce', London Labour Briefing, no. 50, June 1985.

Zubaida, S., Islam, the People and the State. R K P, London, forthcoming 1988.

(B) **THESES**

Crawley, I., 'The London Borough of Tower Hamlets and the Greater London Council's Spitalfields Project, Pt. 2, The Case Study', M.A. dissertation, City of London Polytechnic, 1979.

Leach, J., 'Bengali Immigration in East London: The Historical background and the Situation Today', B.Sc, project, Polytechnic of the South Bank, 1976.

(C) **LOCAL GOVERNMENT DOCUMENTS**

(I)   London Borough of Tower Hamlets

Administration Committee	Equal Opportunities in Employment, 28 September 1982 item 4 (12)
Administration Committee	Public Sector Workshop on 10 November 1984, 4 February 1985, item 7.3.2.
Development Committee	Report of the Spitalfields Working Party. Spitalfields Urban Programme Grants 1983/84.
Ethnic Minorities Committee	Orders of Reference, 3 August 1963.
Ethnic Minorities Committee	The Keeping of Ethnic Records, 20 October 1983, item 3.2.

Ethnic Minorities Committee	Ethnic Minorities Forum, 5 September 1984, item 5.2.1.
Ethnic Minorities Committee	Ethnic Minorities Forum, 24 October 1984, item 5.13.
Ethnic Minorities Committee	Ethnic Minorities Forum, 6 February 1985, items 2.4. and 2.5.
Ethnic Minorities Committee	Meeting with CRE - The Hackney Report, 6 February 1985, item 6.8.
Ethnic Minorities Committee	THARE Conference on Social Services - 17/9/85, 16 October 1985, item 6.7.
Ethnic Minorities Committee	CRE's Code of Practice on Employment Matters, 4 December 1985.
Housing Management Committee	Report of Director of Housing, Housing Allocations - Review, 11-12 September 1984.
Housing Management Special Transfer Sub-Committee	Report from Director of Housing, 12 September 1984, para. 3.12.
Multi-Committee	Joint Report of Chief Executive and Director of Housing, 6-26 February 1985, section 10.12.
Policy Committee	Item 6.5, 5 June 1981.
Policy Committee	Review by Officers' Group of Race Relations in the London Borough of Tower Hamlets, September 1982.
Policy Committee	Tower Hamlets Inner Areas Programme 1985/86, 24 June 1985, pts. 2.3 and 5.2.
Policy Committee	Revenue Budget 1986/7, 24 June 1985, item 4.28, app. A.
Policy Sub-Committee	First Report of Tower Hamlets Working Party on Race Relations, 13 July 1981.
Policy Sub-Committee	Fourth Report of Tower Hamlets Working Party on Race Relations, 13 July 1981.
Policy Sub-Committee	Report of the Policy Sub-Committee - 13 July 1981 - Race Relations Matters, 16 July 1981, item 3, (2).
Policy Sub-Committee	Report of the Policy Sub-Committee -24.3.81, 30 March 1982.

Policy Sub-Committee	Ethnic Monitoring, 10 July 1985, item 3.10, pt. 2.4.
Directorate of Development	Towards a Local Plan for Spitalfields, Interim Report, vol. 2, Feb. 1977.
Directorate of Development	The London Borough of Tower Hamlets, 1981 Census Analysis.
Directorate of Development	A Short Report on the Asian Population of Tower Hamlets, February 1984.
LBTH	1981 Census Information and Analysis. 8, Tower Hamlets within its Inner London Context.
LBTH	Note of Public Consultation Meeting, Thursday, 30 May 1985.

(ii)   Greater London Council

Ethnic Minorities Committee	Race Equality and Ethnic Minorities in London, Future Strategy Report 1983-85, December 1982.
Ethnic Minorities Committee	Anti-Racist Programme of Activities 1983: Objectives and Outline Working Arrangements, EM 270, 10 May 1983.
Housing Committee	Report of the Co-ordinator of Housing Services, 25 January 1982.
Housing Committee	Report of the Co-ordinator of Housing and Technical Services, HG 350, 13 July 1982.
Housing Committee	Report of the Chairman, September 1982.
Housing Committee	Report by the Head of Housing Services, 31 May 1984.
Housing Committee	Monitoring of the Experimental Housing Allocation Scheme for GLC Properties in Tower Hamlets, Report by Dr. D.A. Phillips, 23 November 1984.
Housing Committee	Phillips, D.A., Race and Housing: GLC Policy and Practice in Tower Hamlets.
Housing Management (Tower Hamlets) Sub-Committee, Race and Housing Advisory Group.	Race and the Allocation of Council Housing: A Response to the CRE Investigation in Hackney, 8 March 1984.

Joint Housing Management Committee (JHMC)	Report of GLC Controller of Housing and Technical Services, 6 June 1982.
JHMC	Housing Management - Progress Report, 13 September 1983, item 2.8.
Planning Committee	Report by Controller of Transportation and Development, Community Areas Policy Summary of Grant Applications for Community Area Projects 1983-84, 23 June 1983.
Public Information Branch	Putting The Heart Back Into Spitalfields, 6 October 1977, no. 396.
GLC	London Borough Elections, 6 May 1982.
Housing Department	GLC Lettings, 3 January 1984.

(iii)   Inner London Education Authority

Development Sub-Committee	Advisory Section on Inner City Programmes - Tower Hamlets, ILEA 3526, app. 1, (b).
Development Sub-Committee	Review of Primary and Secondary Accommodation Needs in Tower Hamlets, ILEA 5147, item 3, 3 March 1985.
Policy Co-ordinating Sub-Committee	Memorandum to Head of Legal Branch, 15 Nov. 1984.
Policy Co-ordinating Sub-Committee	Report by Education Officer, ILEA P228, item 5, 7 April 1985.
Education Officer	Report by Education Officer, Tower Hamlets Initiative - Community Education Project, ILEA 3296, 14 June 1983.
Education Officer	Report by Education Officer, Tower Hamlets Initiative Arrangements for Financial Administration and Monitoring Grants, ILEA 3296, 16 June 1983.
Education Officer	Report by Education Officer, Tower Hamlets Inner Area Programme - 1985-86, ILEA 4540, 10 Oct. 1984.

ILEA	Report by Education Officer and Chief Finance Officer, Revenue Estimates 1983-84, ILEA 3296, 16 June 1983.
ILEA	School Governors Handbook, 1977.
ILEA	Race, Sex and Class, 1. Achievement in Schools, 1983.

(D) LABOUR PARTY DOCUMENTS

| Bethnal Green and Stepney CLP | Election Agent's Report: General Election, 9 June 1983. |
| Spitalfields Labour Party | Minutes. November 1984. |

(E) LOCAL ORGANISATIONS

BENTH Bulletin	No.1, May 1983; no.3, July 1983; no.4, Aug. 1983; no.5, Sept. 1983; no. 7, Feb. 1984.
'Brady' BENTH	Bulletin, Oct. 1984; Annual Report 1984.
'Naz' BENTH	Bulletin, nos. 13-14, Sept.-Oct. 1984.
BWA	Annual Report 1981-83.
FBYO	Annual Report 1982-83.
New Voice	14 December 1984.
SHAPRS	New Houses in Spitalfields: The Big Sleep?, Oct. 1979.
SHAPRS	What's happening to West Spitalfields?, May 1980.
SHAPRS	Annual Report, August 1980.
SHAPRS	Bengalis and GLC Housing Allocations in E.1, March 1982.
SHAPRS	Annual Report, December 1983.
SHAPRS	Bengalis and GLC Housing Allocations in E.1, An Update -March 1984.
SHAPRS	Adams, M., 'Blight Caused By Office Development', Panel of Evidence on Tower Hamlets Borough Plan Office Policy, May 30 1984.
SHAPRS	Selby Street: Make it 200 Council Homes, September 1984.
SHAPRS	Training on Housing Allocations, 1985.

SHAPRS and Catholic Housing Aid Society	The Spitalfields Survey: Housing and Social Conditions in 1980, 1981.
Spitalfields Local Committee	Interim Report by the Spitalfields Project Steering Group, 1 June 1977, (v).
Spitalfields Youth Magazine	No. 6, 1984.
THARE News	January 1985.
THARE	Annual Report 1984-1985.
Tower Hamlets Homeless Families Committee	Hotels for the Homeless - Our Way Out, 1983.

(F) NEWSPAPERS AND SIMILAR PUBLICATIONS

East London Advertiser	20 August 1982.
London Labour Briefing	No.41, July 1984 and no.54, Nov. 1985.

Index

Commission for Racial Equality (CRE) 92, 93, 99, 104, 113 n. 39, 123, 177
Communists 40
Community Relations Council (CRC) 13-4, 92
councillors 5-7, 14, 30, 43, 80, 91, 109, 116, 130, 157, 178, 186 passim
Croydon 7
Corbishley, S. 44
Cove, J. 66, 86
Cypriots 27, 125

Damesick, P. 37 n. 1
Davenant St. Estate 126
Dearlove, J. 7, 186
Denning Point 43
Department of the Environment (DoE) 32
Department of Health and Social Security (DHSS) 34, 84
direct action 129-30, 179
Drucker, H. 64 n. 6 and 9
Duncan, S.S. and Gladwin, M. 11, 18 n. 28
Dunkirk 9
Dunleavy, P. 64 n. 6 and 9

East End Community School 45, 51, 153
East London War Against Racism (ELWAR) 69, 87 n. 6, 134
E. 1 116 passim, 131, 133
education 5, 13, 15, 33, 59, 63, 84, Chap. 6
Elboz, A. 43, 44, 54, 65, 66, 74, 81, 82, 83, 85
employment and unemployment 5, 15, 63, 70-1, 75, 84, 102, 104, 146
equal opportunities 98, 99, 101, 102, 104
Ethnic Minority Forum 109 passim, 177
Ethnic Minority Group 78-9 (see also Black Sections)
Ethnic Minority Liaison Group 109 passim, 177
ethnic monitoring 99 passim, 176, 186
ethnicity and ethnic minorities 2, 3, 10, 12, 13, 79, 118, 175, 178 passim, 185 passim

Federation of Bangladeshi Youth Organisations (FBYO) 33, 35-7, 46, 48,51, 63, 89, 90, 106, 107, 127, 130, 143
Feuchtwang, S. 14, 18 n. 35, 142 n. 48, 189
Finsbury Park 83
Fishman, W. 38 n. 6 and 8

Howick, C. 37 n. 1
Huque, Nurul 37, 45-7, 65, 71, 72, 74, 80, 81, 152-6, 165, 183
Huque, Sherajul 49 passim

Independent councillors 44, 45, 52, 72, 171, 174, 183
Inner Area Programme 90, 91
Inner London Education Authority 14, 16, 17, 25, 26, 28, 32-
    4, 37, 41, 90, 93, Chap. 6, 182 passim; adult education 164,
    165; Chief Education Officer 145, 157, 158, 160; Divisional
    Office 165; Equal Opportunities Sub-Committee 144, 145,
    147, 152, 158; Head of Legal Branch 157; Policy Co-
    ordinating Sub-Committee 157; Youth Office 164-5 (see
    also Tower Hamlets Initiative)
interests 2, 3, 6, 7, 11, 13, 178, 181, 185 passim
Irish 27, 125, 142 n. 54
Islam, S. N. 46, 50, 53, 62, 152 passim
Islamic religion 27, 150-2, 182
Islington 94

Jews 23, 26, 28, 44, 103, 125, 142 n. 54
Joganari 152, 156
Joint Consultative Committee (JCC) 92 passim, 107, 108,
    175
Jones, P. 38 n. 15

Kelly, Bill 60, 61
Kensington and Chelsea borough council 94
Key, T. 37 n. 1
Khan, V. Saifullah 2, 3
Khatun, Begum 83
Kobi Nazrul Centre 31, 35, 35, 37, 73, 106, 154, 156, 183

Latif, A. 75
Leach, J. 38 n. 8
Lewisham 94
Liberal Party 42, 43, 44, 50, 59, 61, 69, 80, 87 n. 3 and 5, 95,
    96, 97, 104
Liverpool 80, 86
Livingstone, K. 87 n. 8, 89, 125, 144
local community 55, 75, 78, 172, 189
Local Government Committee (LGC) 83, 84, 87 n. 4, 88 n.
12
Lojkine, J. 7-9

London Docklands Development Corporation (LDDC) 21, 90, 133
London Labour Briefing 66, 80, 86, 87 n. 2, 91
Lowe, S. 18 n. 22

Malik, A. 106
Maltese 125
managerialist thesis 5-6
Manchester 2
Marxism: 4-5, 187; and ideology 5, 7, 11-2; and
  instrumentalism 7-9; and structuralism 8-11
Maxwell, P. 75, 80, 84, 85, 86
meals on wheels 103
McBrearty, T. 87 n. 8
McDuff, R. 76 passim
Mikardo, I. 41, 42, 47, 66, 67, 68
Miliband, R. 7-9, 17 n. 16
Militant Tendency 66, 86, 87 n. 2, 88 n. 9
Millwall ward 21
miners strike 70-1, 173
Montefiore Community Education Centre 16, 25, 37, 45, 47,
  49, 70, 76, 92, 106, 145, 147, 156, 161 passim
Moore, R. 3, 5, 17 n. 3
Morrell, F. 144, 167
Motin, A. 149, 150, 154, 155, 156, 158, 159, 160
Mustafa, G. 45, 46, 50, 60, 61, 74

National Front 41, 42, 56, 67, 68, 69, 71, 173
National Health Service (NHS) 173
National Union of Public Employees (NUPE) 88 n. 13
National Union of Miners (NUM) 88 n. 13
National Union of Railwaymen (NUR) 88 n. 13

Ocean Estate 46
office development 23, 25, 90, 173
outreach workers 34, 46, 83

Pahl, R. 5-6, 10, 17 n. 7 and 8
Pakistani voluntary organisations 2
Pauline House 125
Peggie, A. 2
Pelham Buildings 53
People's Democratic Alliance (PDA) 46, 49 passim, 62 passim
Phillips, D. Chap. 5, 179, 180

Phillips Report 123 passim, 134 passim
Phizacklea, A. 11, 18 n. 29
pluralism 3, 7, 185 passim
police 67, 107
political arena 2, 11, 15, 16, 81, 185 passim
political practices 10, 68, 87, 174, 176, 185
political construction of community and class 15, 185
political representation 2, 3, 6, 12-5, 68
Poplar 40, 162
Poulantzas, N. 9
power 14-5, 174, 178, 179, 181 passim

Race Relations Act (1976) 101
Race and Housing Advisory Group (RHAG) 122
racial discrimination 5, 101, 102, 104, 122, 123, 131, 134,
    136, 139, 148, 181
racial harassment 67-8, 119, 128, 134, 135
racism 11-2, 14, 47, 53, 56, 57, 58, 59, 67, 68, 75, 102, 117,
121,
    124, 125, 134, 142 n. 54, 159, 180-1, 184; direct racism
    127, 131, 136; institutional racism 13, 119, 124, 159
Regional Labour Party 73, 82
residential time points 138, 139 (see also Housing)
resistance 15, 150, 181 passim
Rex, J. 3-5, 10, 17 n. 3 and 4
Reza, M. 37, 147, 149, 150, 154, 156
Rhodes, R. 64 n. 9
Riaz, M. 88 n. 12, 156, 165
Richardson, J. 78
Riley, J. 96
Robert Montefiore Secondary School 26, 28, 29, 57, 58, 106
Roberts, G. 85, 86
Royal Mint Square 120

Samad, A. 37, 154, 156
Saunders, P. 6-7, 9, 13, 17 n. 6, 9 and 14, 35, 64 n. 8, 186
    passim
Section 11 32, 101, 102, 143, 160
Selby St. site 25, 126
Shadwell Gardens 134
Shadwell ward 21, 27, 44, 50
Sharma, S. 2
Shore, P. 41, 47, 66, 73-5, 85, 86, 174
Shukur, A. 38 n. 8
Sivanandan, A. 11

211